String of Thoughts on North East India: An Economist's Perspective

Atul Sarma

AAKAR

String of Thoughts on North East India: An Economist's Perspective
Atul Sarma

First Published 2018

ISBN 978-93-5002-552-9

Published by
AAKAR BOOKS
28 E Pocket IV, Mayur Vihar Phase I
Delhi 110 091 India
aakarbooks@gmail.com

Laser Typeset at
Arpit Printographers, Delhi 110 032

Printed at
D.K. Fine Art Press, Delhi 110 052

For Niva, Nitu, Loni, Mun
Who deserved a lot more than
what I could give them

Contents

Introduction

I am a development economist. I pursued my career in academics in a competitive environment for most part of my active life outside my home state which is Assam. There remained limited scope or opportunity for serious research on the problems that concerned my state/region. However, I was fortunate that the Assam government associated me with the State Planning Board as a member for more than two decades (1978-2000). I was also made a member of the Economic Advisory Council to the Chief Minister, Assam along with the Late scientist, Prof. Raja Ramanna and the Late L.C. Jain by the first AGP government. I would like to confess, however, that I could make precious little contribution to the development of the state. That was largely because the State Planning Board had not played the envisaged role in the economic development in most states and remained in reality an ornamental institution. This was my experience even in the case of the Manipur State Planning Board with which I was associated as a member for five years spreading over the late 1980s and early 90s. I was also associated with a few official committees/task forces (Dinesh Goswami Committee, for example) constituted by the Assam government and task force constituted by the Planning Commission (headed by L.C. Jain, then Member of the Planning Commission) in the later part of the 80s. We worked hard to recommend suitable policy interventions for taking the state to a higher growth trajectory. I do not think, those recommendations had ever been implemented for lack of responsive governance. In fact, such reports gathered dust in the place of the department of origin.

Associations such as the ones I have indicated above were most unlikely to impact the state's development policy. But they helped me in more than one way. They helped me to realize the complexity of the political, social and economic realities of the north east states. They also helped me to reflect on the causes of persistent underdevelopment despite their rich endowments. They further helped me to fathom the underlying paradigm of development interventions by the union government. Furthermore, I realized that for the fundamental fact of geography, if nothing else, seven sister states are an interdependent economic system. Their development challenges lie in discovering/identifying each of their comparative advantages and in chalking out an appropriate strategy for promoting specialization in their respective areas of comparative strength.

My stint as Vice-Chancellor, Rajiv Gandhi (then Arunachal) University (2003-06), Itanagar, Arunachal Pradesh offered me another opportunity to come face to face with the ground realities of a hill economy. I was closely associated with the preparation of the *Human Development Report for Arunachal Pradesh* as also with the State Development Report for the state by the Economics Department of the University. Both these studies provided deep insights into the problems confronting the state as also suggested policy directions in which the state government should act. As expected, the government was hardly responsive to such suggestions. Even so, these studies broadened my own understanding of the constraints and prospects of development of a hill economy.

Yet another opportunity presented itself. I was appointed as a member of the Thirteenth Finance Commission (2007-10). This opened up the possibility to study the official documents and interact closely with the policy makers of the country. I had intensive discussions with the policy makers particularly of the North Eastern states. It also exposed me to the unique institutions and economic systems that exist in the north east hill states. At the same time, I came to understand the type of binding constraints that policy makers face in designing policy in a subsistence agrarian hill economy. With limited financial resources at their command, policy makers tended to address the exigencies in an ad hoc manner rather than pursuing medium or long-term development goals in a well-articulated development framework.

With all these exposures and experiences, I am fully aware that the complex realities and the challenges offered by the region's huge ethnic and other diversities call for studying them in multidisciplinary perspectives including economics, geography, sociology and social anthropology. Even so, I have gathered my thoughts on different issues that concern the development of the region and I have addressed them mostly in an economic perspective, my basic discipline being Economics. I shared most of these thoughts in public forums on one or the other occasion. Most of them have been published in professional journals, conference proceedings or edited volumes.

These articles were prepared over a span of almost one and a half decades (2003-17). Some of them are dated in terms of data used. Yet I have not attempted to revise them. It is because what I attempted was to drive a point rather than mere data analysis. Therefore, I believe that while the data could be dated, thoughts/ ideas arising from the data analysis remain relevant at least in the particular time context. Further, in an emerging economy like ours, growth dynamics are changing with release of the constraints even if gradually as also with changing aspirations of the youths. For example, remoteness of the region has shrunk in more than one way. With an increasing and efficient communication network, with massive outmigration of the youths for studies or career pursuit or even for merely earning a livelihood to a more prosperous states the regional market is increasingly being integrated with the national market. Similarly, with the advances in information, communication technology (ICT), the locational disadvantage of the region is slowly but steadily on the wane. More importantly, a clearly articulated development framework in terms of integrating the north east with the east and South East Asia has edged into the horizon in the wake of the Look (ACT) East Policy. This is a work in progress. Once it reaches the critical minimum in terms of putting in place the enabling conditions, the growth dynamics for the region can be expected to alter significantly.

This book brings together sixteen select articles that I wrote mostly in the last decade and a half on one or another aspect of the economic development of a remote region of India which is North East India. The region in its initial formation comprised seven states,

Sikkim was added later. These articles mostly deal with seven sister states. This region is strategically important, 99.5 per cent of its boundary being with foreign countries. The region accounts for four per cent of India's population and eight per cent of areas. With an overwhelmingly large tribal population and vast expanse of hilly areas, the region is unique in more than one way. Despite being endowed with nature's bounty, the region lags behind the national average in terms of most economic development indicators.

This book does not attempt to develop a coherent set of ideas relating to the economic development of North Eastern region. It brings together the thoughts developed in the form of articles that attempt to understand the process of economic development of the region. Two concerns tie together the articles incorporated in this volume. One relates to the deep concern of the persistent under-development of the region despite its rich endowments in terms of nature's bounties—water, forest, mines and minerals. The other is the economic interdependence of the region even if seven (later added to eight) highly diverse—ecologically, economically, institutionally, culturally and so on—and complex political units make up the region.

I have included in this volume one article, jointly authored with Biswajit Saikia who is no more. He died at an early age. I remember him with a sense of deep sorrow, his energy, enthusiasm and eagerness to complete a task undertaken despite his failing health. I have also included articles, co-authored with Amarendra Sahu, Deepak K. Misra and Vandana Upadhaya and Sushanta K. Nayak. I gratefully acknowledge their contributions.

My thanks are due to the journals which published many of these articles and permitted me to publish them in this volume. Dr. Bhupen Sarmah, Director, OKD Institute for Social Change and Development (OKDISCD), Guwahati took a keen interest in putting these articles together in a book form. In fact, he introduced me to Mr. K.K. Saxena of Aakar Books. I thank him for all this. Dr. Saswati Choudhury, OKDISCD put together the articles scattered over. Dr. Vandana Upadhaya, Rajiv Gandhi University, Itanagar searched for some of the articles which had escaped my attention. I am indeed thankful to both of them. I thank Mr. K.K. Saxena of Aakar Books who willingly agreed to publish this book.

1

Why the North Eastern States Continue to Decelerate*

> Simplified paradigms or maps are indispensable for human thought and action. On the one hand, we may explicitly formulate theories or models and consciously use them to guide our behaviour. Alternatively, we may deny the need for such guides and assume that we will act only in terms of specified "objective" facts dealing with each case "on its merits". If we assume this, however, we delude ourselves. For in the back of our minds are hidden assumptions, biases and prejudices that determine how we perceive reality, what facts we look at, and how we judge their importance and merits.
>
> –*Samuel P. Huntington***

In 1993 two states of the North Eastern region, Arunachal Pradesh and Nagaland had real per capita income (at 1993 prices) above the all-India average. At the end of the decade, 1999-2000, the latest year for which the data except for Mizoram was available, none of the states in the region had real per capita income above the national average—the gap ranging from 13.32 per cent for Nagaland to 42.54 per cent for Assam.

It was during the same period the north eastern region received special economic packages.[1] In October 1996 H.D. Deve Gowda, the then Prime Minister announced an economic package of

---

* Published in *Man and Society, A Journal of North East States* (2005), Vol. 1, No. 1, Spring. The earlier version was presented at the Seminar on "Transforming the Hill Economy of the North East Region: Emerging Challenges and Opportunities" organized by Arunachal University in collaboration with the Institute for Human Development at Itanagar, November 26-28, 2004.

** *The Clash of Civilizations and the Remaking of World Order.*

Rs. 6,100 crore for specific projects in the North East states. He also introduced the North East sub plans in all central ministries for which 10 per cent of their budgets would be earmarked. I.K. Gujaral who followed him as Prime Minister assured the implementation of the package. In January 2000 Atal Bihari Vajpayee, the next Prime Minister further announced a Rs. 10,271.66 crore package for the region.

Why is this paradox? Why did all the north eastern states continue to decelerate even while several special economic packages were put in operation? This chapter attempts to understand what explains this paradox. Finally, it provides an analytical framework to view the problems of development of the North East.

North East: A Heterogeneous and Yet Interdependent Economic System

North East India consisting of seven states in its initial demarcation is landlocked surrounded by foreign countries—China, Myanmar, Bangladesh and Bhutan—with 99.5 per cent international border and only 0.5 per cent border of the region touches the country.[2] Apart from geographical isolation, there are several other features, which stand in sharp contrast to the rest of the country. For example, the North Eastern states, which are, by and large, hilly ones, are characterized by the preponderance of ST and less significantly SC population. As compared to the all India share of 8.6 per cent, the ST population in the North East ranged from 94.4 per cent in Mizoram to 12.4 per cent in Assam in 2001 and also a decade later in 2011.

Secondly, all the states in the region as compared to the rest of the country recorded a high decadal population growth even during 1981-91. In the decade of 1991-2001 also, the population growth (22.16 per cent) in North East was higher than all-India average (21.34 per cent). Significantly, however, the decadal population growth in the hill states apart from Nagaland (where it was negative) was far higher than the all-India average during 2001-11 and it was much lower in Assam and Tripura. Thirdly, the real per capita income of all the states of the region has been much below the all-India average per capita income.

What is more, each of them is far behind the rest of the country in terms of administrative, social and economic infrastructures, be it per capita power consumption, credit deposit ratios, road and railway transport and so on. Another unique feature of the region is that unlike other tribal populations, the rate of literacy is higher than the all-India average in four states despite their predominantly tribal population.

But the states within the region are very dissimilar in several ways. Broadly speaking, the North Eastern states are of two distinct categories: entirely hill states—Arunachal Pradesh, Meghalaya, Mizoram and Nagaland while partially hill states—Assam, Tripura and Manipur with overwhelmingly larger population living in the valley/plain districts. Significantly, however, the latter three states accounted for slightly less than fifty per cent (48.70 per cent approximately) of the Scheduled Tribe population of the region. Population density ranges from 17 per sq kms (Arunachal Pradesh) to 398 per sq km (Assam), higher than the all-India average of 382.

They are also dissimilar in terms of urbanization rate, literacy rate and other demographic characteristics, physical features, stages of economic development, etc. leaving aside the ethnic composition.

Yet the north east states are an inter-dependent economic system, both for historical and geo-political reasons. The North Eastern Council (NEC), which was set up in 1971, was the result of the recognition of this economic interdependence. It was indeed a significant institutional innovation. Its performance over this long period, however, reflects its monumental failure to develop an integrated approach to the economic development of the region.There are several reasons for this failure. Essentially, these can broadly be traced to two sets of factors. One relates to its inability to visualize its role appropriate to the unique characteristics of the region. It is because the NEC being under the administrative control of the ministry of Home Affairs and not under any development ministry or the Planning Commission was conceived less as a development agency and more as an administrative appendage of the Government of India.[3] The other basically following from the first owes to its failure to assess the economic system and institutions and to evolve the right development plan and instruments in the framework of economic interdependence of the region as well as in alignment with the unique features of the region for releasing a dynamic growth process.

Binding Impediments

I would like to submit that five I's—Initial conditions, Infrastructure lag, Insurgency, Imperfection/distortion in factor and product markets and Indifferent governance, though not necessarily in the same order, are still acting as binding constraints on the north east economic development. I will elaborate each of these in greater detail as follows.

1. Initial Conditions: Important initial conditions that continue to act as stumbling blocks are:

(i) **Disruption of Traditional Trade Links:** As is well known, partition led to the disruption of the long existing transport and trade links that the North East was accustomed to. The alternative trade and transport routes that were developed in the post-partition period have been much longer in distance and thus involved much larger transport costs. For example, the distance travelled between Kolkata and Agartala was slightly more than 300 kms in the pre-partition era while it is 1,700 kms in the post-partition period. "To move a 9-ton truck from Guwahati to Kolkata, a distance of 1100 kms today costs around Rs. 20,000. A truck going from Chennai to Kolkata, a distance of 1,600 kms costs only Rs. 16,000. This also reflects on the quality of road connecting the North East with the rest of the country."[4]

In respect of railway links, some areas of the North East are still to have railheads while in the rest even the partial conversion of the meter gauge to broad gauge had taken years. The railway network designed initially by the colonial power to sub-serve its commercial interests is yet to be fully restructured. The extent of transport/market disruption in the region can be inferred from the fact that in the pre-partition days, boats laden with tea, coal and timber reached Kolkata from Dibrugarh in eight days, but now Kolkata-Guwahati shipment takes more than 25 days for lack of night navigation and customs formalities at various points. As the Shukla Commission set up as late as in 1997 succinctly put it:

Partition further isolated an already isolated geo-politically sequestered region. It was left with over 4500 kms of external frontier with Bhutan, China, Myanmar and Bangladesh but no more than a slender 22 km connection with the Indian hinterland through the tenuous Siliguri corridor, the Gateway to the North East. The very considerable market disruption, socio-economic distancing and retardation that resulted has not been adequately appreciated and compensated.[5] The net effect of all this is the weakening of the market linkage of the region with the rest of the country.

(ii) Population Influx: The population influx from across the borders has hugely impacted not only the demographic composition of the North Eastern states but also their polity and economies. As such, this is a highly emotive issue as has been demonstrated by prolonged student uprisings in Assam and other states of the region. But the inability to effectively deal with this problem by the student leaders when they came to power in Assam after a protracted movement against this issue only highlights the extent of complexity of the problem. The fact is that the influx of population that had begun since partition continues to remain at the root of social and political mobilizations leading to a prolonged disturbed situation in several parts of the region. This, in turn, has vitiated its environment for investment and growth. On the other hand, the economic stagnancy that impedes employment and income growth serves as a fertile ground for fortifying and sustaining insurgency. Thus economic stagnancy and insurgency move in a vicious circle.

(iii) Unharnessed Resource Endowments: It is widely recognized that North East India is a highly resource endowed region. The region is endowed with mineral resources such as petroleum, natural gas, coal and limestone, water and forests, fertile soil and so on. Hydel power potential deserves a special mention.As Chief Managing Director, National Hydel Power Corporation stated, the North East has hydropower generation potential of 57,000 MW or 60 per cent of the country's 84,000 MW (at 60 per cent load factor).[6] The region also has large deposits of oil and natural gas. It would be pertinent to mention here that water and mineral resources are in the Union list and hence harnessing the same essentially depends on the priority of the central allocation. On the other, their utilization involves a substantial investment that is beyond the capacity of the state governments particularly of the North East states. The level of investment that is required for harnessing hydropower generation potential can be gauged from the following. The NHPC is currently working on an investment of Rs. 100,000 crore for generation of power with a plant capacity of 25,000 MW. Assuming the same average rate per MW it would involve another Rs. 128,000 crore at 2003 prices if the remaining part of the estimated hydropower potential were to be utilized. But the fact is that enormous hydropower potential as well as oil and gas-based downstream industries still remain undeveloped.

On the other hand, water resources instead of being a source of economic prosperity have continued to be a bane for the region causing flood and erosion,[7] year after year resulting in immense human suffering and loss of lives and property. This has in effect weakened farmers' incentives to invest in farms in these predominantly agricultural economies.

(iv) **Enclave Economy:** Crude oil production and its refining as well as tea plantation and plywood industry are the few old resource-based modern industries in the region. But both oil and tea industries, which have existed for more than one and a half centuries, have not induced any industrial growth based on their backward and forward linkages. For example, tea plantation requires a wide variety of inputs such as fertilizers, insecticides, chappals, umbrellas, small tools, etc. These backward linkage-based industries, despite their large market, did not come up in the region. Instead, the industry is largely dependent on supplies from outside the region.

Similarly, the oil industry had been hesitant for long to develop refineries, and a petrochemical complex, which could have led to developing many downstream industries in the region. On the other hand, the surplus that accrued in these industries year after year was siphoned off to investment activities elsewhere. This has led to an 'enclave economy' in which these few modern industries exist without having any linkage with the much larger segment of traditional activities. For reasons such as these, the resource-based extractive industries have come to be perceived as the symbol of exploitation.[8]

(v) Monopolistic Operations of Deeply Entrenched Trading Interests: It is well known that the North East is greatly dependent for the supply of its requirements on the rest of the country. To indicate the measure of such dependence, Assam's procurement of food items such as food grains, fish edible oils, etc. alone is estimated at Rs. 3,500 crore during the Eighth Plan period.[9] Such vast requirement is available through a trade and distribution network. The trade network was organized on the basis of monopolistic competition. In many situations, traders collude for price advantage. The trade margin being high, the investment on commodity production is understandably not preferred. It is so, particularly because the risk factor is higher in a perennially disturbed environment as well as in a situation where there is a lack of adequate infrastructure, all leading to high transaction costs. What is more, there are instances to suggest that such deeply entrenched mercantile capital militates against the emergence of local entrepreneurship.

2. Infrastructure Lags

There exists a broad consensus that the North East lacks the basic minimum physical, social and administrative infrastructures for unleashing growth dynamics in the region. Physical infrastructures such as power, communications, transport, irrigation, and market access, are grossly inadequate to generate a dynamic growth process. The High Level Commission (1997) constituted to examine 'Tackling Backlogs in Basic Minimum Services and Infrastructure Needs' for the North East estimated the requirement for infrastructure—power, roads, railways, irrigation flood control and inland water—placed at Rs. 93,619.01 crore in addition to the Ninth Plan requirement of Rs. 17,995.42 crore.[10] A study conducted in 2004, ranked Assam 15th among the major states, while all six smaller states were at the bottom among the small states of the country.[11] Inadequate infrastructure particularly in the context of hill states where market institutions such as land market have not developed has resulted in poor market incentives and this in turn contributed to low productivity and growth in different sectors of the economies of the region. As also obvious, poor infrastructure is not conducive to attracting private investment.

The creation of some of the crucial infrastructures has two important dimensions. First, because of the interdependence of the economies of the region, the essential criterion is to develop a good network of inter-state transport and communication in addition to developing intra state market and basic service accessibility. The remoteness and hilly terrain involves larger unit cost as well as maintenance cost. For example, cost of construction of a one km road in the hilly areas of the region is five times higher than that in the plains; two and a half times the number of primary schools or primary health centres in the plains is required to provide the equivalent population coverage in Arunachal hills.[12] Apart from developing the intra-regional connectivity it is equally important that effective border road and water transport networks are required to be developed for trade and transport links in liaison with the neighbouring countries of Myanmar, South East Asia, Bangladesh and South China. Second, the full utilization of the power potentials of the region and also effectively controlling the flooding problems in the region not only requires heavy investment as mentioned earlier but also mutual understanding and cooperation of the individual units of the North East as well as the neighbouring countries like Bangladesh and China.

3. Insurgency

Beginning from the NSCN led militancy for independence in Nagaland to ULFA in Assam it has been a long story of an uninterrupted disturbed situation in most parts of the North East.[13] Without delving into the historicity of the genesis of the problems and their possible solution, a few points still remain crucial for the region. First, the socio-political disturbance that the region has been exposed to over long years adds to already high transaction cost that discourages private investment and impinges development. The measure of the burden of corruption of all kinds and extortion by different underground groups imposed on transport cost which increases the transaction cost even within the region can be realized from the following example. "A moving truckload of goods from Moreh to Dimapur, a distance of 316 kms, costs Rs. 50,000. .....Traders claim that to move a truck from Imphal to Guwahati (487 kms) costs Rs. 35,000."[14] Second, rapid population growth unaccompanied by economic growth in the North East has led to impoverishment and growing unemployment in the region. To illustrate, in Assam alone nearly 22 lakhs of the population (approximately 10 per cent) are unemployed. Seventy per cent of the unemployed are educated looking for jobs.[15] Other North East states have similar problems. What is important to underline is that insurgency and high youth unemployment resulting from poor economic development feed on each other.

Added to the phenomenon of insurgency, numerous civil society protests in the form of bandhs and strikes, partial or total at the slightest provocation have become frequent phenomena, particularly in Assam, the gateway to all other North East states. The Federation of Industries in the North Eastern Region has estimated and published recently in a local newspaper that one-day's strike causes a loss of Rs. 50 crore due to disruption of economic activities. Such disruptions being frequent, one can well imagine the extent of direct annual loss to the North East economies and negative impact on the economic environment.

4. Imperfection/Distortion in Factor and Commodity Markets

In the North East states both commodity and factor markets are working to their disadvantage. With low production base and heavy dependence on the rest of the country for their requirements, local demand generated within the region induces income and employment generation in the states with larger production base. Similarly, due to an inhospitable investment environment, savings arising in the region finds its way out into the more investment-friendly region. This largely explains very low credit-deposit ratio in the North Eastern states. Such asymmetrical market integration—a large inflow of goods into the region and outflow of savings from the region—has impeded the pace of growth in the region.

Besides, the absence of a land market particularly in the hill states acts as a serious impediment to investment. The labour market has also been hugely distorted by heavy population influx. With supply side factors being inhospitable, integrated product and credit market accompanied by the distorted labour market and non-existence of land market in the hill states of the North East region have led to reverse flow of resources from the region to the more developed state economies. The outcome of this process is low growth despite special dispensation by the central government.

5. Indifferent Governance

Why have some states in India developed faster than their counterparts elsewhere? Widely perceived factors such as resource endowments and closeness to national market do not offer adequate explanations. For example, Bihar or the states of North East India or Orissa with resource abundance are some of the least developed states in the country. In contrast, Gujarat with no great claim on such resources has grown faster than most other states. The broadly observed inverse relation between resource endowment of states and their respective level of development should be considered in the following perspective. Constitutionally the responsibility of using major minerals and water resources rests with the central government. Their utilization also involves large-scale investment. This holds true especially for hydro power development. Therefore, their utilization has to be built into macro plans. Another problem is that extractive industries such as coal, aluminium and oil have weak backward linkage while their forward linkage is with the larger production bases located elsewhere. The economic backwardness of vastly resource endowed Bihar, Orissa and states of North East India could perhaps be understood in this perspective.

This leads us to the question whether the closeness to the national market induced the growth process in states like Gujarat? But the paradox lies in the fact that states like UP or MP which are in the heartland of the national market failed to record high growth. On the other hand, Karnataka and Tamil Nadu even though away from the national market have grown faster. Even Haryana, which had poor infrastructure at the time of its creation in 1966, is one of the fastest growing states.The moot point is that widely recognized factors such as resource endowments, closeness to national market, and so on are by themselves not sufficient conditions to spur growth.

It can be hypothesized that consistent pursuit of clearly defined priorities in a development perspective contributes to growth. How does it work? Development policies with well-articulated thrusts pursued over a long period percolate down to economic agents, who start demanding the state machinery to address their problems and thus lead to better delivery system. In the process both the political leadership and the bureaucrats over time become accountable to the economic operators for better delivery, which eventually induces growth.

Lack of such prioritized thrusts, in the case of North East India is reflected in the poor delivery system even in their limited areas of operation. Widespread corruption and cynicism of the bureaucracy is both cause and effect of the casual approach to development.

Explanatory Hypothesis

The foregoing discussions on the spatial and economic frontiers of the North East drives home the point that the North East with only 0.5 per cent of its territorial boundary with the rest of the country and the remaining with foreign countries, was loosely fitted in the macro development perspective of India. It was because the development initiatives for North East India were largely anchored on two perspectives. One is the security perspective rather than a well articulated development perspective and the other is the perspective based on least interference in traditional institutions and practices.[16] Incidentally, infrastructure like the railways developed in the colonial period linked the areas associated with tea, oil, coal and plywood but not any of the traditional urban centres. Similarly, Stillwell Road that linked North East India with Myanmar constructed during the Second World War period was intended to serve as a defence supply line and not as any market linkage. The importance of the road weaned away in the post-independence period.

The security centric thrust towards the region continued in the post-independence period.In the early mid 1950s with finding of large crude oil reserves, the Government of India (GoI) considered setting up of an oil refinery. The Expert Committee constituted for selection of the site, did not find a place in North East India suitable for setting up an oil refinery for strategic reasons. It is a different matter that eventually in response to prolonged agitation a toy oil refinery was eventually set up in Guwahati and at least four times larger one in Baruini in Bihar. Again, the Armed Forces Special Powers Act (Assam and Manipur) against which Manipuris have been agitating over the years was enacted in 1958 when apart from Naga hostilities there was no other insurgency that warranted such a draconian law to be enforced in the region.

Another important initiative that the GoI took gives an insight into its strategic obsession. Considering the interdependence of the seven North East economies, the establishment of the North East Council (NEC) was a significant institutional innovation. But even this was designed to subserve more a security interest than to promote an integrated development approach to the North East. It is clear from the fact that the NEC was placed under the administrative control of the Ministry of Home, Government of India (GoI) and under the Chairmanship of one of the Governors of the North East states rather than under any development ministries or the Planning Commission.

On the other hand, major development projects were more in response to public agitation. There are numerous examples to show that many critical projects such as the first bridge over the Brahmaputra, conversion of railways into broad gauge, setting up of the second oil refinery and that of IIT were the products of ad hoc responses to public agitation. For far too long the GoI's development initiatives were more the outcome of strategic/ security consideration and ad hoc responses to public agitation rather than following from a development perspective.The other perspective on which the development initiatives were anchored especially in the hills states/regions was the least intervention in the traditional system and institutions. The requirement of inner line permit for entry into most parts of the hill states and ban on the land ownership by non-tribals are the evidence of the attempt to preserve the traditional system and institutions. What perceptions and forces that shaped this perspective or whether there exists any justifiability are beyond the scope of this paper. But the fact remains that product and money markets are being integrated with the national and regional markets in the hill regions as well, e.g. varieties of industrial goods, say shampoo pouches, soaps and detergents have entered the consumption basket even in the remotest part of these regions but the traditional production system associated with low productivity and self-sufficiency can hardly sustain the changing consumption pattern requiring more cash transactions. Under the emerging scenario the traditional system and institutions have to grapple with the challenges of a market economy. On the other hand, even if marketable surplus is produced, farmers can barely obtain any price incentives for their disposable produce due to lack of easy and viable market access. Similarly, in the traditional system prevailing in large parts of the hills region, the land market does not exist, land being owned by the community. The absence of land market is a serious impediment to the flow of investment, particularly from outside. This is also an impediment to the flow of formal credit particularly in the rural sector because land cannot serve as collateral and there does not exist any substitutable asset. Even the functioning of the labour market is constrained. In a traditional system the concept of wage labour rarely exists. As a result, for development projects such as construction of roads and bridges, much greater reliance has to be placed on migrant labour from across the border rather than on local labour. This has induced inflow of migrant labour in great magnitude. Its impact is outflow of labour income, at least a part of it and at another level a source of conflict as has been witnessed in several parts of the North East.

All this clearly suggests that the traditional systems and institutions are not compatible with product, factor and credit market integration. To put it the other way round, the traditional systems and institutions are not sustainable if the development process leading to market integration as is generally envisaged is to be promoted. How to resolve this contradiction is precisely where the major challenges to transforming the hill economy lie.

Concluding Remarks

The chapter has summarized the situations in five I's—Initial conditions, Infrastructure, Insurgency, Imperfection/distortion in factor and product markets and Indifferent governance that still stand even at the end of more than five decades of planning as binding constraints on the economic development of the North East region. I have submitted two paradigms. One relates to overstress on security/strategic consideration rather than a development perspective in development efforts. The other relates to the minimum intervention in traditional systems and institutions of the hill economy, which has led to their non-compatibility while market integration is at work at least to an extent. These paradigms underlined the strategies and action of the Government of India. Since the mid-1990s, the economic development of the North East began to find place in the collective psyche of the development activists in India. This has been reflected in the debates, deliberations and discourse at the national level as well as in the announcement of special economic packages for the economic development of the region. With the articulation of 'Look East Policy' in the early 1990s, a new vision in development perspective as a gateway to dynamic East Asian economies has been unfurled.

What followed is an attempt to revamp the NEC recognizing explicitly the economic interdependence of the constituent states of the region. Only in February 2005, the NEC had been restructured more as a regional planning body rather than an administrative unit with the overtone of strategic consideration. With the emergence of an economic perspective, a shift in policy thrust on the part of GoI, is clearly visible. Attention has been directed towards road connectivity among the North East states,[17] connectivity and communication between the region and the rest of the country, other infrastructure, harnessing the resources of the region, potential areas of development such as tourism and paving the way for large trade with the East and South East Asian countries and flow of funds with specified objectives thereby indicating initiatives within a framework of development perspective. Development activism in civil society has also played an important role in recent times.

It is not to argue, however, that all the binding constraints discussed earlier have been adequately addressed. There are several areas of concern: such as governance, sensitive issues like influx of people from across the border and burgeoning mass of unemployed youths who are attracted by numerous militant groups. As the situation stands now, one can only wonder whether it is the beginning of the end of the long and dark tunnel.

NOTES

1. A high level Commission, "Transforming the North East" was constituted under the Chairmanship of Shri S.P. Shukla following the Prime Minister's announcement of 'New Initiatives for the North Eastern Region' on October 27, 1996 and the Report was submitted in

March 1997. Prior to that, the Planning Commission constituted a Working Group on the Development of the North Eastern Region during the Seventh Five Year Plan, 1985-90 under the Chairmanship of P.H. Trivedi, Secretary, NEC. Also, the Planning Commission at the instance of the Union Home Ministry constituted a Committee under the Chairmanship of L.C. Jain, then Member, Planning Commission to look into the question of economic development of Assam under Clause Seven of the Assam Accord and the Report was submitted in April 1990.

2. Planning Commission, GoI, (1997), High Level Commission, Transforming the Noth East-Tackling Backlogs in Basic Minimum Services and Infrastctural Needs, p. I.
3. Only in December 2004, it was announced in both Houses of Parliament that the revamped NEC in the pursuance of an Expert Committee was going to have the Minister, Development of North Eastern India as its Chairman even as the NEC was all set to activate its role as security agency. Earlier in 2002 the NEC Act was amended to enable the NEC to function as the regional planning body and to formulate specific projects and schemes that would benefit two or more states. *The Assam Tribune*, December 7, 2004.
4. Planning Commission, GoI (1997), Assam Development Report (Draft), p. 6.
5. Planning Commission, GoI (1997), High Level Commission, Transforming the Noth East-Tackling Backlogs in Basic Minimum Services and Infrastructural Needs, p. I.
6. The estimate of hydropower potential of the North East widely varies. For example, the Central Electricity Authority places the total hydropower potential of the region at 34,920 MW against the all-India potential of 84,044 MW (*The Times of India*, February 28, 2005). According to the Brahmaputra Board, the hydropower potential of the Brahmaputra alone is about 40,000 MW.
7. Assam is losing on an average 20 sq. kms every year due to erosion by the Brahmaputra. Other allied problems relate to severe drainage congestion, urban floods and devastation of agriculture, Nayan Sharma, an IIT, Roorkee-based scientist at a seminar on Problems and Prospects in Linking the Indian Rivers organized at Gauhati University on March 28, 2005, *The Sentinel*, Guwahati, March 29, 2005.
8. For further elaboration, see, Report of The Task Force on Economic Development of Assam, Vol. 1, April 5, 1988, Para 3.5, p. 12.
9. Planning Commission, GoI, Economic Development of Assam: Report of the Committee on Clause Seven of Assam Accord, 1990, p. 2.
10. *India Today* (Special Issue), India's Best and Worst States August 16,

2004. Also see, Ministry of Finance, Government of India, Report of the Eleventh Finance Commission (2000-05), June 2000, p. 218.

11. Worked out on the basis of data available in the *Human Development Report, Arunachal Pradesh, 2003* (unpublished) prepared by Arunachal Uinversity, 2004.
12. More than a hundred groups are said to have been engaged in militant activities in the North East. Most of these are essentially ethnic in character. The genesis of insurgencies, however, cannot be traced to any single factor particularly because there are more than 100 militant groups operating in the region for different motivations under different objective conditions. For useful discussion and many relevant references on around the issue, for detailed discussion, see H. Srikanth, Insurgency and Counter–Insurgency, Agenda for Peace in India's North East, in C.J. Thomas (ed.) (2005) *Polity and Economy: Agenda for Contemporary North East India*, Regency Publications, New Delhi, pp. 1-24.
13. Planning Commission, GoI (1997), Assam Development Report (Draft), p. 6.
14. North Eastern Development Finance Corporation Ltd.
15. For similar observations in another context, see Amar Yumnam, "Regional Cooperation and Development: Strategy for Development in a Conflict Zone" (Unpublished). Presented at the Conference entitled Towards a New Asia Transnationalism and North East India organized by CENIAS Forum, OKD Institute of Social Change and Development, Guwahati on September 10 and 11, 2004, p. 3.
16. The GoI has recently cleared a multilane North East Express Highway linking all the capitals of North East states spanning 6,907 kms towards connectivity within and between different units of the region, infrastructure development (4,464 kms national highways, 2,050 kms of newly declared highways and 393 kms of NEC roads).

2

Unique Institution of Governance in the North East: Its Relevance in the Present Context*

Here we may briefly recall how each of the seven states of the NER have come into existence. Assam has come to its present form after being forced to give up its original territory several times. First, most of its Sylethet district was to be transferred to East Pakistan (now Bangladesh) as part of operationalizing the Boundary Commission headed by Sir Cyril Radcliffe.

In 1957 Naga Hills district of Assam and Tuensang Frontier division were brought under the Union administration and later in 1963, this union territory was given statehood naming it as Nagaland under the 'State of Nagaland Act 1962'.

Under the Assam Reorganization (Meghalaya) Act, 1969, Meghalaya comprising Khasi and Jaintia Hills district and the Garo Hills district was formed as an autonomous state within the state of Assam while the European ward, Police bazaar ward and Shillong Cantonment remained with Assam. Later under the North Eastern Area (Reorganization) Act 1971 (Act No 81 of 1971) of Parliament, the autonomous state of Meghalaya was given statehood.

Under the same act, the Union Mizo Hills district of Assam

---

* Revised version of the 9th Tarlok Singh Memorial Lecture published in the Journal of Indian Association of Social Science Institutions (IASSI) Quarterly, *Contributions to Indian Social Sciences,* Vol. 34. No. 1-4 (January-December), 2015, pp. 5-25. Also included the unrevised version in Sarma, Atul and Debabani Chakravarty (2016), *Integrating the Third Tier in the Indian Federal System,* Palgrave Macmillan.

was accorded the status of a union territory known as the Union Territory of Mizoram in 1971. Thus the territory under the newly formed state of Meghalaya and the Union Territory of Mizoram as in the case of Nagaland since 1957 ceased to be parts of Assam.

For decades the area of the North East Frontier was under the North East Frontier Areas (Administration) Regulation. In 1954 the entire North East Frontier Area (NEFA) was designated as North East Frontier Agency and made a union territory. NEFA was renamed as Arunachal Pradesh under the North Eastern Areas (Reorganization) Act 1971. Arunachal Pradesh became a full-fledged state in 1987.

Tripura, a feudatory state of Bengal, earlier known as Hill Tipperah was a princely state till October 1949. It was merged into the Indian Union and became a Part-C State, under the Government of India. Tripura became a full-fledged state in 1972 (January 21).

Manipur was a princely state till 1891. The Anglo-Manipur war of 1891 brought it under British rule. After independence, its princely status was restored. In 1949, Manipur was merged into the Indian Union. It was a Union Territory during 1949-1972. Manipur became a full-fledged state in 1972.

To sum up, three states of the North East, Nagaland, Meghalaya and Mizoram were carved out of Assam. Manipur and Tripura had their own existence while North East frontier tracts eventually formed the state of Arunachal Pradesh.

2. Evolution of a System of Governance

Colonial Backdrop

The governing mechanism evolved by the colonial government for the inhabitants of hills in the NER was anchored on the policy of seclusion. The evidence of this policy could be found in the Garo Hills Act, 1869 that had sought to exclude Garo Hill district from the general administrative set up of Bengal and to place it as special duties of the Lt. Governor.The management of Assam was transferred from the Lt. Governor of Bengal to a Chief Commissioner in 1874. In the same year the Scheduled Districts Act 1874 was enacted to declare a few territories under Assam as scheduled areas.

Subsequently the Government of India Act 1919 under Section 52 A (2) empowered the Governor General in Council to declare any territory under British India as a backward tract. Under this provision nine tracts (a) Garo Hills district; (b) The British portion of Khasi and Jaintia Hills district other than the Shillong Municipality and cantonment; (c) The Mikir hills in Nowgong and Sibsagar districts; (d) The North Cachar hills in Cachar district; (e) The Naga hills district; (f) The Lushai Hills district; (g) The Sadia Frontier Tract; (h) Balipara Frontier Tract and (i) The Lakshimpur Frontier Tract) in the province of Assam were declared backward tracts.

The Government of India Act, 1935 replaced the terminology of Backward Tracts by Excluded Areas and Partially Excluded Areas. The basic difference in the governance of these two areas was that Excluded Areas were to be administered by the Governor himself in his discretion while Partially Excluded Areas were to be his special responsibilities meaning he was empowered to override the advice of the ministers, whereas in regard to the matters within the Governor's discretion, the ministry's advice was not required. Under Section 91(1) of the Government of India Act 1935, the Excluded Areas declared were: 1) The North East Frontier (Sadiya, Balipara, Lakhimpur Tracts); 2) The Naga Hills district; 3) The Lushai Hills District and 4) The North Cachar Hills subdivision of Cachar district while the areas declared as Partially Excluded were: 1) The Garo Hills district; 2) the Mikir hills (in Nowgong and Sibsagar districts) and 3) the British portion of Khasi and Jaintia Hills district other than the Shillong municipality and cantonment.

It will be useful to note that prior to the Government of India Act 1935, the Indian Statutory Commission 1930, known as the Simon Commission which examined the position prevailing in these areas observed: "The stage of development reached by the inhabitants of these areas prevents the possibility of applying to them methods of representation adopted elsewhere. They do not ask for self-determination, but for security of land tenure, freedom in the pursuit of the traditional methods of livelihood and the reasonable exercise of their ancestral customs".

Another evidence of the policy of seclusion relates to the inner line demarcation[3]. In 1873, Lord Curzon introduced the inner line demarcation under the Bengal Frontier Provision Act, 1873. Its rationale could be understood in the context of what Lord Curzon described as "the frontier system" of the British Empire. The frontier was classified into three categories: an administrative border, a frontier of active protection and an outer or advanced strategic frontier. The British established direct rule only in the areas of the "administrative" border.

Most of the present Assam which was resource rich in terms of promising new economy of tea, oil and coal reserves was the area within the administrative border of the colonial Assam. In the course of exploiting these potentials in the latter half of the 19th century, the colonial government established a modern legal and administrative system and property rights and thus created an enclave in alignment with the global capitalism. Beyond the inner line to the Frontier Tracts lay "the tribal areas" which Curzon described as the zone of "active protection". The Frontier Tracts comprising Sadiya, Balipra and Lakhimpur were described as "frontier areas inhabited by tribes in an early stage of development"[4] (as quoted in the Bordoloi Sub-Committee Report on the North East Frontier (Assam) Tribal and Excluded Areas). The British with their revenue maximization motivation had no interest in establishing modern institutions beyond the administrative border.

Post-Independence Era

The Constituent Assembly while considering the issue of designing the mechanism of governance for the hill areas of Assam appointed a Sub-Committee under the chairmanship of Gopinath Bordoloi, then Prime Minister of Assam on February 27, 1947 to report on a scheme of administration for the Excluded and Partially Excluded Areas of Assam. The Committee while preparing the Report kept in view: i) the colonial mechanism of governance that had evolved; (ii) aspirations and concerns of the 'tribal people' inhabiting the different hills of the then Assam, (iii) positive social customs and traditions of the tribals in these areas and (iv) the socio-economic and political conditions prevailing in these areas. The provisions of the Draft Sixth Schedule were based on the recommendations of the Sub-Committee. It was this Draft Sixth Schedule to the

Constitution of India on which the Constituent Assembly debates took place.

The debates in the Constituent Assembly reflected sharply divided views on the philosophy underlying the Sixth Schedule that laid down the administrative mechanism for the hill areas of Assam. Interestingly, both the supporters and opponents of the Sixth Schedule had similar concerns: how to address the problem of bringing the people of the hills and plains together. Huge differences arose however in their approach. One view upholding the philosophy underlying the Sixth Schedule recognized explicitly the distinctness of the tribals of Assam as compared to those in the rest of the country and argued for a different sort of scheme of governance for the hill areas of Assam securing the willing cooperation of the hill people. The other view reflecting fears and apprehensions was that instead of perpetuating the segregation and isolation of the hill people as is the case in the colonial period, the people of hills in Assam should be integrated with the rest of the country using the method of force, if need be. While explaining the background of the recommendations of the Advisory Sub-Committee constituted by the Constituent Assembly, Gopinath Bordoloi posed the dilemma confronting the Sub-Committee as: "Whether for the purpose of integration the methods of force, the methods of the use of Assam Rifles and the military forces, should be used, or a method should be used in which the cooperation of these people could be obtained for the purpose of governing these areas."[5] The Sixth Schedule was anchored on the latter course. The guiding principle of the Sixth Schedule as articulated by Nicholas Roy, one of the members of the Sub-Committee was to give a certain measure of self-government to these hill areas that would make the people of the hills feel that nothing would be forced on them to destroy their culture and customs. At the same time the laws and regulations to be made by the District Councils were subject to the control and assent of the Governor of Assam. This would thus be "the best method of allowing people to grow according to their culture and according to their genius and at the same time to become unified with the whole of India."[6] The Sixth schedule was designed towards this end and provided for District Councils for the Hills districts of Assam and Regional Councils for the pocket of the tribes other than the main tribe residing in the Naga Hills, in the North Cachar Hills and other hills, Regional Councils have limited powers, limited to their customary law and management of their land and villages.

Articulating eloquently the basic philosophy behind the Sixth Schedule, Dr. Ambedkar argued as follows: "The tribal people in areas other than Assam are more or less Hinduized, more or less assimilated with the civilization and culture of the majority of the people in whose midst they live. With regard to the tribals of Assam that is not the case. Their roots are still in their own civilization and their own culture. They have not adopted, mainly or in a large part, either the modes or the manners of the Hindus who surround them. Their laws of inheritance, laws of marriage, customs and so on are quite different from the Hindus. I think that is the main distinction which influenced us to have a different sort of scheme for Assam from the one we have provided for other territories."[7]

In contrast, several members of the Constituent Assembly expressed apprehensions and doubts about the provisions of the Sixth Schedule in regard to its efficacy in safeguarding the national interests. One member (Rohini Kumar Choudhury) went to the extent of saying: "This autonomous district is a weapon whereby steps are taken to keep the tribal people perpetually away from the non-tribal and the bond of friendship which we expect to come into being after the attainment of independence torn under."[8] Several other members also shared the view that the Sixth Schedule would stand as an impediment to the process of assimilation of the tribal and non-tribal people and to the process of nation building and national integration.

Addressing the fears and apprehensions of perpetuating segregation as voiced by some members, Dr. Ambedkar elaborated the following provisions of the Constitution which would serve as binding factors and those which would nullify the segregation. First, the executive authority of the Assam government would be exercised even in the areas included in the autonomous district councils. Dr. Ambedkar explained that the binding factor would rest in the fact that barring certain specified law making functions which would be exercised by the village panchayats or the Regional Councils or the District Councils, the authority of Parliament as well as that of the Assam Legislature would extend over the Regional Councils and the District Councils.

The other binding influence remains in the fact that the laws made by Parliament and the laws made by the Assam Legislature would automatically apply to the Regional/District Councils unless the Governor thinks otherwise. Dr Ambedkar further clarified that barring such functions as law-making in certain specified fields such as moneylending, land and so on, and barring certain judicial functions which were to be exercised in the village panchayats or the Regional Councils or the District Councils, the authority of Parliament as well as the authority of the Assam Legislature would extend over the Regional Councils and the District Councils; they were not immune from the authority of Parliament in the matter of law-making nor were they immune from the jurisdiction of the High Court or the Supreme Court. At another level, the tribal people having Regional Councils and District Councils would have representation in the Legislature of Assam as well as in Parliament so that they could play their part in making laws for Assam as also in making laws for the whole country. These cycles of participation were meant to unify the Regional Councils and the District Councils with the political life of the province as a whole.

3. Unique Institution of Self-Governance Under the Sixth Schedule

For the purpose of administration, the tribal population of a little above 104 million (2011) was grouped under two categories: (i) those who are inhabitants of North Eastern states (then Assam) and (ii) those who are inhabitants in states numbering nine other than North Eastern states. The Constitution of India has made provisions for the administration of the latter category under the Fifth Schedule to the Constitution of India while for the larger part of the former under the Sixth Schedule.

Article 244 (2) of the Constitution provides for the Sixth Schedule which shall apply to the administration of the tribal areas in the states of Assam, Meghalaya, Mizoram and Tripura. Para 20 of the Sixth Schedule lists the following tribal areas in three parts[9].

Part I (Assam)

1. The North Cachar Hills District

2. The Karbi Anglong District
3. The Bodoland Territorial Area District

Part II (Meghalaya)

1. Khasi Hills District
2. Jaintia Hills District
3. The Garo Hills District

Part II (A) (Tripura)

1. Tripura Tribal Areas District

Part III (Mizoram)

1. The Chakma District
2. The Mara District
3. The Lai District

For each of the Districts under the Sixth Schedule to the Constitution of India, there shall be an Autonomous District Council (ADC). If an autonomous district is inhabited by different Scheduled Tribes, the Governor may, by a public notification divide the areas inhabited by them into autonomous regions; for each autonomous region, there shall be a separate Regional Council (RC). The District Council or the Regional Council after its first constitution may make rules with the approval of the Governor with regard to inter-alia (a) the formation of subordinate local councils or boards and their procedure and conduct of their business; and (b) generally all matters pertaining to the administration of the district or the region as the case may be.

Each District Council or each Regional Council under the Sixth Schedule is a corporate body having perpetual succession and common seal. A District Council consists of no more than thirty members of which no more than four shall be nominated by the Governor while the rest elected on the basis of adult suffrage for a period of five years. The elected members of the District Council elect a Chairman and a Deputy Chairman who preside over the Council sessions.

The rules framed under the Sixth Schedule provide for an Executive Committee of a District Council.[10] The EC comprises the Chief Executive Member and two or more other members. The elected members of the District Council elect the Chief Executive while other members are appointed from amongst the members of the District Council by the Governor on the recommendations of the Chief Executive Member. The Executive Committee is like a cabinet system in a parliamentary democracy. It carries out the executive functions of the District Council. The Chief Executive Member allocates certain functions to each member. The member who is allocated financial affairs is in charge of the District Fund; he also prepares the budget of the District Council and gets it passed. The EC is collectively responsible for all executive decisions and policies as also implementation of development schemes in an autonomous district. The Chief Executive Member appoints a Secretary to the Executive Council who is not a member of the District Council. If and when the Chief Executive Member resigns, the Executive Committee gets dissolved. The civil administrations of an autonomous council as provided under the Sixth Schedule rest with two authorities, the Deputy Commissioner representing the state government and the Executive Committee the District Council.

Powers and Functions[11]

A. Legislative Powers of the District Councils and Regional Councils

The District Council/Regional Council shall have the power to make laws for its jurisdiction in regard to (a) allotment, occupation or use, or the setting apart of land, other than any land, which is reserved forest—reserved forest under the Assam Forest Regulation, 1891—for the purpose of agriculture, or grazing or residential or other non-agricultural purposes or for any purpose likely to promote the interest of the inhabitants of any village or town.It is, however provided that nothing in such laws shall prevent compulsory acquisition of any land for public purposes by the concerned state government in accordance with the law in force authorizing such acquisition; (b) the management of a forest not being a reserved forest; (c) the use of any canal or water course for the purpose of agriculture; (d) the regulation of the practice of Jhum or other forms of shifting cultivation; (e) the establishment of village or town committees of the councils and their powers; (f) any other matters relating to town or village administration, including village or town police and public health and sanitation; (g) the appointment or sucession of chiefs or headmen; (h) the inheritance of property; (i) marriage and divorce; and (j) social customs.

All laws by ADC/RC pertaining to the above subjects shall come into effect only after obtaining the Governor's assent.

B. Judicial Powers

The Regional and District Councils are conferred the power to constitute village councils or courts within their respective jurisdictions for the trial of suits and cases except those mentioned in the schedule between the parties all of whom belong to Scheduled Tribes. The District Council and the Regional Council shall exercise the powers of a court of appeal in respect of all suits and cases triable by a village council or court. The High Court shall have and exercise jurisdiction over the suits and cases specified by the Governor from time to time.

C. Executive Powers

The District Council for an autonomous district is given the power to establish, construct or manage primary schools, dispensaries, markets, cattle pounds, ferries, fisheries, roads, road transport, and waterways. With the prior approval of the Governor, the District Council may prescribe the language and the manner in which primary education shall be imparted.

D. Financial Powers

1. The Regional Council and District Council within their respective jurisdictions have the power to assess and collect revenue in respect of lands in accordance with the principles followed by the state government in assessing lands for the purpose of land revenue in the state generally.

2. The Regional Council and District Council have the power to levy and collect taxes on lands and buildings and tolls on persons residing within their respective areas.

3. The District Council for an autonomous district shall have the power to levy and collect the following taxes within its jurisdiction:

(a) Taxes on professions, trades, callings and employments.
(b) Taxes on animals, vehicles and boats.
(c) Taxes on the entry of goods into a market for sale therein and tolls on passengers and goods in ferries.
(d) Taxes for the maintenance of schools, dispensaries or roads.

4. Royalties accruing from the licenses or leases for the purpose of prospecting for or the extraction of minerals in respect of any area within an autonomous district shall be shared between the state government and the District Council as agreed upon between them. If any dispute arises in this regard, the matter shall be referred to the Governor and the decision of the Governor shall be final.

E. Regulatory Powers

The District Council has the power to make regulations for the control of moneylending and trading by non-tribals within the district. But regulations made shall come into effect only after the Governor accords his assent.

F. District and Regional Funds

A District Fund for each autonomous district and a Regional Fund for each autonomous region shall be constituted for crediting all moneys received by the District Council and Regional Council respectively. The Governor may make rules for the management fund as also procedure to be followed in respect of payment of payment into the above funds and withdrawal of moneys therefrom. The accounts of these funds shall be maintained in such form as the Comptroller and Auditor-General of India, with the approval of the President, may prescribe.

G. Autonomy

The Sixth Schedule provides that the Acts of the Parliament and the state legislature do not normally apply on the subjects assigned to the DCsand RCs (under Para 12B) and thus the DCs and RCs enjoy autonomy in their respective assigned spheres. Even in the subjects other than those assigned to them, the Governor is empowered to direct that any Act of Parliament or of the State Legislature shall not apply to an autonomous district or an autonomous region or shall apply subject to certain exceptions or modifications, as may be notified.

H. Role of Governor

In the scheme of the District Council as provided in the Sixth Schedule, the Governor of the state has been assigned numerous roles in its functioning. The Sixth Schedule has provided as many as 27 major or minor roles that the Governor of the state may be required to play in the functioning of a District Council[12].Just to illustrate, a few highly significant provisions can be mentioned. One such provision relates to empowering the Governor under paragraph 16 to dissolve a District Council or a Regional Council and to assume himself all the powers on the recommendation of a Commission appointed under paragraph 14 of the Schedule. Again, Para 16 (2) empowers the Governor to dissolve a District Council or a Regional Council and takes over all or any of the powers and functions for a certain period if any time the Governor is satisfied that the administration of the autonomous district or a region cannot be carried out in accordance with the provisions of the Sixth Schedule. The Governor is also empowered to alter laws or rules passed by the District Council if found violating the provisions of the Sixth Schedule. Thus the Sixth Schedule has placed the Governor as the head of the ADC/RC.

To sum up, the Sixth Schedule clearly laid down the manner of constituting the Regional Councils and District Councils, their powers and functions, the role of the Governor in their functioning, their relations with the state legislature and the contour of autonomy that they enjoy in self-governance.

4. Working of Autonomous Councils

The Regional and District Councils have been in operation for more than six decades (since 1952). They were subject to many limitations. Some serious limitations/challenges that they faced are highlighted below.

1. It is argued that the provisions of the Sixth Schedule accommodated the community process but the institutions created thereunder were subordinate to the state government. As such, they tended to derive their legitimacy mainly from the state process rather than the community process.[13] It appears that there has been an attitude of disharmony between the bureaucrats of the state government and the leadership and officials of the District Councils.

2. The provisions under the Sixth Schedule do not ensure financial independence of the Autonomous Councils. As a result, they have to depend on the respective state governments for their financial allocations.Several studies have noted that there has been reluctance on the part of the state government even to release their legitimate share. For example, one important source for the ADCs is grants-in aid under Article 275 of the Constitution. While the Union government releases the grants through the state government, the ADCs receive a part or the whole of the amount after a huge time lag.

3. Similarly, even from the shared sources such as royalty on licenses and leases granted by the state government for the purpose of prospecting for or extraction of minerals in certain areas within the District Council, District Councils often allege that the state government does not pay their share regularly. Obviously all this has an adverse impact on their performance in service delivery.

4. Even on the part of the autonomous councils, there is laxity in resource mobilization from the sources assigned to them. The ADCs are empowered to levy and collect taxes such as those on profession, trade callings and employment and vehicles. But they do not levy at all or even if they do, they do not enforce it effectively.

5. The relationship between the autonomous councils and the state government as laid down in the Sixth Schedule is not conformable to the efficient and accountable fund utilization. For example, there is no provision for coordination of the activities of autonomous councils and the state government. Similarly, the state is vested with the power to sanction grants and loans for development schemes of the autonomous councils but not with the power to assess and review their working. One recent study has observed in this regard as "Within the Councils, over a period of time, due to large development funds available, a nexus has emerged between the neo-rich middle class, rich traders, contractors and bureaucrats who have emerged from within the tribal society of the region. This emerging socio-economic power structure in the tribal areas does not allow the benefits of the Sixth Schedule to percolate down to the weaker sections of the society."[14]

6. Under para 7 (2), the Governor may make rules for the management of the District Fund/Regional Fund. Since such rules

do not seem to have been made, various financial irregularities have been committed by the Councils, grants-in aids have not been properly used and in several autonomous councils even the audit has failed to curb extravagances and wastage of public funds.

7. Autonomous District Councils have not been able to evolve an institutional mechanism for overall development of the district.

8. As for gender justice, no political space has been given for women in the autonomous district councils.

9. And finally while the Sixth Schedule could ensure decentralization at the district level, it did not provide for decentralization to percolate below.

5. Comparison Between District Councils and Panchayati Raj Institutions

The 73rd Amendment of the Constitution, 1992 which mandated the establishment of three-tier panchayats at the village level, intermediate and district levels included the Eleventh Schedule that listed 29 subjects coming under the jurisdiction of panchayats[15].

The legislature of a state is vested with powers to endow the panchayats with such powers and authority as may be necessary to enable them to function as institutions of self-government such as preparation of plans and their implementation for economic development and social justice regarding the 29 subjects listed in the Eleventh Schedule.

Twenty-nine subjects that come within the jurisdiction of the panchayats as under the Eleventh Schedule are: (1) Agriculture, including agricultural extension; (2) Land improvement, implantation of land reforms; (3) Minor irrigation, water management and watershed development; (4) Animal husbandry, dairying and poultry; (5) Fisheries; (6) Social forestry and farm forestry; (7) Minor forest produce; (8) Small-scale industries including food processing industries; (9) Khadi, village and cottage industries; (10) Rural housing; (11) Drinking water; (12) Fuel and fodder; (13) Roads, culverts, bridges, ferries, waterways and other means of communication; (14) Rural electrification, including distribution of electricity; (15) Non-conventional energy sources; (16) Poverty alleviation programme; (17) Education including primary and secondary schools; (18) Technical training and vocational education; (19) Adult and non-formal education; (20) Libraries; (21) Cultural activities; (22) Markets and fairs; (23) Health and sanitation, including hospitals, primary health centres and dispensaries; (24) Family welfare; (25) Women and child development; (26) Social welfare, including welfare of the handicapped and mentally retarded; (27) Welfare of the weaker sections, and in particular, of the sccheduled Castes and the Scheduled Tribes; (28) Public distribution system and (29) Maintenance of community assets.

Two important distinctions between the powers and functions of panchayats and those of autonomous districts and autonomous regions are: First, in the case of the latter, the Sixth Schedule of the Constitution directly assigned the powers and functions while in the case of the former, the legislature of a state is vested with the powers to transfer the subjects listed in the Eleventh Schedule of the Constitution. Second, the powers given to the autonomous councils are mostly of a regulatory nature while those of panchayats mostly relate to economic and social development.

One can argue that the functions and responsibilities as listed under the Eleventh Schedule are essentially anchored on the theory of decentralization. The theory of decentralization holds that a decentralized system enhances efficiency and minimizes transaction costs in public service provisioning, encourages innovation by inducing intergovernmental competition and ensures greater participation of the people in the decision-making process[16]. Decentralization as enshrined in the Constitution gives the ownership of inextinguishable constitutional powers[17]. Ownership of powers is important for the sub-national governments as it enables them to exercise unfettered choice in their assigned domain and provide public services according to citizens' preferences.

In the three-tier panchayati system, powers percolate down to the village level while in autonomous councils the powers are concentrated at the district level leaving limited scope for empowerment at the grassroot level. At another level, women's representation is neglected in the autonomous councils while there is reservation of seats for women in panchayat bodies.

The 73[rd]amendment also provides for the constitution of a State

Finance Commission every fifth year to review the financial position of panchayats and to recommend to the Governor as to

(a) The principles which should govern (i) the distribution between the state and the panchayats of the net proceeds of the taxes, duties, tolls, and fees leviable by the state which may be divided between the panchayats at all levels their respective shares of such proceeds; (ii) the determination of the taxes, duties, tolls and fees which may be assigned to or appropriated by the panchayats; (iii) the grants-in-aid to the panchayats from the consolidated fund of the state.
(b) The measures needed to improve the financial position of the panchayats.
(c) Any other matter referred to the Finance Commission in the interests of sound finance of the panchayats.

When the powers, scope of function and financial support as provided to the panchayats under various provisions of the 73rd amendment are compared with those provided to the Autonomous District Councils under the Sixth Schedule, the following observations can be made. First, the ADCs have more regulatory powers while panchayats have more developmental functions. Second, Autonomous Councils are to depend hugely on the state government for the exercise of developmental functions while a large number of developmental functions fall within the operational jurisdiction of panchayats. Third, in several cases, the scope of operations is higher for the panchayats. For example, primary schools come within the jurisdiction of Autonomous District Councils while the panchayat's functional jurisdiction extends to secondary schools. Similarly, Autonomous District Councils may establish dispensaries while primary health centres and hospitals also fall within the operational jurisdiction of panchayats. Fourth, Even though the sources of finance for autonomous councils appear to be more diversified, the state government's intervening role squeeze their actual access. In the case of panchayats, the establishment of a quinquennial Finance Commission provides a useful safeguard for financial viability.

Further, panchayati bodies have an edge over the Autonomous Councils in regard to their dissolution. In the case of panchayats, the 73rd Amendment stipulates that if the panchayat bodies are dissolved, they must be reconstituted within a period of six months from the date of dissolution. In the case of autonomous councils, fresh elections shall be held for its reconstitution subject to the approval of the state legislature within a period not exceeding twelve months.

In short, comparing carefully the provisions of the Sixth Schedule with the 73rd Amendment of the Constitution, Roy Burman concluded: "While the Damocles' sword of the state power is moving closer and closer to the Autonomous Councils, a liberalization process has been set in motion in respect of panchayati bodies."[18] He further added: "If the panchayati bodies under the Amendment Act are not introduced in the Sixth Schedule and (also Fifth Schedule areas where existing panchayats have limited statutorily laid down development functions) these areas will enjoy less power of self-government (in the development aspect) than the rest of the country."[19]

6. Concluding Observations

The autonomous councils could be viewed as an institutional innovation of effecting self-rule of tribal peoples with distinct customs and traditional institutions devolving powers under the Constitution. These have "succeeded in bringing about transformation of the traditional tribal society into a legally defined and structured one, fit for having a representative form of government in a formal constitutional way at the district level and in some cases at the village level."[20]

But over time the Sixth Schedule has lost its relevance in its present form. The autonomous councils had come into existence in 1952. North East India had witnessed many changes since then. Three hill states, Meghalaya, Mizoram and Nagaland had been carved out of Assam. All these states are predominantly tribal. The main motivating factor to provide for autonomous councils for the tribal districts of erstwhile Assam was to protect the interests of the tribal population inhabiting these areas and to protect and preserve their customs and traditional institutions. It was thought that a legislature dominated by Plains people might not fulfil all these needs. Now that the legislatures function mostly with the tribals, even if they do not belong to a homogeneous tribe, there is no room for earlier apprehensions. Therefore, autonomous councils in its present form have become both redundant and irrelevant.

Another reality then was that tribals residing in remote and isolated areas were not at all integrated with the rest of the country. The situation has drastically altered since. With improved connectivity in terms of road and communication ensuring higher connectivity and mobility, much higher level of interactions at the institutional level as well as at the inter-personal level, the extent of remoteness and isolation has receded considerably.

At another level, the three markets, viz. commodity, labour and money markets have penetrated all over the country including the autonomous districts, to a varying degree though. Even the tribal population residing in the autonomous districts has been participating in these markets to an extent. In this sense local commodity, labour and money markets have been integrated to some degree with the regional and national markets. To gain more from market integration, market compliant institutions are called for. This makes a case for a reappraisal of the institutional design under the Sixth Schedule. What is more, while market integration is in progress, the inner line permit which was introduced by the colonial government as a way of fencing tea plantations and other capital investments against the marauding raids of "barbarians" acts as impediments to maximizing benefits from market dynamism as well as removal of segregation of the tribal areas from the rest of the country.[21]

As we have noted above, the autonomous councils have been functioning under several constraints and have not been able to deliver the desired outcomes.We have also noted that the panchayati bodies as provided under the 73rd Amendment have a distinct edge over the present form of autonomous councils in several respects, e.g. larger thrust on economic operations, gender representation, higher financial independence, decentralization to the village level, etc.

While a long history of tribal struggle for identity assertion as also the need for the tribal society to evolve according to its own genius cannot be ignored, it should be possible to synthesize the positive features of the institutional arrangement under the Sixth

Schedule and those under the 73rd Amendment of the Constitution and their respective functioning and put in place a more appropriate Sixth Schedule[22] which could truly emerge as decentralized institutions of governance.

NOTES

1. Planning Commission, GoI, (1997), High Level Commission, Transforming the Noth East-Tackling Backlogs in Basic Minimum Services and Infrastctural Needs, p. 1.
2. Only in December 2004, it was announced in both Houses of Parliament that the revamped NEC in the pursuance of an Expert Committee was going to have the Minister, Development of North Eastern India as its Chairman even as the NEC was all set to activate its role as security agency. Earlier in 2002 the NEC Act was amended to enable the NEC to function as the regional planning body and to formulate specific projects and schemes that would benefit two or more states. *The Assam Tribune*, December 7, 2004.
3. Its motivation and for related details, see Roy Burman, B.K., Prefatory Introduction in Alexander Mackenzie (2003), *The North East Frontier of India*, Mittal Publications, New Delhi, pp. 4-6.
4. As quoted in the Bordoloi Sub-Committee Report on the North East Frontier (Assam) Tribal and Excluded Areas.
5. *Constituent Assembly of India*, Vol. IX, Tuesday, September 6, 1949.
6. Ibid.
7. Ibid.
8. Ibid.
9. Manipur with its one-third population in the hill districts was seeking Sixth Schedule status for its hill districts. While it was not conceded, an Act of Parliament, viz.The Manipur (Hill Areas) District Act, 1971 was passed and it provided for establishment of six Autonomous District Councils in Manipur. In accordance with the powers vested in the Governor, six Autonomous District Councils were constituted on February 14, 1972. They were: (1) Churachandpur ADC; (2) Chandel ADC; (3) Senapati ADC; (4) Sadar Hills ADC; (5) Tamenglong ADC and (6) Ukhrul ADC. They do not enjoy any real powers and have several regulatory powers subject to state control. As for development functions, with highly limited financial powers they are greatly dependent on the state government.
10. For detailed discussion on the constitution and functions, see Prasad, R.N., Analysis of the Framework and Operation of the Sixth Schedule to the Constitution of India in L.S. Gassah (ed.) (1997), *Autonomous*

District Council, Omsons Publications, New Delhi, pp. 60-62.

11. It should be noted that the Sixth Schedule to the Constitution (Amendment) Act, 1995 assigned additional powers to the North Cachar Hills Autonomous Council and the Karbi Anglong Autonomous Council. It may be mentioned that the North Cachar Hills sub-division of the United Mikirand Cachar Hills was upgraded to district in 1970. The Mikir Hills District section was renamed as Karbi Anglong in 1976.

    Similarly, the Sixth Schedule to the Constitution (Amendment) Act, 2003 assigned additional powers to the Bodoland Territorial Council to make laws with respect to forty subjects.
12. See, Sarmah, Bhupen (2014), *Sixth Schedule to the Constitution of India: A Preliminary Note* (Mimeo).
13. See, Roy Burman, B.K. (1997), op. cit., p. 22.
14. Sarmah Bhupen, op. cit.
15. A large part of North East India is governed under the Sixth Schedule of the Constitution. The Panchayats (Extension to the Scheduled Areas) Act, 1996 extends the 73rd Amendment to the Fifth Schedule areas. Meghalaya, the Sixth Schedule areas in Assam, Mizoram and Nagaland fall outside the purview of the 73rd Amendment.
16. Bretton, A. (1995), *Competitive Governments: An Economic Politics and Public Finance*, New York: Cambridge University Press.
17. Bretton, A. (2000), "Federalism and Decentralization: Ownership Rights and Superiority of Federalism", *Publius: The Journal of Federalism*, Vol. 30, No. 2, pp. 1-16.
18. Roy Burman, B.K. (1997), Sixth Schedule of the Constitution in L.S. Gassah (ed), *The Autonomous District Councils*, Omsons Publications, New Delhi, p. 30.
19. Roy Burman, op. cit., p. 31.
20. Ganguly, J.B., (1997), The Relevance of the Autonomous District Councils, in L.S. Gassah (ed), *The Autonomous District Councils*, Omsons Publications, New Delhi, p. 332.
21. For detailed discussion of the issue, see, Baruah, Sanjib, "Dividing Line", *Indian Express*, New Delhi Edition, October 3, 2014.
22. For similar views see Roy Burman, B.K., op. cit., p. 32.

3

North East as the Gateway to South East Asia: Big Dream and Home Truths*

A recent study[1] argued that development initiatives in North East India lacked a well-articulated policy framework. Two paradigms dominated the Government of India's North East India policy. One relates to overstress on security/strategic consideration rather than on development efforts in a development perspective. The other relates to the minimum intervention in traditional systems and institutions of the hill economy, which is what has led to their non-compatibility with the functioning of the market system. Since the mid-1990s, however, uninterrupted disorder and its relation with persistent underdevelopment of the North East began to find a place in the mainstream collective psyche as reflected in the growing national level debate, deliberations and discourse as well as pronouncement of special economic packages for the North East economic development.

With the articulation of 'Look East Policy' in the early 1990s, a new vision for the North East as a gateway to dynamic South East Asian economies is taking shape. The underlying thrust on 'A New Asia' makes one think of 'a New North East' too. A vision or a development framework for North East India is absolutely necessary simply because there was none in the past. It is now envisaged that "with the recent softening of geo-political rigidities following understandings with China, then Myanmar and, most

---

* Published in *Man and Development* (2006), Vol. 28, No. 2, June—revised version of the Presidential address delivered at the Seventh Annual Conference of the North Eastern Economic Association held at Rajiv Gandhi (Arunachal) University.

especially, with Bangladesh, the North East is no more a burdensome peripheral region somewhere out there, but is poised once again to resume its dynamic role as a bridge to the booming economies of South East Asia and South West China to mutual benefit."[2] The economic rationale that lies behind this vision is: The landlocked North East in the aftermath of partition will have wider market access, that too with some of the fastest growing South East Asian and East Asian economies. This market integration would boost trade with those countries with the North East serving as the gateway. Trade would thus serve as a driver of rapid economic development of the region.

Extensive deliberations and discourses have followed in different forums resulting in the emergence of a considerable literature in the past few years. Policy makers, economists, political scientists, journalists and others have all made contributions on this issue. A cursory look at these contributions suggests that by and large, non-economists such as journalists and historians, are rather euphoric about it while economists seem somewhat cautious in their expectation of North East linkage with South East Asia as driver of its economic resurgence.

This chapter attempts to take a close look at the proposition of North East India's integration with East and South East Asian countries and the possible gains to the region. It addresses itself to the following questions: How does market integration work? How did internationalization of the Assam economy in the past work and what lessons did we learn from such experiences in the past? How have informal and formal trade flows with South East Asia in the recent past impacted the North East economies? What are the required facilitating policy environment and physical infrastructure for trade linkage to yield gains? What initiatives should the North East take to maximize the economic gains as and when the vision of its integration with the South East Asia becomes a reality?

How Does Market Integration Work?

Market integration leads to both trade creation, i.e. the emergence of new trade and industry and trade destruction, i.e. the exit of inefficient activities due to competition from more efficient competitors from the integrating countries. This process stimulates specialization depending on the respective region's comparative advantage and eventually higher growth and welfare through scale economies resulting from a lager market linkage. This is the theoretical reasoning that has spurred regional integration in different parts of the world. Notable examples are the European Union and Association of East Asian Nations (ASEAN).

The inspired advocacy for the integration of the North Eastern region with the dynamic South East Asian countries could be anchored on this theoretical postulation. It is empirically true that "Opening up to international trade has helped many countries grow far more quickly than they would otherwise have done. International trade helps economic development when a country's exports drive its economic growth. Export led growth was the centrepiece of the industrial policy that enriched much of Asia and left millions of people there far better off."[3]

What Do We Learn from the Past Internationalization of Assam's Economy?

Assam has a long history of internationalization. Broadly speaking, Assam, for that matter, North East passed through three phases of internationalization of its economy and society: (i) ancient Assam till the end of the Ahom rule; (ii) colonial period and (iii) post-independence period with two sub periods—pre and post-reform (1991) periods. But the nature, characteristics and impact on the economy in different phases were widely different.

The first phase began with the establishment of the Ahom kingdom by Sukapha, the first Ahom conqueror of Assam (a Tai Shan from Burma) in 1228, and the Ahom rule continued uninterrupted for almost 600 years till the British wrested it from the Ahom rulers in 1826. This period was characterized by political stability.

Historical evidences suggest that apart from the Patkai route through which Sukapha with his men and materials entered Assam, there were several other routes to China via Burma, Bhutan and Tibet through which ancient Assam had trade access. There were also many other passes through which the northern mountains of Assam led to China, Afghanistan, and the West through Bhutan and Tibet.[4]

The trade that took place through these routes was considerable. Ray (2005) on the basis of historical evidences summed up the degree of openness of ancient Assam as follows: "Assam's and for that matter, North East India's prosperity was closely related to the high level of development of its local handicrafts, natural products, silk and other textile products, forest products, etc. as well as its easy access to the different parts of India in the west to Myanmar and South West China in the east, to the north through tribal intermediaries, and to the south through a direct sea route".[5]

"North East India's trade with Tibet was disrupted whenever the Chinese asserted their role in the latter. Since their occupation of Lasha, they closed Tibet to the inhabitants of India, and the inhabitants of the neighbouring countries like Bhutan ... Such sanctions undermined border trade. Gradual expansion of the Muslim rule to the North Eastern part of India in the medieval period did the same damage to trade".[6]

It should be noted, however, that although the Ahoms encouraged trade, political considerations received precedence over trade. In reality, the external trade and its pattern were essentially governed by the absolute domestic requirement, on the one hand and the isolationist policy of Ahom rulers, on the other.[7]

The second phase of internalization began with the British colonization in 1826. The Charter of 1833 that stripped the East India Company monopoly over the British trade to China led to the formation of 'The Assam Company' with virtual monopoly over tea production in Assam during the first decade. With the success of the company in tea production and government patronage, tea plantation received a huge boost. But the important point to note is that the growth and expansion of the tea industry was almost entirely dependent on the external market.

Alongside the tea industry, a few other resource-based industries such as the coal, petroleum and plywood industry also came up. Infrastructure was essentially built to give support to the modern industry sector mostly catering to the external market. For example, the railway system that was developed in the 19th century did not link many important centres of habitation. Similarly, the total investment in the organized economic sector of Assam was estimated at Rs. 200 million during 1881-1901 and the average annual investment at Rs. 10 million.[8] But the investment and infrastructure that came up by the end of the 19th century bypassed the traditional sector.

At another level, largely due to labour shortages in Assam and partly due to aversion of indigenous people to take up plantation-related wage employment, the tea industry essentially had to rely "on the famine-stricken tribal areas of the rest of India for steady labour supply".[9] The inputs and other requirements for the plantation sector were also procured from large suppliers from outside the state.

The overall result had been that the tea and other resource-based modern industry of Assam had limited linkage with the domestic local commodity, factor and money markets. In the process the tea industry that largely catered to the international market induced minimal investment in forward and backward linkage based industries in the state while the surplus accruing to the industry was ploughed back in the industry or siphoned off elsewhere. In essence, investment, consumption, output and employment multipliers did not work to the advantage of the domestic economy since the modern economic sector had negligible interactions with the traditional sector. On the top of it, import of cheap industrial products from Great Britain undermined the indigenous handloom and handicraft industries, the mainstay of the Assam economy.

The important point to stress is that the internationalization of the Assam economy with the growth of the export market oriented tea industry did not emerge as the driver of its growth and prosperity. The other point to note is that this phase of internationalization of the Assam economy was characterized by a basic difference from that of the earlier phase. The earlier phase witnessed a much closer link of the pattern of traded goods with the indigenous sectors of the state economy while the later phase functioned almost in isolation from the traditional economic activities of the state. As a result, the gains from trade were far more perceptible in the earlier phase.

While this phase continued till India's independence and partition, the new phase began with the incalculable damage caused to the North East region by disruption of its traditional transport and communication links and the resultant trade links. As the Shukla Commission noted, "Partition further isolated an already geo-politically sequestered region. It was left with over 4,500 kms of external frontier with Bhutan, China, Myanmar but no more than the 22 km connection with the Indian heartland through the tenuous Siliguri corridor, the Gateway to the North East. The very considerable market disruption, socio-economic distancing and retardation that resulted has not been adequately appreciated or compensated".[10]

With foreign countries on all sides[11] of the North East region, one could expect robust trade ties with the neighbouring countries. But that depends on political relations and policy environment.

The erstwhile East Pakistan and now Bangladesh is crucially important for the North East's inland and surface transport link. But the country's political relations with it was one of overt or covert hostility, except for a brief period following the independence of Bangladesh. More important, Bangladesh poses a demographic threat to the region even if it is not a security threat to India.

On the north east border remain Tibet (now the Tibet Autonomous Region of China) and Myanmar. The McMahon line that the British drew as boundary between British India in the North Eastern Frontier Tracts (Arunachal Pradesh) and Tibet was never accepted by China. It still remained the bone of contention between India and China. The 1962 India-China war reinforced China's hostility towards India.

India-Myanmar relations from the beginning were friendly since the early 1950s. Even with the military government of Myanmar (State Law and Order Revolutionary Council or SLORC) India's relations with Myanmar have improved since 1993. Similarly, India's relation with Bhutan are friendly, the latter being India's protectorate.

Given the political relationship with the neighbouring countries as above, the actual realization of trade potentials is constrained. There are many other constraints as well. The most important among them are policy environment at home and enabling conditions such as supporting trade infrastructure and transport and communication connectivity with the possible trading partners.

The inward looking policy that India pursued in the post-independence period never viewed trade as a driver of the economy. The trade that took place during this period was mostly with the developed Western countries for the simple reason that India's thrust was to develop the key and basic heavy industries and the required plant and equipment as well as basic raw materials were to be imported from developed countries. Not many trade possibilities were explored with the neighbourng Asian countries during this period. Nevertheless, the North East continued to have informal trade with its neighbours. For example, illegal border trade with Myanmar is said to comprise goods like precious metals, wood, spices, vehicles, consumer goods such as electronic goods, fabrics and drugs.

The North East's formal and informal trade with Bangladesh through Assam (Mankachar and Karimganj routes), Tripura (Agartala) and Meghalaya (Western Meghalaya-Baghmara and Chibbari) largely comprised farm and animal husbandry products, agro-processed products like sugar and manufacturing products such as medicines, cosmetics, motor parts and bicycles as exports and jewellery, electronic goods and jute and cotton textiles as imports from Bangladesh.[12] Interestingly, very few of the manufacturing exports relate to products of local origin. What is more, while the export of bicycles and bicycle parts to Bangladesh was thriving, the only bicycle factory at Guwahati was closed down and the export requirement was met from elsewhere despite high transport costs. It is also noteworthy that some of these trade routes facilitated informal import of hashish, heroin and other narcotic drugs, foreign exchange and unskilled labour from Bangladesh.

How India's 'Look East Policy' Shaped a Vision for the North East?

With the shift in policy framework towards the market driven system and integration of the Indian economy with the global economy in the early 1990s, external trade came to play an important role. With it followed the Narasimha Rao government's articulation of 'Look East Policy'. The successive Indian governments supported the policy and built on it. It is in this process that a new vision was shaped for the North East region to serve as the gateway to South East and East Asia. Jairam Ramesh forcefully argued, "...political integration with the rest of India and economic integration with East and South East Asia particularly is certainly one direction that this region must be looking to as a new way of development".[13]

A number of bilateral and multilateral agreements have provided the foundation for India's growing sub-regional cooperation with South East Asia. The Ganga-Mekong subregion and the Bangladesh-China-India-Myanmar, Sri Lanka Thailand Economic Cooperation (BIMST-EC-December 1997) are notable examples of multilateral relations. The Kunming Initiative[14] of 1999 in which ASEAN and India stressed deeper integration of ASEAN and Indian economies also led to the Bangladesh-China-India-Myanmar Regional Economic Forum (BCIM Forum).

India is now one of the four summit level partners of ASEAN, the other three being China, Japan and Korea. It has signed a free trade agreement (FTA) each with Thailand and Singapore. There are plans to do so with Indonesia, Malaysia and Brunei by 2011 and with the remaining ASEAN countries—the Philippines, Cambodia, Laos, Myanmar and Vietnam by 2016. Furthermore, former Prime Minister Dr. Manmohan Singh made a proposal at the third ASEAN-India summit for an Asian economic community including ASEAN, China, Japan, Korea and India.

The most significant bilateral relations from the perspective of cross border trade potential between the North East region and its eastern neighbour is India's relations with Myanmar. A Border Trade Agreement with Myanmar, which was signed on January 21, 1994, came into effect from April 12, 1995 when Indo-Myanmar border trade was officially declared open at Moreh in Manipur. The 160-km Tamu-Kaewa-Kalemo road constructed with Rs. 90 crore by the Border Road Organization as India's gift to Myanmar holds out promises. While inaugurating the road in 2001, the then Minister, External Affairs observed: "The natural movement of goods, people and services for the North East is not through Calcutta" and stressed the importance of "opening up the natural outlet of the North East". Expressing similar enthusiasm, Myanmar's Construction Minister, Major General Saw Tun said that the "road will become a vital section of the designated Asian Highway running from Singapore to Istanbul passing through Myanmar and India". Subsequently, the Indian government opened its second trade route with

Myanmar through Zokhawahar (Rih) located in Mizoram. In December 2003 there was a meeting of the Foreign Ministers of Myanmar, Thailand and India in Delhi to discuss the technical and funding issues relating to the 1,400 km transnational highway.[15]

But India has no such agreement yet with Bangladesh that has a long border with the North East. The economic cooperation with Bangladesh is expected to hugely benefit the North East. The Indo-Bangla Joint Commission has not been able to settle the thorny socio-political and border issues that exist between the two countries and thus pave the way for economic cooperation. The proposed Indo-Bangla Free Trade Agreement is expected to strengthen economic cooperation between the two countries. India has also improved its economic relations with China, the other important neighbour of North East India.

What Kind of Connectivity is Required for the North East to be the Gateway to East and South East Asia?

It is in the above backdrop of trading environment that the prospect of North East India's gains from India's 'Look East Policy' should be considered. It is important to note, however, that while a favourable trading environment is an enabling condition, physical connectivity assumes a critical role in the realization of gains from trade.

Revolution in information and communication technology (ICT) has drastically changed the very concept of connectivity. It has reduced distances and made possible the dispersion of business operations to take advantage of differentials in wages, natural and other resource endowments thus bringing down dramatically the production cost.

Even so, the physical connectivity has to accompany ICT connectivity. For, goods have to be shipped to the market destination by water, road, and railway or by air, rather by inter-modal transport, to use the jargon of the world of transportation to emphasize the integration of different modes of transport system. For a landlocked North East, intermodal transport would require the integration of road, railways, air and water.

It is envisaged that the reconstruction of the Stilwell Road (also known as Burma Road)[16] constructed during the Second World War period (1942-45) as Trans-Asian Express Way together with

Trans-Asian Railway could link Myanmar, South West Chinese trading centres and the entire South East Asian region.

Goswami and Gogoi[17] elaborated the scheme as follows: Stilwell Road constructed during the Second World War period (1942-45) connected India with Myanmar and China. It passed through Ledo, Lekhapani and Pangshu Pass in India, Myitkyina and Lashio in Myanmar, and Kunming, the capital of Yunnan province of South China. The stretch from Ledo to Myitkyina, 160-232 kms, requires rebuilding while from Myitkyina to Kunming is well developed. Lashio is well connected by rail and road with provinces of south and central Myanmar bordering Laos, Thailand, Malaysia and Singapore. Indian exports by the Stilwell Road could move from the easternmost border of Arunachal Pradesh to Kunming in South China (1,736 kms) in two days, to Tangoon in Myanmar in two and a half days, to Bangkok in Thailand in four days and to Singapore in six days.

Another possible route is: if the Tamu-Kalewa-Kalemy road (160 kms) that was opened in 2001 is extended by 250-300 kms to join the Stilwell Road at Bhamo in Myanmar, which is well connected with Kunming. This road could also be extended from Manipur by 300 kms through southern Assam to the Bangladesh border.[18] If this happens, as compared to Kolkata port, Chittagong port would be within a shorter distance from Agartala, Guwahati or Shillong.

If such connectivity could be put in place, the operationalization of South Asian Free Trade Area (SAFTA) from January 2006 as agreed upon by the leaders of the South Asian Association for Regional Cooperation (SAARC) in January 2004 would open up great possibilities for the development of the North East. In such a scenario, the region "could emerge as a business transit centre for both the SAARC and ASEAN groups of nations."[19]

The above is a neat outline of physical network that could enable the North East to truly emerge as the gateway to the dynamic East and South East Asain economies. Once rebuilt, Stilwell Road could be advantageous for India's trade with China. Today, India's trade with China makes a long and laborious 6,000 km trip through the Straits of Malacca while Stilwell Road could shorten the trip to less than one third. But the fact is, as Jairam Ramesh puts it, "The approximately 1,700-km-long road (of which about 60 kms are in

India, about 1,000 kms in Myanmar and the rest in China) still exists but in a state of extreme dilapidation."[20] Yet the implementation of such a scheme would encounter hurdles of the following type.

First of all, the Government of India's commitment to the vision of North East India's economic integration with its geographically, historically and ethnically closer East and South East Asian countries has to be firm for the simple reason that the capital cost involved is enormous apart from several other hurdles. But India's participation in the Asian highway does not reflect the centrality of the North East in its scheme of integration of India with South East Asia and beyond. Nor does one see any initiatives on the part of the GoI to take up the reconstruction of the Stilwell Road. On the contrary, the GoI has shown greater interest in building a 1,360 km trilateral highway from Moreh in Manipur to MaeSoi in Thailand via Bajan in Myanmar "taking a more southern route away from the emerging Yunnan-Northern Myanmar-South East Asia corridor."[21]

The Indian government's hesitation to project the North East in its Look East Policy can be traced to five factors. First, overstress on security/strategic consideration rather than a development perspective in development efforts was all along one of the dominant paradigms of the Indian government in dealing with North East India in the post-independent period.[22] Second, prolonged and uninterrupted militancy led by groups like the National Socialist Council of Nagaland (NSCN), United Liberation Front of Assam (ULFA), People's Liberation Army, National Democratic Front of Bodoland and so on weighs heavily in rebuilding the Stilwell Road across the thick hills and mountains of Myanmar. This could turn out to be a haven for numerous militant groups of the North East and thus involve a high security risk. Third, aggressive economic expansion of China to South East Asian countries[23] like Myanmar is perceived as a threat in terms of flooding the Indian market with cheap Chinese goods. Fourth, it is also apprehended that the road could facilitate import of vices such as drugs and aids/HIVs. Finally, the mainland India's trade with South East Asian countries has traditionally been by sea. Even now, it is cheaper and easier to trade with these countries by sea rather than by land.

While some of these concerns are not entirely unfounded, long run gains from integrating the North East with East and South East

Asia heavily outweigh the risks involved. As expressed aptly by sociologist, Anthony Giddens: "The positive embrace of risk is the very essence of that energy which creates wealth in a modern economy. Risk is the mobilizing dynamic of a society bent on change, that wants to determine its own future rather than leaving it to religion, tradition or the vagaries of nature."[24]

What Look East Policy Meant to the North East So Far?

One can observe a wide divergence between the official rhetoric of the North East as the centre in the 'Look East Policy' and the facts that have unfolded themselves. Rajiv Sikri, former Secretary (East), Ministry of Foreign Affairs, Government of India said: "The 'Look East Policy' envisages the North Eastern region not as the periphery of India, but as the centre of a thriving and integrated economic space linking two dynamic regions with a network of highways, railways, pipelines, transmission lines crisscrossing the region."[25] Against this enthusiastic formulation, one should recall the GoI initiatives so far as flagged above and the trade statistics below.

With the outward looking policy, India's foreign trade shot up to US $140 billion by 2003 from below US $ 40 billion in the early 90s. Foreign trade as a ratio to GDP rose to more than 23% in 2003 from 12% in the early 1990s. With it also rose developing countries' as well as Asia's share in India's trade (Table 1). About one quarter of India's foreign trade is with Asia. North East neighbours' share in India's trade also more than trebled since 1992-93 though it is still very small and far below the potential.

Table 1: India's Trade with Asia and North East Neighbours*

India's Total Trade (US $ b)	29.24	40.42	76.49	140.49
Percentage Share of	1987-88	1992-93	1997-98	2003-04(P)
Developing Countries	16	21.1	26.1	30.3
Asia	12	16.5	19.9	24.2.
SAARC	1.3	2.3	2.4	3.3
NE Neighbours	1.7	2.6	4.6	8.0

*North East neighbours include Bhutan, Nepal, Bangladesh, China and Thailand.

Source: Sushil Khanna, (2004), "Will 'Look East' Policy Usher an Era of Growth and Prosperity?" Paper presented at the SENISEAS Forum "Towards a New Asia: Transnationalism and North East India", Guwahati, September 10-11, 2004.

What is noteworthy is that while India's trade with North East neighbours witnessed a dramatic rise from 1.7% to 8%, the trade through the Manipur-Myanmar route has remained small and insignificant at a mere 0.49% of India's trade with Myanmar in 2001-02 (Table 2). It only suggests that the bulk of increase in trade has been shipped through traditional maritime routes. In other words, India's booming trade with its eastern neighbours in the wake of the regime of Preferential Trade Arrangements with SAARC/SAPTA members (50% less custom duty levied on import) in the 90s and Free Trade Agreements with Nepal, Bangladesh, Sri Lanka, Myanmar and Thailand has not been hindered[26] by non-opening up of more North East borders or non-development of continental trade route with its neighbours through the North East. In fact, it has almost bypassed the North East.

Table 2: Indo-Myanmar Border Trade (Through the Moreh Route)

Rs. Million

Year	*Export*	*Import*	*Total*
1998-99	50.6	37.4	88.0
1999-2000	32.6	36.8	69.4
2000-01	52.9	1.9	54.8
2001-02	12.5	82.9	95.4

Source: Government of Manipur website as presented by Sushil Khanna (2004): See Table 1

The regions that have gained are the hinterlands of Chennai, Vizag and Kolkata port on the eastern side. It is hardly surprising that with closed borders, open ports and absence of proper infrastructure and connectivity, North East India is not part of India's trade expansion strategy with the east.[27] It means that the possibility of the North East serving as the entrepot for the entire hinterland of India is nowhere in sight.

Is North East Ready?

Having said this, one could pose the following question. Assume for a moment that the envisaged connectivity with South East Asia is put in place. What does the North East trade?

We have discussed earlier that Assam, for that matter, the North

East passed through three phases of internationalization of its economy. We observed that external trade did exist in Assam even in its long past. Ancient Assam's trade was governed by absolute domestic requirement, on the one hand and the isolationist policy of Ahom rulers, on the other. Yet there was correspondence between the domestic production pattern and external trade thus yielding higher trade gains even in a non-expansionist regime.

But the external trade from the region in the colonial period thrived in isolation thus limiting the gains to only colonial producers such as tea planters. In the post-independence era, the export basket comprised resource-based products like tea as in the colonial period and the North East continued to have informal trade with the neighbouring countries. With the thrust on external integration of the Indian economy in the reform period, trade with Asia recorded a huge expansion but the North East was only a marginal player.

Even the limited export, particularly of industrial products from the North East to its neighbouring countries through both formal and informal channels had little correspondence with its local production pattern. Nor has such trade induced any perceptible growth impulses apart from developing a few commercial centres near borders. This is more so even with fast rising Indian aggregate exports to the East and South East Asian countries in the recent years. This means, therefore, that static gains from trade to the North East are limited though it could be much larger if it emerges as an entrepot. But the dynamic gains could be enormous under a favourable environment.

It is generally argued that the North East's exports could "emanate from agricultural produce, mainly processed fruits, vegetables and spices; floricultural produce (mainly flowers and orchids) and varieties of handlooms and handicrafts in which the region has established a substantial production base."[28] Similarly, it is argued that the North East's bio-diversities and heritage sites could be a great tourist attraction. It is further pointed out that with regional cooperation with South East Asia, Assam's age-old tea industry could find new outlets for exports.[29]

The North East has also vast hydro-power potential. Once harnessed, power could be exported to neighbouring countries.

As the Shukla Commission argued eloquently and many more before and after it: "The region is bountifully endowed with bio-diversity, hydro-potential oil and gas, coal, limestone and forest wealth. It is ideally suited to produce and process a whole range of plantation crops, spices, fruit and vegetables, flowers and herbs, much of which could be processed and exported to the rest of the country and worldwide."[30]

But the point to note is that such development potentials that essentially relate to the region's natural endowments not only existed but were also widely recognized for long. Yet neither is its trade booming nor has its vast natural endowments become a great source of growth. On the contrary, its growth continued to decelerate. The per capita income of Assam, for instance, slumped from its initial advantage of 4% above the nation's average per capita income in 1951 to 45% below it in 2004.[31] Why so?

The discussion on development potentials in term of resource endowments is based on the supply side of a market. But to unleash the development process calls for creating enabling conditions both for demand and supply sides of a market to interact efficiently. At the same time, it should be recognized that the utilization of resources involves huge lumpsum investment that is beyond the capacity of the North East states. The level of investment that is required for harnessing hydropower generation potential, for example, can be gauged from the following. The NHPC has estimated the financial involvement at Rs. 100,000 crores for power producing capacity of 25,000 MW. Assuming the same average cost per MW, it would involve another Rs. 128,000 at 2003 prices if the remaining part of the estimated hydropower potential were to be used. It adds up to an investment of Rs. 228,000 crores for full utilization of the hydel power potential of the region. No wonder, therefore, enormous hydropower potential and similar such resource potentials remained untapped and thus a mere theoretical possibility.

In the same way, the development infrastructure required to unleash a dynamic growth process in the region involves an investment of massive scale. The High Level Commission estimated the indicative requirement of funds at Rs. 93,619.01 crores at 1996-97 prices.[32] This estimate is very much on the lower side as can be guessed from the indicative level of investment required for harnessing hydro power potential given above.

On the other hand, despite special economic packages by the successive Prime Ministers since 1996 and the submission of the High Level Commission to the Prime Minister on 'Tackling Backlogs in Basic Minimum Services and Infrastructural Needs' the North East has not witnessed any significant improvement in its infrastructure. A recent study[33] ranked Assam 15th among the major states in 2004 and one place down (16th) in 2005[34] while all six smaller states at the bottom among the small states of the country. In terms of the Human Development Index as well, Assam ranked 26th among 32 states and union territories both in 1981 and 1991 while small North Eastern states except for Arunachal Pradesh, and Meghalaya were above the national average score.[35] The short point is that resource endowment by itself is not enough to unleash a dynamic process of economic development. It is possible only if enabling conditions are created.

It inevitably follows that the North East has to address itself first to remove the binding constraints[36] on its economies in terms of its initial conditions, infrastructure lag, insurgency, imperfection/distortion in factor and product markets and indifferent governance. For, all these constraints result in high transaction cost and thus in huge inefficiency. Only then would the North East have a chance to benefit from its possible integration with the East and South East Asia. It should not lose sight of the fact that these countries are highly efficient and competitive. Again, the flow of current or past informal trade avoiding custom barriers and duties is no indication of viability of formal trade that would face custom duties or barriers.

At another level, the North East with 38 million people, larger than many high-income countries in the world, must aim at unifying it as a common market with an efficient transport and communication network. Even this would benefit the North East economies enormously while serving as a preparatory step for reaping benefits from its integration with the East and South East Asian countries as and when it takes a concrete shape.

To conclude, the North East as a gateway to South East and East Asian countries is undoubtedly a great vision for this landlocked region. But for it to edge into reality would inevitably involve a considerable time frame even if the GoI were serious about it. The right strategy would be to pursue this vision vigorously while the North Eastern states individually and collectively focus on removing market rigidities and other impediments within each constituent and between them. This strategy would bring down the high transaction cost of doing business and thus improve efficiency and business environment. It would yield higher growth in the immediate future while ensuring better preparedness to take full advantage of market integration. Without such preparedness, the North East would remain on the periphery even if the connectivity with the neighbouring countries were put in place.

NOTES

1. Atul Sarma (2005), "Why the North Eastern States Continue to Decelerate," *Man and Society*, Vol. II, No. 1, Spring 2005, pp. 1-20.
2. Transforming the North East: Tackling Backlogs in Basic Minimum Services and Infrastructural Needs, High Level Commission Report to the Prime Minister, New Delhi, March 7, 1997, p. 8.
3. Joseph Stiglitz (2002), *Globalization and its Discontents*, Allen Lane, an imprint of Penguin Books, p. 4.
4. For detailed historical records, see, Hariprasad Ray, "The Silk Route from North East India to China and the Bay of Bengal: Some New Lights" (pp. 43-65) in Alokesh Barua (ed.) (2005), *India's North East Developmental Issues in a Historical Perspective.*
5. Op. cit., p. 57.
6. Op. cit., p. 63.
7. For further details, see, Alokesh Barua, "The Rise and Decline of the Ahom Dynastic Rule: A Suggestive Interpretation" in Alokesh Barua (ed.), op cit., p. 105.
8. Amalendu Guha (1991), "A Big Push without a Take-Off: A Case Study of Assam 1871-1901" in Alokesh Barua (ed.) op.cit., p. 144.
9. Op. cit., p. 148.
10. Transforming the North East (1997), op. cit., p. 1.
11. Assam, Tripura and Meghalaya share a border with Bangladesh while Mizoram, Manipur and Nagaland with Myanmar. Assam has a border with Bhutan, too. Tibet region of China and Myanmar border Arunachal Pradesh.
12. Based on a survey conducted by Srinath Barua in 1996. See also

Niranjan Roy (2005), "Indo-Bangladesh Trade Through Karimganj: Problems and Prospects" (unpublished), Presented at the International Seminar, Indo-Bangladesh Border Trade, organized by Shillong ICSSR on July 12-13.

13. Jairam Ramesh (2005), "North East India in a New Asia" in Gateway to the East—A Symposium on North East India and Look East Policy, *Seminar* 500, June, p. 4.
14. This envisages investment and trade cooperation between Yunnan, Bangladesh, Myanmar and India's North East. But it has not made much progress yet.
15. This paragraph has been paraphrased from Sanjib Barua (2004), "The Look East Policy and North East India", CENISEAS, OKD Institute for Social Change and Development, Guwahati.
16. The Stilwell Road which was built by Chinese labourers, Indian soldiers and American engineers and named after American General, Joe Stilwell, provided a vital support to China's besieged army as it fought Japanese occupation. The road transported 50,000 tonnes of bullets, guns and food in a brief period of 10 months. This was once the southern silk route, taking jade, silk, amber, spices, tea and Buddhism across ancient Asia. *Times of India*, September 18, 2005.
17. Homeswar Goswami and Jayanta Gogoi, "Trading Across China, Myanmar, Bangladesh: Impact on North East India" in Alokesh Barua (ed.) (2005).
18. The Governments of India and Bangladesh seem to have proposed this recently.
19. Goswami and Gogoi, op. cit., p. 461.
20. Jairam Ramesh (2005), *Making Sense of Chindia, Reflections on China and India*, India Research Press, p. 44.
21. Sanjib Barua (2004), op. cit., p. 16.
22. For further explanation, see, Atul Sarma, "Why the North Eastern States Continue to Decelerate", in *Man and Society*, A Journal of North East Studies, Vol. II, No. 1, Spring 2005, pp. 12-14.
23. Eyeing the vast potential of the South Asian market, and trying to attract investment to its South West, China already began to repair the old Burma Road to turn the 679 km stretch from Kunming to Myanmar into a six lane highway and to help Myanmar to rebuild the road in its jurisdiction.
24. Anthony Giddens (1999), 'Runaway World: How Globalization is Reshaping Our Lives', BBC Reith Lectures, Lecture 2, "Risk", Hong Kong as quoted in Sanjib Barua 2004.
25. In the CENISEAS Forum, Towards a New Asia, Transnationalism and North East India held on September 10 and 11, 2004.

26. It is non-trade barriers like restrictions on transit, visas and custom regulations that have hindered further expansion of trade with them.
27. For further elaboration, see, Sushil Khanna (2004), op. cit., p. 19.
28. Parliament of India, Rajya Sabha, Department Related Parliamentary Standing Committee on Commerce (1998-99), Thirty-Sixth Report on Development Potential of Commerce in the North Eastern Region, p. 4. See also, Goswami and Gogoi (2005), op. cit., p. 462.
29. Ibid.
30. Op. cit., p. 2.
31. In 1993 two states of the North Eastern region—Arunachal Pradesh and Nagaland had real per capita income (at 1993 prices) above the all-India average per capita income. At the end of the decade, 1999-2000, the latest year for which the data except for Mizoram are available, none of the states in the region had real per capita income above the national average—the gap ranging from 13.32% for Nagaland to 42.54% for Assam.
32. Transforming the North East, op. cit., p. 87-A.
33. *India Today* (Special Issue), India's Best and Worst States, August 16, 2004. Also see, Ministry of Finance, Government of India, *Report of the Eleventh Finance Commission (2000-05)*, June 2000, p. 218.
34. *India Today* (Special Issue), India's Best and Worst States, August 15, 2005.
35. UNDP, *Human Development Report 2001, The State of Human Development*.
36. For detailed discussion on how exactly these constraints have impeded the economic development of the region. See, Atul Sarma (2005).

4

Economic Development of the North Eastern States in the Context of Globalization*

The shift of economic policy from the physical control regime to a market driven system mildly from the mid-80s and more drastically from mid 1991 would have an important impact both at the macro as well as the regional levels. The thrust of the current economic reforms is on upgrading and modernizing technology through globalization of the Indian economy and achieving thereby rapid growth relying more on market forces. In response to such policy reforms, private investment, both domestic and external, is expected to rise at a faster rate in different sectors of the economy. The flow of private investment to different states of the country would, however, depend on the level and quality of administrative, social and economic infrastructures that are obtained in different states. Such differential flow would also lead to higher or lower growth depending on their respective capacity to induce private investment. On the other hand, the central government has now much fewer instruments to direct resources for correcting such imbalances in the changed policy environment.

It is in this context that this chaper first highlights some of the major North Eastern economic realities and their implications on the pace and performance of these economies. Then the chapter discusses the policy options that the North Eastern states have in the new regime.

---

* Published "Economic Development of the North Eastern States in the Context of Globalization" in V.S. Jafa (ed.), (2001), *Liberalization in India: The Road Ahead*, New Century Publications, New Delhi.

Major Challenges

North East as a Distinct Region: North East India consisting of seven states is a distinct economic region. Apart from geographical isolation, there are several other features, which stand in sharp contrast to the rest of the country. The North East states, which are, by and large, hilly ones, are characterized by the preponderance of ST and less significantly SC population. As compared to the all-India share of 22.80%, the SC and ST population in the North East ranged from 94.5% in Mizoram to 19.3% in Assam in 2001 (Table 1). Second, all states in the region compared to the rest of the country recorded a high decadal population growth even during 1981-91. Third, except for Mizoram, the real per capita income is much below the all-India average per capita income (Table 2). What is more, each of them is far behind the rest of the country in terms of administrative, social and economic infrastructures, be it per capita power consumption, credit deposit ratios, road and railway transport or whatever. Another unique feature of the region is that unlike other tribal population, the rate of literacy is way above the all-India average in four states despite the preponderance of tribal population (Table 1).

But the states within the region are dissimilar as well in several ways. They are dissimilar in terms of population size varying from 0.9 million in Mizoram to 26.6 million in Assam. Population density ranges from 13 per sq km (Arunachal Pradesh) to 340 per sq km (Assam). They are also dissimilar in terms of urbanization rate, literacy rates and other demographic characteristics, physical features, stages of economic development and so on, apart from the ethnic composition.

An Interdependent System: It is important to recognize that the North East states are an interdependent economic system, both for historical and geo-political reasons. The North East Council, which was set up about three decades ago, was the result of the recognition of this. Its performance over this long period, however, reflects its monumental failure to develop an integrated approach to the economic development of the region. There are many reasons for this failure. Essentially, these can broadly be traced to two sets of factors. One relates to its inability to visualize its role appropriate to the unique characteristics of the region. The other basically following from the first owes to its failure to assess the economic system and institutions and to evolve right instruments in alignment with unique features of the region for releasing a dynamic growth process.

Unharnessed Resource Endowments: It is widely recognized that the North East is a highly resource endowed region. Undoubtedly, the region is endowed with mines and minerals, water and forest resources, fertile soil, etc. In fact, crude oil production and its refining as well as tea plantation and plywood industry are the few resource-based modern industries in the region. But both oil and tea industries, which have existed for a century or so, have not induced the industries that could have been developed on the basis of their backward and forward linkages. For example, tea plantation requires a wide variety of inputs such as fertilizers, chappals, umbrellas, small tools, etc. None of these backward linkage-based industries, though economically viable, was set up in the region. Instead, the industry depended on supplies from outside the region. This long dependence on trading has given rise to well entrenched vested interests, which work against the emergence of local entrepreneurship. Similarly, the oil industry had been hesitant for long to develop refineries, and petrochemical complex, which could have led to developing many downstream industries in the region. On the other hand, the surplus that accrued in these industries year after year was siphoned off to investment activities elsewhere. This has led to an 'enclave economy' in which these few modern industries exist without having any linkage with the stagnant traditional activities. For reasons such as these, the resource-based extractive industries have come to be perceived as the symbol of exploitation.

There are several other types of resources potentials, which are yet to be realized. Water resources and natural gas call for a special mention. Hydel power potential of the North East (38,000 MW or 30% of the country's hydel potential) is large enough to meet a sizeable part of the requirement of even the eastern states for many years to come. Natural gas-based industries are also feasible. But water resources instead of being a source of economic prosperity have continued to cause flood havoc year after year with immense human sufferings and loss of lives and property as a result. But harnessing water for irrigation and hydel power generation as also economic utilization of natural gas and other resources involves large lumpsum investment, which the North Eastern states with their stagnant economics, and narrow tax base cannot provide. The resources available in terms of plan assistance to these states can hardly be earmarked for such projects, as this type of investment cannot be made in doses. Nor do these projects find place in the Central Plan. As a result, these important resources, which should have been the base of vibrant economies, have remained a source of uncertainty, human suffering and property loss. The state governments continue with fire fighting operations and provide flood/natural calamity relief causing a heavy drain on their otherwise meagre resources. Farmers, on their part, do not make farm investment for the fear of its being washed away by impending floods while the rest of the country perceive this reluctance as the manifestation of their indolence.

Disruption of Traditional Trade Links: Partition led to the disruption of the long existing trade links and infrastructure that the North East was accustomed to. The alternative trade routes and infrastructures that we developed in the post-partition period have remained for long a makeshift arrangement, as it were. The conversion of the meter gauge to broad gauge took years. A large part of the North East is yet to have railheads. The railway network linking the places only to exploit the commercial interests of the colonial power is still to be restructured for even growth. The net effect has been that people pay higher prices for their purchase originating in the rest of the country. Producers do not get right prices for their products such as fruits, potatoes, ginger or the exquisite handicrafts and handloom products. The income generation that has taken place, even if at a modest rate leaks out to producers elsewhere through consumption linkage for these economies being unable to produce income induced consumption goods. They thus remain heavily dependent on the rest of the country for their most day-to- day requirements.

The geographical isolation coupled with inadequate infrastructures is certainly a major stumbling block to growth. But an appropriate development strategy could use this disadvantage to the maximum advantage. For such disadvantages act, in fact, as barriers to trade and to that extent, provide protection to the local entrepreneurs for undertaking a right mix of activities.

Population Influx: The population influx from across borders has huge implications both on the polity and economies of the North Eastern states. As such, this is a highly emotive issue as has been demonstrated by student uprisings in Assam and other North Eastern states. But the inability to effectively deal with this problem by the student leaders when they came to power after a protracted movement against this issue only highlights the extent of complexity that it is associated with.

This problem should be clearly understood, and its realistic solution should be sought. Without going into great details of the migrant population from across borders, the following points can be flagged. First, the flow of immigrants, which continued much beyond the aftermath of partition, has presumably been induced by economic considerations. This means that most of these immigrants have moved out of their hearth and home in search of better means of living, which sparsely populated North Eastern states, might offer. Second, these immigrants who are uneducated and unskilled, sought to be absorbed in agriculture and related sectors. These sectors being of an informal nature, they were not very visible until the growing mass started having an impact on the polity of the states. The extreme example of this presence was felt in Tripura where migrant population marginalized the local inhabitants in power sharing. Third, complete uprooting of the vast immigrant population is not feasible as the student leaders of Assam realized being saddled in power for almost two terms of five years each.

Having noted the above points, one should seek a solution to the problem of population influx in the following perspective. The problem of immigrants should first be bifurcated between the existing stock and the future flow. The existing stock reckoning from a cut off date should be given the status of economic migrants. This status would entitle them to earn their living but not to property acquisition and political rights. This practice seems to be prevalent in Germany.

In order to arrest the future flow, a strategy with a longer time perspective needs to be adopted. This strategy should clearly recognize that fencing the vast border is neither easy nor is foolproof vigilance practicable. Even developed countries found it difficult to stop illegal migrants. It should also recognize that there exists an element of schizophrenic attitude among local inhabitants: In private they prefer cheap and pliant immigrants as farm labour while in public they discard them. This makes the problem more complex.

Therefore, a longer term strategy should aim at altering the objective conditions. There should be a well designed attractive scheme of settling landless local inhabitants along the borders. They would greatly reinforce the existing vigilant force. Such a scheme at the same time would provide a viable means of sustenance to the landless poor. The other part of the strategy should be to upgrade technology in farms and other sectors. Such technology upgradation would necessitate higher skill, which immigrants do not have. Simultaneous efforts to impart the required skill at the local level would meet the new demand while at the same time minimizing the opportunities for immigrant labour. With the expansion of the modern organized sector, the scope for absorption of immigrant labour will be shrunk. More so, when the land providing job avenues for immigrants as was the case before, does not exist any more. Thus a strategy of introducing new technology simultaneous with generating the required skill at the local level would provide the longer term solution to the much vexed problem of population influx. The success of the Bangladeshi mass literacy and other development programmes with rising employment opportunities at home would further enhance the efficacy of the above strategy.

Infrastructure Lags: There exists a broad consensus that the North East lacks the basic minimum physical, social and administrative infrastructures for unleashing growth dynamics in the region. Physical infrastructures such as power, communications, transport, irrigation, market access, etc. are grossly inadequate to generate a dynamic growth process. Inadequacy of all this is reflected in poor market incentives and thus in low productivity and growth in different sectors of the economies of the region. But the creation of some of the crucial infrastructures has two important dimensions. First, because of the interdependence of the economic systems of the North East, it is essential to develop a good network of inter-state transport and communication in addition to developing intra-state market and basic service accessibility. The remoteness and hilly terrain involves larger unit cost as well as maintenance cost. Again, for longer run connectivity and effective trade links, it is necessary to develop border road and water transport network in liaison with the neighbouring countries like Myanmar, South East Asia, Bangladesh and South China, which are very close to the region. Such infrastructure creation would obviously involve imaginative initiatives of the Government of India.

The other is that the full utilization of the power potentials of the region or effective flood controls not only requires heavy lumpsum investment as mentioned earlier but also mutual understanding and cooperation of the individual units of the North East.

As for social infrastructure, it should be noted that several of the major changes in the 1990s, collapse of the socialist world and the emergence of a unipolar world order and globalization are all essentially technology driven. The thrust on continuous skill upgradation, which would facilitate technology assimilation, absorption and innovation, would, therefore, be the best survival strategy for a developing country like India. This is all the more important for the North East region with its unique features and problems requiring appropriate technological solution and with rich resources needing their economic utilization.

By now the states have established many educational and skill generating institutions. At one level, these institutions should be strengthened in terms of equipping them adequately with advanced training facilities and teaching aids. At another level, there should be networking with similar institutions of excellence located elsewhere. Administrative infrastructure will be taken up later with the issue of governance.

Deeply Entrenched Interests: The availability of various types of infrastructure is a necessary but not a sufficient condition for spurring economic growth. Their utilization depends on the response of the economic agents. For far too long, the North East is dependent for the supply of most of its requirements on the rest of the country. The extent of such dependence is estimated at Rs. 2,500 crore annually. This vast requirement is available through a trading and distribution network. The trading network was organized on the basis of monopolistic competition. In many situations, traders collude for price advantage. The trading margin being high, the investment on commodity production is understandably not preferred. It is so, particularly because the risk factor is higher in a perennially disturbed environment as well as in a situation where there is a lacd of adequate infrastructure. What is more, there are instances to show that such deeply entrenched mercantile capital militates against the emergence of local entrepreneurship. All this eventually means that the economies do not stir and fail to meet the growing aspirations of the people, particularly the younger generation. This, in turn, provides a fertile ground for grooming various militant groups or a spurt of popular uprisings. In some sense, lack of growth and disturbed environment feed on each other. This is exactly what is happening in most of the North Eastern states.

Unaccountable Governance: Why have some states in India developed faster than some of their other counterparts? It is certainly not because of resource endowments. Bihar or the North East or Orissa with resource abundance are some of the least developed states. In contrast, Gujarat with no great claim on resources has grown faster than most other states. Is it then due to closeness to the national market? Why have not then the UP or MP being at the centre of the national market recorded high growth? On the other hand, Karnataka and Punjab even though away from the national market have grown faster. Even Haryana, which had poor infrastructure at the time of its creation in 1996, is one of the fastest growing states. The point is that widely recognized factors such as resource endowments, closeness to the national market, etc. are by themselves not sufficient to spur growth.

It can be hypothesized that consistent pursuit of clearly defined priorities over a long period percolates down to the economic agents, who start demanding the state machinery to address their problems quickly and thus lead to a more effective delivery system. In the process both the political masters and correspondingly bureaucrats over time become accountable to the economic operators for better delivery, which eventually induces growth

Lack of such prioritized thrusts, as indeed is the case in the North East is reflected in the poor delivery system even in their limited areas of operation. Widespread cynicism of the bureaucracy is both cause and effect of the nonchalant approach to development.

The Minor Role of Manufacturing: State economies within the region do not reflect in several respects the general development pattern of the country. For example, compared to the all-India average, the contribution of agriculture to the NSDP was considerably higher in most of the states in 1980-81 and remained so even at the end of 1988-89. Interestingly, the role of agriculture in income generation was considerably low in a few hill states such as Nagaland and Mizoram in 1980-81 and further declined in the subsequent years (Table 3). Again, in constrast to the general pattern, the share of agriculture in NSDP remained almost steady or increased over the years in a few states such as Tripura and Mizoram. Further, the contribution of Banking and Insurance to NSDP was substantially lower than the all-India average in 1980-81. Even with some increase over the years, the relative position did not alter substantially.

The structure of state income varied from state to state within the region. States like Assam, Meghalaya and Mizoram derived a considerably larger proportion of income from mining and quarrying (ranging from 2.01% in Mizoram to 4.3 in Assam as against 1.23% for all-India in 1988-89) than what the country as a whole did. This clearly indicates rich endowment of mining resources in these states. Similarly, the contribution of construction was substantially higher than the all-India average in all the states except for Assam. Much higher than the all-India average share in the total income was also derived from real estate, ownership of dwelling and business service by the states. More important, public administration contributed a much larger share to NSDP in all the states.

It is important to note that trade, hotels and restaurants generated a considerable income even in the hill states although the sector's share tended to decline over the years in most of them.

The manufacturing sector, in contrast, contributed far less share to NSDP ranging from 1.9% in ACP to 12.78 in Assam as against the all-India average of 19.6% in 1988-89. Its share declined from

3.1% in 1980-81 to 2.1% in Nagaland. Although the registered manufacturing sector's share in NSDP tended to increase in the states other than Nagaland, its contribution was far less than the all-India average in all the units.

Even regarding the unregistered manufacturing sector, its share in NSDP was much lower than the all-India average level. But two important points may be made in this regard. First, the importance of unregistered manufacturing for income generation was overwhelmingly higher compared to the registered sector in all the states except Assam. Second, in contrast to the rising share of the unregistered sector of the country as a whole, the sector's share in NSDP remained steady or declined over the years in the states other than Manipur and Mizoram. Thus it emerges that the region is lagging far behind the all-India average level of industrialization as reflected in the manufacturing sector's contribution to NSDP.

Leading Industrial Sectors: The industrial base of Assam constituted, as in 1980-81, in manufacture of food products and sugar, wood and wood products, gas and steam and repair services. Over the years, i.e in 1988-89, two additional sectors, viz. manufacture of rubber, plastic, petroleum and coal products and manufacture of non-metallic mineral products were added to the industrial base of the state. But repair services lost its importance over the years.

The industrial base of Manipur in 1980-81 comprised manufacture of food products, wood and wood products, paper and paper products and repair services. The only industrial sector that emerged by 1987 was 'other manufacturing' while food products became insignificant.

In Meghalaya wood and wood products, paper and paper products, non-metallic mineral products and repair services made up the industrial base. One other industry, i.e. 'other manufacturing' was added to the industrial base by 1987-88 while the non-metallic mineral sector lost its significance.

Tripura had six important factory level industries, viz. beverages, tobacco or tobacco products, wood and wood products non-metallic mineral products, metal products and parts except machinery and transport equipment, water works and supply and repair services. By 1987-88 jute textiles and other manufacturing emerged while beverages, wood products and metal products paled into insignificance.

The required data to identify the industrial base of Nagaland, Arunachal Pradesh and Mizoram are not available.

Considering the four North Eastern states together, we can make the following broad observations. First, the industrial base comprising significant factory level industries is very narrow.

Second, the industrial sectors mainly consist of first stage processing industries such as grain mills, wood and wood products based on local resources and demand induced industry like repair services. Third, the few modern industries such as non-metallic mineral products and gas and steam that have come up in certain parts of the region are also resource-based. Finally, except for the growth of some miscellaneous type of industries, the factory level industrial had not been significantly altered even in 1987-88.

Production Linkages[1]: It is possible to argue that the lead industries identified in respect of four of the state economies would suggest the type of industries that can be developed on the basis of production linkages, backward and forward. State economies being highly open, this approach to industrialization is subject to severe limitations.

Nevertheless, we have attempted to suggest in an illustrative manner the industrial sectors that can be developed on the basis of backward and forward linkages of the lead sectors indicated earlier.

Of the four lead sectors in the Assam economy, only two, viz. the manufacture of food products and manufacture of wood and wood products, furniture and fixtures reveal high backward employment linkages. This suggests that an increase in output of these two sectors would lead to high employment generation in the industries supplying inputs to them. But only one of the leading industries, which happens to be wood and wood products, has also high forward employment linkages.

In Manipur and Meghalaya also, the wood and wood products sector shows high backward and forward linkages. In both these economies, this is the only sector, which has high linkages.

This discussion on production linkages should be qualified. As mentioned earlier, production linkages based on national reference technology may not be necessarily relevant to a state economy, at least not to the same extent to all state economies. Secondly, it is possible that there are industries other than the revealed leading industries, which may have higher backward and forward linkages but does not get captured in our analysis. Finally, backward and forward linkages indicate only the direction of demand. But supply factors may be more critical for industrial development.

Some Reflections on Constraints

There are many factors, which facilitate or inhibit the economic development of a state. These factors can be classified into two sub-sets: One relates to the supply side while the other to demand side. Resource endowment, infrastructure support, evolution of the right type of institutions, access to market, availability of human capital in the form of entrepreneurship and skilled labour, credit availability, etc are all important determinants affecting the supply side. The income level and its distribution are important factors operating on the demand side. Both sets of factors need not be binding for the development of a state, which is a highly open economy. However, the working of the national economy over the past 50 years has favoured some and differentiated against several other state economies. In the process of evolution of the national economy, product and money/credit market got integrated faster with the national market while labour market integration was hindered by several rigidities emerging especially from labour surplus situations. This led to a larger inflow of goods into and outflow of savings from the region.

When supply side factors are not equally conducive to all states, integrated product and credit market unaccompanied by similarly integrated labour market has led to reverse flow of resources from the less developed to the more developed state economies. More importantly, such asymmetry results in an adverse effect on local industries by way of introducing competition from technologically superior counterparts. This process is eminently discernible in the context of the entire North East.

The important reasons why some states have developed faster than others are as follows: First, there were differences in the initial level of capital accumulation, human capital and infrastructure in some states. Second, and more importantly, as explained earlier, some states succeeded in identifying and pursuing clear priorities and developing a mechanism for better participation of economic agents particularly in the prioritized sectors. This generated pressure from below for better delivery.

This probably helped to develop a higher level of infrastructures as also a responsive and an accountable system that led to their more efficient utilization. This was particularly important in the policy regime with the public sector directing the limited resources for providing infrastructures while private sectors use them. To illustrate, Punjab and Haryana accorded consistently high priorities to agricultural development. When these priorities got trickled down to the farmers, they created pressures for releasing the operational constraints faced by them. Industrial development in Gujarat and Maharashtra, and the high level of social services and their efficient delivery in Kerala can similarly be attributed to clear prioritization and the development of a mechanism that ensures powerful feedback system between the decision-makers and the economic agents.

In addition to this general approach to development, it will be useful to take note of certain features that are inherent in the economic systems or in the past growth process of the states in the region. Some illustrations are given below. The economic base of the North East hill states is very narrow. More importantly, they are characterized by activities, which are carried on with primitive technology. This presents two fold problems.

On the one hand, the administrative, social and economic infrastructure as also human capital needs to be developed fast. On the other hand, the narrow economic base stands as a great impediment to mobilizing resources for developing the required infrastructure.

There is also some ambiguity in the perception of needs and goals of economic development in a hill state predominantly inhabited by tribal population. It is argued that tribal identities need to be retained in the development process. But mainly because of relatively larger public expenditure in these states as pointed out earlier, there is a perceptible change in the level and composition of consumption baskets of at least the segment of the population directly and indirectly associated with government operations. Demonstration effect must have resulted in an inroad of modern products into the consumption basket of others as well. It should be recognized that the activities carried on with primitive technology cannot enable the people at large to sustain a higher level of consumption. Therefore, there is a need for reorganization of economic activities with better technology, which will inevitably lead to changes in the ways of people's lives. If rapid economic development is the goal, the so-called tribal identity should be left to be evolved by the people themselves.

There are also other important issues. First, the narrow economic base and limited use of tax instruments for resource mobilization in hill states have also imposed restrictions on Assam's manoeuvrability. It has done so in the following manner. Assam being surrounded by hill states finds it difficult to levy high taxes for the fear of diversion of economic activities to the neighbouring states, which are virtually tax havens.

Second, the major industrial activities that have come up in Assam are essentially resource based, viz. oil and plantation in Assam. The backward linkages of these industries are rather limited while their forward linkages are with industries located in the big metropolises elsewhere. The result has been the emergence of an enclave type economy, i.e., a few modern industries in the midst of traditional industries with limited or no interactions between the two.

Third, as mentioned earlier, with an increasingly greater degree of integration of the product market, the development of traditional industries which essentially make up the industrial profile of the states in the region is no longer feasible; more so, in the context of the present liberalized framework. They can be developed only if the productivity can be raised using superior technology.

Development Strategy

The development strategy for the North East has to be based on the explicit recognition of the following:

- The seven states that comprise the region are essentially interdependent sub systems both in terms of historical background and geographical location. This calls for an integrated approach to development for the entire region.
- Geographical isolation from the rest of the country has put the region at a great disadvantage. This coupled with unique

features of hill economies has made the states highly dependent on the rest of the country for the supply of final goods.

- Third, the unique features of most of these economies make it difficult to adopt a development strategy entirely based on the experiences of the rest of the country. It is, therefore, important to evolve an appropriate development strategy taking into account the objective conditions inclusive of socio-cultural backgrounds.
- Though most of these state economies are somewhat associated with primitive technology, they have enormous hydel power potential, forest reserves and potential for agro horticulture. Hydel power potentials, if realized even partially, could be a source of attraction for power intensive but cleaner industries or at least a source of revenue from power export.
- This region has all the important attractions such as hill resorts, pollution free environment, water, natural game sanctuary, etc which, together provide an excellent potential for an important tourist destinationt. Tourism, if developed properly will contribute to income and employment generation directly in tourism-related sectors and indirectly in the well developed labour intensive handloom and handicrafts. NEDFI can take the initiative of preparing a master plan for tourism development in the North East.
- Concerted efforts are required to equip adequately the existing educational and technical institutions and build new institutions for generating marketable skills, on the one hand and to build the capability to adopt and absorb new technologies. On the other hand, equally important is to evolve the existing economic institutions and agents to make them technology-friendly.
- The present mercantile capital should be encouraged to invest in linkage-based industries and in those whose products have markets in the neighbouring countries such as Bangladesh, Bhutan and South East Asian countries.
- One of the major handicaps for this region is the weak transport and communication system both between the

states as well as with the rest of the country.

- The North East Council if revamped appropriately could provide a forum for these states to cooperate and collaborate in their efforts to develop a mutually supportive economic system.
- To sum up, having lagged behind in terms of the level and quality of administrative, social and economic infrastructures, these states will not attract immediately private investment flows in the new regime. In the immediate future, therefore, the public sector has to play a much greater role in these economies.
- Finally, while these states have been passing through political and social upheavals in the process of a search for an ethnic identity, the rapid economic development may offer an escape opportunity to restore normalcy.

NOTES

1. Based on the author's earlier study entitled 'Industrialization in North Eastern and Eastern Zones' jointly with Amarendra Sahoo.

5

Growth Experiences of the North Eastern States: Post-Reform Period*

Introduction

The economic reform process that had begun since 1991 and the Government of India's North East policy that followed gave rise to the following paradox. In the year 1993-94, three states of the North Eastern region[1], namely Arunachal Pradesh, Nagaland and Mizoram had real per capita income above the all-India average. In 2005-06, none of the North Eastern states had real per capita income above the national average (Table 2). However, the gap is narrowing in the states of Arunachal, Manipur, Nagaland and, Tripura, while widening in Meghalaya, Mizoram and Assam in recent times.Thus, over time the region is diverging away from the national average in terms of share innational income as the largest state of the region, Assam with a population share of 70 per cent of the region was experiencing a low growth rate in real per capita income of 0.22 per cent in 1993-99 and 3.74 per cent in 1999-2006, in contrast to the national growth of 4.58 and 5.44 per cent in the respective periods.

Paradoxically, during the same period, the North Eastern region received special economic packages.[2] In October 1996 H.D. Deve Gowda, the then Prime Minister announced an economic package of Rs. 6,100 crore for specific projects in North Eastern states. He also introduced the North East sub plans in all central ministries for which 10 per cent of their budgets would be earmarked. Mr. I.K. Gujaral who followed him as Prime Minister

---

* Jointly with Sushanta Nayak, Professor of Economics, Rajiv Gandhi University.

assured the implementation of the package. In January 2000 Atal Bihari Vajpayee, the next Prime Minister further announced a Rs. 10,271.66 crore package for the region. Further, during the Tenth Plan period more than 80 thousand crore of rupees was invested in the region through different schemes. It is in this background that this chapter addresses the following questions:

(i) What have been the growth experiences of the North East states in the post-reform period?
(ii) What are the major outcomes?
(iii) How have the variables such as infrastructure, power, transport, communication and investment that determine the pace of growth and its outcome moved?
(iv) How can one explain the performance of the North East state economies the way they have done?

SECTION I: ECONOMIC GROWTH

This section attempts to understand the growth profile of the NER over the last two and a half decades.[3]

Table 1 provides the trend rate of growth of GSDP at different time periods: 1980-81 to 1992-93 is taken as the pre-liberalization period and 1993-94 to 1998-99 as post-liberalization, phase-I and 1999-2000 to 2005-06 as the post-liberalization, phase-II period.[4]

In the pre-liberalization period, all the North East states other than Assam experienced a growth rate of more than 5 per cent per annum. In fact, four states, viz. Arunachal Pradesh, Meghalaya, Nagaland and Tripura witnessed even a growth higher than the national average of 5.57 per cent. In the post-liberalization (Phase-I) period the states other than Assam and Arunachal Pradesh continued to grow at a rate above 5 per cent while Tripura and Meghalaya could even surpass the national average of 6.53 per cent. In Phase II of the post-liberalization period, four states, namely Arunachal, Manipur, Nagaland and Tripura grew at a rate higher than the national average of 7.06 per cent. However, growth rates of Meghalaya, Mizoram and Assam were less than the national average. Thus, in the period, 1999-2006 the growth performance of four North East states were keeping pace with or even surpassed the national average growth while the biggest North East state which is Assam along with two other smaller states were lagging behind..

Table 1: Growth Rate of GSDP and its Components of Population

		Arunachal	*Manipur*	*Meghalaya*	*Nagaland*	*Tripura*	*Mizoram*	*Assam*	*India*
Agriculture	Pre-Liberalization	7.65	2.32	0.89	5.7	2.76	NA	2.24	3.03
Agriculture	Post-Liberalization, Phase-I	-3.53	3.35	5.94	6.85	4.06	3.82	0.65	3.16
Agriculture	Post-Liberalization, Phase-II	0.75	5.17	4.29	12.64	4.24	1.45	1.95	2.73
Industry	Pre-Liberalization	7.44	7.34	6.56	12.74	5.17		3.54	6.84
Industry	Post-Liberalization, Phase-I	12.46	2.74	5.70	7.64	9.34	-11.38	2.25	7.46
Industry	Post-Liberalization, Phase-II	19.01	2.50	8.14	8.94	3.68	5.08	7.73	6.84
Service	Pre-Liberalization	8.76	6.7	7.88	5.17	9.09		4.85	6.25
Service	Post-Liberalization, Phase-I	5.66	6.44	6.79	4.81	9.84	8.31	3.01	8.06
Service	Post-Liberalization, Phase-II	8.39	10.69	5.47	8.50	9.51	7.23	6.37	8.69
SDP/GDP	Pre-Liberalization	7.95	5.05	5.61	6.96	5.77		3.57	5.23
SDP/GDP	Post-Liberalization, Phase-I	2.75	5.00	6.44	5.55	7.97	5.86	1.98	6.53
SDP/GDP	Post-Liberalization, Phase-II	7.26	8.52	5.67	9.79	7.77	6.20	5.24	7.06
Population	Pre-Liberalization	2.74	2.54	2.98	4.21	2.92		2.18	
Population	Post-Liberalization, Phase-I	2.34	2.22	2.62	4.85	1.50	4.85	1.76	1.94
Population	Post-Liberalization, Phase-II	1.42	2.04	1.42	3.41	1.11	2.53	1.50	1.59
PCSDP	Pre-Liberalization	2.74	2.54	2.98	4.21	2.92		2.18	3.24
PCSDP	Post-Liberalization, Phase-I	0.41	2.78	3.81	0.70	6.47	1.01	0.22	4.58
PCSDP	Post-Liberalization, Phase-II	5.82	6.48	4.25	6.35	6.66	6.02	3.74	5.44

Source: Computed from GSDP data of CSO as provided in their website for the period 1993-2002 and from the period 1981-93 SDP data has been taken from the EPW Research Foundation (2003)

In per capita terms, however, only Nagaland had per capita GSDP growth rate above the national average in the pre-liberalisation period. In the post-liberalization (Phase-I) period Nagaland dipped due to high population growth while Tripura recorded more than the national average growth. On the other hand, the per capita income growth was abysmally low in Arunachal Pradesh, Assam and Mizoram at 0.41, 0.22 and 1.01 per cent respectively. In this period, some improvement in per capita income growth took place in Manipur and Meghalaya. In the post-liberalization (Phase-II) period, all the states except Meghalaya and Assam witnessed higher than the national average of 5.44 per cent. Even so, as Table 2 shows, barring Arunachal Pradesh in the early years of liberalization and Mizoram in the first five years of the second phase of liberalization, each state had percapita income lower than the national average per capita income, to a varying extent.

Table 2: PCGSDP of Different States of North Eastern States as a Percentage of National Average

	Arunachal	*Manipur*	*Meghalaya*	*Nagaland*	*Tripura*	*Mizoram*	*Assam*
1993-94	109.52	76.41	90.84	114.54	69.34	109.32	73.31
1994-95	100.72	69.36	87.28	112.2	64.4	NA	70.31
1995-96	106.64	97.96	89.24	109	65.19	NA	67.36
1996-97	93.65	67.51	85.22	105.08	67.16	NA	64.38
1997-98	91.76	69.91	85.7	105.37	71.12	NA	62.23
1998-99	88.76	66.88	87.78	90.05	74.06	NA	58.61
1999-00	84.91	81.99	91.12	84.80	85.64	101.32	74.88
2000-01	87.87	73.37	91.25	93.27	88.01	101.16	74.04
2001-02	95.88	73.98	92.12	94.12	96.67	101.34	71.89
2002-03	89.25	70.57	92.36	94.78	98.77	106.61	74.04
2003-04	91.21	71.70	91.58	92.93	96.58	100.38	72.37
2004-05	95.55	82.66	91.04	99.47	97.51	96.36	70.91
2005-06	91.37	83.37	87.93	96.86	96.86	93.38	68.81
2006-07	NA	84.05	84.96	NA	NA	90.64	67.58

Source: Same as Table 1

Examining the sectoral growth across the states as presented in Table 1, the following observations can be made.

Agriculture: In the pre-liberalization period, Arunachal

Pradesh and Nagaland recorded higher growth in agriculture than the all-India average. In the post-liberalization (Phase-I) period, the growth rate at the national level declined by 0.43 percentage points as it did in Arunachal and Assam. But in Manipur, Meghalaya, Nagaland, Mizoram and Tripura, the growth rate in the post-liberalization (Phase-I) period was higher than the national average and except for Mizoram, the performance of these states was better than the pre-liberalization period. In the post-liberalization (Phase-II) period, the performance of agriculture improved in all states except in Meghalaya and Mizoram.

Industry: In the pre-liberalization period, five states,viz. Arunachal, Manipur, Meghalaya, Nagaland and Tripura witnessed the industrial growth rate above 5 per cent, which was comparable to the national average of 6.84 per cent (excluding Tripura). In the post-liberalization (Phase-I) period, these states other than Arunachal, Nagaland and Tripura had recorded growth lower than the national average ranging from (—) 11.38% in Mizoram to 2.25% in Assam. Only Arunachal, Nagaland and Tripura had higher growth than the national average in the post-liberalization (Phase-I) period. Thus a sharp acceleration in industrial growth took place in Arunachal and Tripura, and a deceleration in Nagaland, Manipur, Assam and Meghalaya. In the post-liberalization (Phase-II) period further acceleration took place in Arunachal (mainly due to electricity), Meghalaya, Nagaland, Mizoram and Assam and deceleration in Manipur and Tripura.

Service Sector: At the national level the service sector grew at a higher rate in the post-liberalization period compared to the previous period. The service sector growth in the pre-liberalization period was higher in four and lower in two North Eastern states, than the national average. In the post-liberalization (Phase-I) period the service sector decelerated in Arunachal, Manipur, Meghalaya, Nagaland and Assam and accelerated in Tripura. Tripura and Mizoram had even recorded the growth rate above the national average. In the post-liberalization (Phase-II) period it accelerated in all states except in Meghalaya and Mizoram. Even states like Arunachal, Manipur and Tripura recorded higher growth compared to the national average in the post-liberalization (Phase-II) period.

On the whole, the North Eastern states witnessed a varying sectoral growth pattern of the following type:

(i) Low GSDP growth in Arunachal Pradesh and Assam in the post-liberalization (Phase-I) period was mainly due to poor performance of agriculture and industry. In contrast, better performance of agriculture led to higher SDP growth in Meghalaya and Nagaland. In Phase-II agriculture performed better in all North Eastern states except Mizoram

(ii) The deceleration in the industrial sector in phase-I contributed to stagnancy in the GSDP growth of Manipur, and deceleration in Assam. Deceleration in the industrial sector continued in Manipur and Tripura in Phase-II of the post-reform era.

(iii) In Mizoram, both agriculture and service in Phase-I and industry and service in Phase-II were the driving force behind the growth of SDP.

(iv) Better performance of growth in Tripura could be attributed to all round development of the agriculture, industry and service sector in Phase-I and in Phase-II, which is because of agriculture and service.

Decomposing growth as reported in Table 3, it is observed:

The contribution to growth by the agriculture sector turned negative in Arunachal Pradesh in the post-liberalization (phase-I) period and that of industry improved. In contrast, the contribution of the service sector to growth rose to 110.87 per cent in the post-liberalization (Phase-I) period. In Phase-II the contribution of agriculture was positive (2.83 per cent), whereas the contribution of industry declined sharply. In Manipur the contribution of the service sector rose consistently over the three periods, while that of agriculture and industry declined. In the case of Meghalaya the contribution of the agriculture sector first increased in Phase-I and then it declined in Phase-II of the post-reform period.The industry contribution declined in Phase-I and then rose in Phase-II and the contribution of the service sector decreased consistently. In Nagaland, agriculture and the service sector's contribution increased substantially while industries' slumped by 39.55 points between the pre and post-reform (Phase-II) period. Tripura, witnessed a decline in the contribution of agriculture and industry and a rise in service in Phase-II of the post-reform period to the extent of 83.13 per cent. Assam witnessed a falling contribution of agriculture while a moderately rising contribution of industry and a stagnant services' contribution around 66 to 67 per cent in the entire post-reform period. For Mizoram, the pre-liberalization data are not available. Clearly, in the post-reform period (Phase-I) the service sector provided the major growth impulse of 92.76 per cent while Industry's contribution was negative and agriculture's was just 17.75 per cent. In phase-II the contribution of agriculture drastically fell and that of industry improved marginally, but the contribution of service continued to dominate in Mizoram in the Phase-II period (90.66%).

Thus, the overall conclusions are: (i) except for Meghalaya, Mizoram and Assam, the other four states recorded a contribution of the industry sector to their respective GSDP growth in Phase-II, and (ii) five states witnessed declining contribution of agriculture sector in the second phase of the post-liberalization. The most important point that emerged was that the service sector was the driver of growth in almost all the North Eastern states, contributing more than 60 per cent to their GSDP growth. In Arunachal, Manipur, Tripura, Mizoram and Assam, its contribution went beyond 70 per cent which was disproportionately higher than their respective sectoral share in GSDP. Thus the North Eastern states were rapidly moving towards tertiarization at the cost of industry and agriculture. Therefore, it is important to examine the broad components within the service sector that have contributed to its growing dominance.

The service sector can be decomposed into two categories: infrastructure and other services.The infrastructure sector includes sectors like construction, trade, hotels, transport and communication; and financing, insurance, real estate and business services. The other services comprise community, social and personal services. This classification seems to be meaningful in the sense that the infrastructure sector plays a crucial role in the growth of industry and agriculture. Table 4, gives the contribution of these two sectors to the growth of the service sector in the North Eastern state economics.

Table 3: Contribution of Different Sectors to the Growth of GSDP of Different States

		Arunachal	*Manipur*	*Meghalaya*	*Nagaland*	*Tripura*	*Mizoram*	*Assam*	*India*
Agriculture	Pre-Liberalization	43.92	17.73	4.5	23.72	20.87		25.24	20.02
	Post-Liberalization Phase-I	-49.72	22.11	23.49	30.65	16.11	17.75	12.48	13.65
	Post-Liberalization Phase-II	2.83	16.05	16.32	40.88	13.92	4.27	11.64	8.06
Industry	Pre-Liberalization	21.72	18.09	23.58	42.44	8.21		16.94	26.28
	Post-Liberalization Phase-I	38.85	5.90	12.04	10.31	5.04	-10.51	20.37	25.45
	Post-Liberalization Phase-II	24.50	2.72	24.68	2.89	2.94	5.07	22.05	18.87
Service	Pre-Liberalization	34.32	64.97	72.29	35.54	75.2		58.00	53.66
	Post-Liberalization Phase-I	110.87	71.99	64.48	59.07	78.85	92.76	67.15	60.90
	Post-Liberalization Phase-II	72.67	81.24	59.00	56.23	83.13	90.66	66.31	73.07

Source: Same as Table 1.

Table 4 reveals the contribution by different sub components of the service sector to the growth of the service sector in different periods. In the post reform phase-II period the contribution by infrastructure sector to the service sector growth underwent significant positive changes. Within the service, construction emerged as the dominant sector in Arunachal, Manipur, Nagaland and Tripura. The leading sector in Assam and Meghalaya was Trade, Hotels and Restaurants.

Some of the other components under the infrastructure category of Service like Transport by other means, Banking and Insurance, and real estate ownership contributed significantly in Arunachal; Banking and Insurance in Assam; transport by other means, communication, trade, hotel and restaurants, real estate ownership in Manipur; trades hotel and restaurants in Meghalaya; construction and real estate ownership in Nagaland; Trade hotels restaurants and banking in Tripura. It is noteworthy that the banking and insurance in Mizoram tended to decline in terms of its contribution to the service sector growth in the later years of the post-reform period. Thus, this pattern of growth of the components of the service sector in the North Eastern states resulted in a mixed pattern of growth in agriculture and industry. Better performance of agriculture and industry in Arunachal, Assam and Nagaland could be attributed to better performance of infrastructure components under the service sector. The better performance of agriculture and poor performance of industry in Manipur and Tripura could perhaps be attributed to the poor performance of all infrastructures other than construction. In Meghalaya and Mizoram the decline in agriculture could perhaps be related to a decline in storage and better performance of industry to better performance of the industry-related infrastructure.

Table 4: Contribution of Different Sub Sectors to the Growth of the Service Sector During the Post-Liberalization Period

	Arunachal		*Assam*		*Manipur*	
	1993-99 Con grth	*1999-06 Con grth*	*1993-99*	*1999-06 Con grth*	*1993-99 Con grth*	*1999-06*
Construction	-9.00	53.06	17.43	11.25	33.52	81.99
Railways	-0.03	0.13	3.37	5.01	0.00	0.00
Transport by Other Means	17.09	2.51	-6.07	0.00	5.60	1.16
Storage	0.00	0.01	0.00	4.71	0.00	0.01
Communication	2.20	3.75	4.60	5.74	3.74	0.09
Trade, Hotels and Restaurants	-6.21	4.68	-25.45	32.89	18.35	5.49
Banking & Insurance	7.28	2.60	40.86	4.17	3.25	2.08
Real Estate, Ownership of Dwellings and Business Services	4.67	2.00	3.59	2.41	5.24	1.47
Public Administration	44.45	19.57	24.48	8.39	16.56	6.18
Other Services	39.56	11.68	37.18	25.41	13.74	1.54
Non-Infrastructure	84.01	31.25	61.66	33.80	30.30	7.72

	Meghalaya		*Nagaland*		*Tripura*		*Mizoram*	
	1993-99	*1999-06*	*1993-99*	*1999-06*	*1993-99*	*1999-06*	*1993-99*	*1999-06*
	con grth		*Con grth*		*Con grth*		*Con grth*	
Construction	24.86	17.58	38.46	23.26	27.39	37.75	19.16	18.27
Railways	0.00	0.00	0.06	0.15	0.00	0.05	0.00	0.04
Transport by Other Means	5.69	14.63	13.82	17.26	3.17	2.28	4.45	3.02
Storage	0.01	0.04	0.03	0.06	0.25	0.01	0.00	0.02
Communication	1.39	6.71	0.82	1.09	3.35	4.59	0.51	1.68
Trade, Hotels and Restaurants	23.16	18.06	7.12	8.30	19.23	9.49	7.36	2.37
Banking & Insurance	7.38	7.34	2.38	3.49	4.04	2.55	2.91	6.67
Real Estate, Ownership of Dwellings and Business Services	7.69	7.96	16.10	19.82	3.73	7.98	18.99	26.11

Public Administration	19.55	20.25	7.48	16.33	26.72	14.18	20.57	37.78
Other Services	10.28	7.44	13.73	10.24	12.11	21.13	26.04	4.05
Non-Infrastructure	29.83	27.69	21.21	26.57	38.83	35.31	46.61	41.83

Source: Same as Table 1

SECTION II: MAJOR OUTCOMES

Poverty and Calorie Deficiency

Table 5 reveals the incidence of poverty[5] in the North Eastern region. Between 1993-94 and 2004-05, only in Tripura witnessed an increase in poverty while the remaining states saw a substantial decline in the poverty level. Paradoxically, while the poverty level declined, there was a sharp increase in the proportion of calorie deficient households in the region (Table 5.1). This contrasting trend was mainly because of the faulty methodology adopted in calculation of poverty for the region (for lack of the required data for most other North Eastern states, Assam's statistics were used to estimate the poverty level in those states).

Table 5: Poverty Incidence in NER (1993-94 and 2004-05)

	50th Round			*61st Round*		
State	*Rural*	*Urban*	*Total*	*Rural*	*Urban*	*Total*
Arunachal Pradesh	41.20	6.02	37.00	10.85	2.58	9.90
Assam	45.20	7.92	41.40	22.09	3.64	20.38
Manipur	18.86	6.83	15.54	4.22	0.67	3.35
Meghalaya	24.37	1.82	21.29	3.57	0.06	3.11
Mizoram	6.24	0.00	4.26	2.80	0.00	1.69
Nagaland	2.29	0.00	1.68	0.00	0.00	0.00
Tripura	23.63	5.97	21.29	34.59	5.57	30.52
All-India	**36.85**	**32.86**	**35.86**	**28.04**	**25.81**	**27.47**

Source: Dubey and Pala (2008)

Table 5.1: State-wise Proportion of Calorie Deficient Households

State	*50th Round (1993-94)* Rural	Urban	Total	*61st Round (2004-05)* Rural	Urban	Total
Arunachal Pradesh	64.08	26.75	58.69	64.78	47.50	62.30
Assam	74.64	44.04	71.01	72.99	41.16	69.17
Manipur	60.40	49.65	57.36	75.08	27.69	63.02
Meghalaya	83.94	37.30	76.90	93.50	62.22	88.90
Mizoram	74.32	37.86	62.12	73.81	46.82	62.84
Nagaland	52.86	35.02	47.88	82.82	39.26	69.09
Tripura	71.88	51.93	69.16	86.50	44.70	80.04
All-India	**61.32**	**41.45**	**56.23**	68.34	52.60	64.01

Source: Dubey and Pala (2008)

Inequality in Per Capita Consumption Expenditure

Between 1993-94 and 1999-00, the rural urban combined consumption expenditure at the all-India level rose by Rs.13.75 (Table 6). It increased much higher in the five hill states with the exception of the urban areas of Arunachal Pradesh which saw a decline in consumption expenditure. On the other hand, Assam and Tripura recorded an increase of only Rs.2.95 and Rs.6.39 respectively as against the national level rise of Rs. 13.75. Much higher rise in consumption expenditure in the hill states could be due to higher dependency of the population on forest products for food items coupled with a substantial growth of the tertiary sector.

Table 6: Inflation Inequality Adjusted Per Capita Consumption Expenditure (Rupees)

	1993-94 Rural	Urban	Combined		*1999-2000* Rural	Urban	Combined
Arunachal	94.02	164.47	104.71	Arunachal	123.42	152.35	129.38
Assam	90.13	150.54	96.86	Assam	91.59	158.94	99.81
Manipur	108.02	124.19	112.89	Manipur	116.97	157.27	130.88
Meghalaya	110.28	185.27	124.55	Meghalaya	128.99	219.1	145.65
Mizoram	137.88	208.36	174.47	Mizoram	157.64	228.69	202.99
Nagaland	158.43	188.51	164.15	Nagaland	213.98	279.52	228.04
Sikkim	100.32	178.66	108.29	Sikkim	111.49	190.96	117.52
Tripura	111.35	162.16	119.53	Tripura	115.36	175.41	125.92
All India	87.9	124.27	97.53	All India	98.48	143.49	111.28

Source: National HDR 2001

The changing inequality in consumption expenditure can also be evaluated by examining the Gini co-efficient of per capita consumption expenditure over time, which is given in Table 7.

Table 7: Gini Coefficients of Per Capita Consumption Expenditure

	Rural 1993-94	*Rural 99-00*	*Change 94-99*		*Urban 1993-94*	*Urban 99-00*	*Change 94-99*
Arunachal	0.3	0.292	-0.008	Arunachal	0.275	0.298	0.023
Assam	0.176	0.201	0.025	Assam	0.285	0.311	0.026
Manipur	0.149	0.192	0.043	Manipur	0.153	0.216	0.063
Meghalaya	0.271	0.149	-0.122	Meghalaya	0.239	0.205	-0.034
Mizoram	0.165	0.188	0.023	Mizoram	0.174	0.237	0.063
Nagaland	0.153	0.155	0.002	Nagaland	0.195	0.206	0.011
Tripura	0.236	0.189	-0.047	Tripura	0.279	0.294	0.015
All India	0.282	0.258	-0.024	All India	0.34	0.341	0.001

Source: National HDR 2001

During the period 1993-94 to 1999-2000, the Gini coefficient declined by 2.4% in rural areas at the all-India level. In three of the North Eastern states, viz. Arunachal Pradesh, Meghalaya and Tripura, the coefficient declined in rural areas, to a varying degree while it declined in urban areas of only Meghalaya. In the other four states, it increased. The decline in inequality in Arunachal was mainly due to substantial dependency on common property resources (CPR) and substantial shift in occupational structure from the primary to tertiary sector while the decline in Tripura was because of increase in the overall growth in SDP as well as growth in three sectors. In Meghalaya the decline could be attributed to increase in the growth of the agriculture sector.

In other states like Nagaland, Mizoram and Manipur the increase in inequality could be attributed to (i) decline in the industrial sector (this is also evidenced in the decline in growth rate of enterprise and workers) (ii) low growth of agriculture, and (iii) fast growth of the service sector. Thus in rural areas of four states and in urban areas of six states, there had been an increase in inequality, which was mainly due to the poor performance of the economy, particularly of the agriculture and industrial sectors.

What emerged was that the majority of the states in the region experienced poverty reduction while at the same time an increase in inequalities. However, even with the increase in inequality, the level remained below the national average (except rural Arunachal). Thus, the economy of the North East was more egalitarian than the national average.

Employment

Changing Structure of Employment vs. GSDP

It was observed earlier that all the North Eastern states were fast moving towards tertiarization. In this context it is important to analyse the changing employment structure so as to assess the sustainability of the process. Table 8 shows the change in the sectoral share in GSDP and total employment[6].

The share of the agriculture sector in income and employment generation declined in Arunachal, Assam, Meghalaya, Mizoram and Tripura as also there had been deceleration in growth in agriculture in the 1990s. But a disproportionately larger decline in employment compared to the decline in sectoral share in GSDP occurred in Assam, Manipur and Mizoram while the opposite happened in Arunachal Pradesh, Meghalaya Nagaland and Tripura. In Manipur, the share of the agriculture sector in GSDP declined but the share of employment rose disproportionately, which was a case of reverse occupational shift from industry and service to agriculture. The decline in agriculture sector employment was accompanied by an increase in service sector employment in Arunachal, Assam, Meghalaya, Mizoram and Tripura though the income share of the service sector in GSDP was not proportionate except for Arunachal. In Manipur the share of the service sector in GSDP increased but that of employment declined. In Nagaland, the share of the service sector both in GSDP and employment declined while employment share in agriculture moved up.

In Manipur,Meghalaya,Mizoram and Nagaland the share of industry in GSDP declined, which resulted in decline in employment in Manipur and Meghalaya, but in an increase in Mizoram and Nagaland. In Arunachal, Assam and Tripura though industry's share in GSDP increased, the share in employment declined. Thus in five states the share of industry in employment

Table 8: Change in the Sectoral Share of Different Sectors in GSDP and Employment

(In Percentage points)

State	*Agriculture*	*Industry*	*Service*		*Employ-*	
	Employment	*GSDP*	*Employment*	*GSDP*	*ment*	*GSDP*
Arunachal	-1.25	-6.03	-0.64	1.38	2.09	4.65
Assam	-10.89	-4.29	-0.56	0.62	11.54	3.67
Manipur	9.77	-3.73	-4.66	-0.45	-5.01	4.18
Meghalaya	-0.79	-1.41	-0.06	-0.71	0.89	2.11
Mizoram	-8.64	-4.12	0.70	-3.81	8.05	7.93
Nagaland	3.98	5.73	0.52	-4.86	-4.56	-0.87
Tripura	-2.86	-5.89	-2.24	1.56	5.51	4.32
All India	-3.86	-5.40	0.15	-0.32	3.87	5.72

Note: -ve means decline and +ve means increase in period 1999-00 compared to 1993-94.

Source: Changing GSDP is computed from the CSO website and the changing employment is computed from NSSO.[7]

had declined while in Mizoram and Nagaland it increased marginally. Perhaps inability of the industrial sector to absorb more labour force was responsible for the low industrial wage rate in the region (Table 15).

It could therefore be argued that the shift of the workforce from the agriculture to service sector in these states was the result of distress-driven because of poor agriculture performance rather than demand driven. The high rate of occupational shift from agriculture to service sector could be explained by low Net Irrigated Area as percentage of Net Sown Area and land scarcity for sustenance. This has resulted in a faster tertiarization process in the North Eastern region. The reverse process had taken place in Manipur and Nagaland because of poor performance of industry in generating employment accompanied by low industrial wage rate. In Manipur better irrigation facilities and better technology adoption could absorb partially the incremental labour force. Since agriculture was not that remunerative, the educated labour tended to out migrate to other states.Thus, the outcome of this process was abnormally large out-migration from the states of Manipur and Nagaland and more female out-migrants from Nagaland (Table 16).

Incidence of Unemployment

Between 1993-94 and 1999-2000, the rural unemployment rate declined in three states and increased in states like Manipur, Meghalaya and Nagaland. Urban unemployment rate rose in all the North Eastern states except in Tripura. The incidence of unemployment in 2004 in Assam and the North Eastern states together were higher than the national average. Rural unemployment rate in Assam, North Eastern states and India were 3.62, 4.63 and 1.60 per cent and urban unemployment rate 6.61, 7.11 and 4.58 per cent respectively.[8]

Table 9: Unemployment Rate

	Rural 93-94 %	99-00 %	*Change*		*Urban* 93-94 %	99-00 %	*Change*
Arunachal	0.9	0.5	-0.4	Arunachal	1.4	3	1.6
Assam	5.3	4	-1.3	Assam	8.7	9.8	1.1
Manipur	0.9	2	1.1	Manipur	4.2	6.7	2.5
Meghalaya	0.2	0.4	0.2	Meghalaya	1.7	4.5	2.8
Mizoram	1.1	0.9	-0.2	Mizoram	0.4	2.9	2.5
Nagaland	1.5	2.4	0.9	Nagaland	6.7	9.2	2.5
Tripura	2.4	1.2	-1.2	Tripura	8.4	5.8	-2.6
Northeast				North East			
All India	1.2	1.5	0.3	All India	4.6	4.8	0.2

Source: National HDR 2001

The increase in the unemployment rate in many of the states could be attributed to the decline in the growth of total enterprises and workers as can be seen from Tables 10 and 11.

As Table 10 shows, the growth rate of the total number of enterprises in the rural sector declined compared to the 1980s, in all states except for Mizoram and Tripura (comparable data are not available for Assam) in the 1990s. Urban enterprise growth also slumped in all the states in the 1990s. With the exception of Nagaland, the employment growth also declined in all the North Eastern states. This suggests that the increase in the unemployment rate in the 1990s was partly due to low growth in the number of enterprises in the post-reform period.

Table 10: Growth of Number of Enterprise

State	Rural		Urban		Combined	
	1980-90	1990-2005	1980-90	1990-2005	1980-90	1990-2005
Arunachal	5.72	1.07	10.25	4.86	6.61	2.15
Assam	-	3.90	-	4.91	-	4.26
Manipur	6.01	3.71	5.62	3.48	5.84	3.61
Meghalaya	4.44	3.81	4.43	3.18	4.44	3.59
Mizoram	2.23	4.34	8.77	5.33	5.53	4.94
Nagaland	3.91	3.34	4.64	2.96	4.24	3.17
Tripura	4.41	5.52	5.72	5.12	4.77	5.41
All-India	2.69	3.76	3.55	3.07	3.04	3.49

Source: Central Statistical Organization (2001), Fifth Economic Census and other Economic Census as reported in *Economic and Political Weekly*, June 30, 2006.

Table 11: Growth in Number of Workers

State	Rural		Urban		Combined	
	1980-90	1990-2005	1980-90	1990-2005	1980-90	1990-2005
Arunachal	6.97	2.27	9.65	1.16	7.80	1.85
Assam	-	3.18	-	3.42	-	3.26
Manipur	5.26	3.03	3.16	2.36	4.13	2.70
Meghalaya	5.55	3.28	3.71	1.54	4.58	2.46
Mizoram	1.27	2.91	6.51	1.99	4.67	2.27
Nagaland	2.44	2.65	5.46	2.17	5.70	2.35
Tripura	4.80	4.34	5.50	2.58	5.07	3.68
All-India	2.88	2.72	2.81	1.49	2.84	2.08

Source: Central Statistical Organization (2001), Economic Census 1998 as reported in *Economic and Political Weekly*, December 29, 2001 and some issues of *EPW* in 2007.

Educated Unemployment

Table12 shows the extent of educated unemployment in the North Eastern states excluding Assam for which the data are not available.

Column 4 in the Table shows the vacancies notified in employment exchanges as a percentage of the total registered candidates. The percentage of candidates as against the notified vacancies was higher than the national average in Arunachal, Manipur and Mizoram while lower in the other three states for

Table 12: Registration with and Notified Vacancies by Employment Exchange

States	*No. of Registration (thousand)*	*Vacancies Notified (thousand)*	*% of Vacancies Notified to Total Number of Registration*	*Submission of Applications (thousand)*	*% of Applications to Vacancies*
Arunachal	7.4	0.4	5.41	1.6	400
Assam	-	-	-	-	-
Manipur	10.5	0.7	6.67	11.9	1700
Meghalaya	11.8	0.4	3.39	3.4	850
Mizoram	15.2	0.8	5.26	10	1250
Nagaland	9.4	0.2	2.13	1.5	750
Tripura	23.8	0.3	1.26	3.6	1200
All India	5904.8	279	4.72	2273.2	814

Source: *Economic and Political Weekly*, December 21, 2002, p. 5063.

which the data are available. The problem is more acute in Tripura, Nagaland and Meghalaya, where the job aspirants were much more than the vacancies notified. The last column of Table 12 shows the vacancies notified as a percentage of the applications submitted. In the states other than Arunachal Pradesh, the percentage of frustrated aspirants was alarmingly high. It was the highest in Manipur (1,700) followed by Tripura (1,200) and Mizoram (1,250). High literacy rate in several states unaccompanied by job opportunities led to this acute educated unemployment situation.

Employment in Public and Private Sector

Table 13 brings out that at the national level public and private sector respectively accounted for 60 and 40 per cent of the total employment in 2004-05 and that the private sector employment share significantly rose from 31 per cent in 1999-2000 to 39 per cent in 2004-05.

In Assam, the share of private sector employment was above 50 per cent of the total employment in 1999-2000 and 2004-05. In the rest of the North Eastern states (excluding Assam) the private sector played only a minor role in employment generation while the public sector contributed close to 90 per cent or more employment In the states like Manipur, Mizoram and Tripura the

Table 13: Employment in Public and Private Sector

States	*Public Sector (%)*			*Private Sector (%)*			*Total Employment (in thousands)*		
	1987-88	*1999-00*	*2004-05*	*1987-88*	*1999-00*	*2004-05*	*1987-88*	*1999-00*	*2004-05*
Arunachal		-			-			-	
Assam	82.07	49.38	46.61	17.93	50.62	53.39	664.8	1084.5	1112.2
Manipur	94.05	96.84	96.44	5.95	3.16	3.56	48.7	82.1	80.6
Meghalaya	89.4	88.64	88.64	10.6	11.35	11.36	61.3	81.9	81.9
Mizoram	94	96.63	96.63	6	3.37	3.37	25	41.5	41.5
Nagaland	97.55	95.97	94.33	2.45	4.03	5.67	69.3	76.9	72.3
Tripura	87.63	89.54	89.62	12.37	10.46	10.38	89.7	123.3	123.3
All-India	62.6	69.08	60.05	37.4	30.92	39.95	25748	27959.7	26458.4

Source: Statistical Abstract, *Statistical Abstract India* (various issues) CSO, Department of Statistics, Ministry of Planning, Government of India.

share of the private sector employment declined over time (Table 13). Thus the low private sector role in employment generation had resulted in high pressure on the government to create more jobs. Perhaps this was the main reason why there had been overstaffing in most of the states in the region.

Quality of Employment in Factory Sector

The Annual Survey of Industries gives the status of the workers employed in the factory sector. The definition of factory in other states of India refers to those factories where more than 100 workers are employed. In the case of the North East, all factories irrespective of the number of the workers are taken. Therefore, the data of the North East are not comparable with other major states of India and would be on the higher side.

North Eastern states accounted for 0.39 per cent of the total workers employed in the factory sector of India. At the all-India level, out of the total workers in the factory sector, 17.57 per cent were employed in the public and joint sector in 2001-02 (Table 14). In states like Assam and Meghalaya, public and joint sectors employed a much higher proportion than the national level. However, in Manipur and Nagaland the figure was abysmally low indicating the fact that the private sector played a major role in employing workers in the factory sector. In Meghalaya, Nagaland and Tripura the percentage of contract workers was disproportionately high compared to the national average.

The only state where per worker value added was higher than the national average was Meghalaya and in the remaining states, it was much lower. This low level of per worker value added was reflected in the low level of wage and salary they received.The distance between the state level wage as a percentage of the national level wages and salaries at the state and the national levels declined in all the North Eastern states between 1980-81 and 1991-92. During the post-reform period the distance widened substantially in all the states except for Assam where it stagnated around 55 per cent between 1991-92 and in 2001-02. The distance varied from 23 to 27 per cent in case of Manipur, Nagaland and Tripura and from 51 to 55 per cent in the case of Meghalaya and Assam. The striking fact is that the distance from the national average was rising over time

Table 14: Status of Workers Employed in the Factory Sector (2001-02)

	Total Workers	*Public & Joint Sector*	*% in Private Sector*	*Directly Employed %*	*Contract Labour %*	*Labour Cost Per Man Days*	*Per Worker Wages and Salaries (Rs.)*	*Column 7 as a % of All India Average*	*Per Worker Value Added (Rs Lakhs)*
	1	*2*	*3*	*4*	*5*	*6*	*7*	*8*	*9*
Assam	60127	20.35	79.67	92.5	7.5	159.4	45884	55.37	7.08
Manipur	992	7.26	92.74	99.7	0.3	60.62	19714	23.79	1.52
Meghalaya	1282	22.77	77.23	49.5	50.47	101.76	42520	51.31	13.02
Nagaland	2278	1.36	98.64	53.21	46.79	75.76	22372	27.00	3.64
Tripura	9162	14.72	85.28	32.27	67.73	95.85	22280	26.89	2.81
North East	13947	18.93	81.07	83.64	16.36		41819	50.46	
All-India	3535771	17.57	82.43	78.5	21.5	242.36	82864	100	11.88

Source: Annual Survey of Industries 2001-02, Vol. II, as reproduced in *Economic and Political Weekly*, November 12, 2005 and October 11, 2003.

(Table 15). This particular trend suggests that the low level of investment in the region had resulted in low demand of qualified labour and an increase in the demand of casual workers. The process had resulted in a high share of contract workers to total workers and the end result is the persistence of low wage rate in the region.

Table 15: Wage and Salaries of the Workers in the Factory Sector

	Wage and Salaries Per Worker (Rs)	*As a Percentage of National Average*	*Wage and Salaries Per Worker (Rs)*	*As a Percentage of National Average*	*Wage and Salaries Per Worker (Rs)*	*As a Percentage of National Average*
	1980-81	*1980-81*	*1991-92*	*1991-92*	*2001-02*	*2001-02*
Assam	2293	45.65	8915	54.61	45884	55.37
Manipur	2598	51.72	8452	51.77	19714	23.79
Meghalaya	3350	66.69	20330	124.53	42520	51.31
Nagaland	n.a	n.a	9315	57.06	22372	27.00
Tripura	2124	42.29	9854	60.36	22280	26.89
NE	n.a	n.a	n.a	n.a	41819	50.47
All-India	5023	100.00	16325	100.00	82864	100.00

Source: Computed from Table 14 and *Annual Survey of Industries 1973-1997-98: A Database on the Industrial Sector in India*, EPW Research Foundation, Sameeksha Trust 2002.

Migration

Most of the states of this region have achieved high literacy.With persistent low quality employment opportunities, people started migrating to other parts of the country. Table 16 shows the out migration rate[9] from the North Eastern region.

Table 16 reveals that in the entire North Eastern region the female out migration rate was higher than the males. This was true in the case of Arunachal, Nagaland, Meghalaya and Assam. In Nagaland females' out-migration rate was much higher than the males. In Nagaland (female) and Mizoram (both female and male) migration rate was higher than the national average. A similar trend was also observed in the population in the age groups, 15-24 and 25-34. The point that needs a close scrutiny is the abnormally high rate of female out migration from Nagaland in both the age

Table 16: Out-Migration Rate 2001 (%)

State	*All Age Groups*			*Age Group 15-24*			*Age Group 25-35*		
	Total	*Male*	*Female*	*Total*	*Male*	*Female*	*Total*	*Male*	*Female*
Arunachal	3.35	3.19	3.51	3.59	2.69	4.50	2.27	2.00	2.56
Assam	2.63	2.15	3.12	4.14	2.96	5.27	2.61	1.99	3.27
Manipur	3.38	3.72	3.04	3.37	3.23	3.51	2.43	2.50	2.36
Mizoram	4.85	4.96	4.74	4.36	4.22	4.51	4.17	4.20	4.14
Tripura	1.68	1.77	1.60	3.07	2.92	3.21	2.40	2.37	2.42
Meghalaya	2.13	1.88	2.38	3.93	3.26	4.56	2.27	2.06	2.49
Nagaland	6.27	3.17	9.43	13.42	5.30	20.48	7.29	3.49	11.68
North East	2.88	2.36	3.42	4.44	3.12	5.73	2.86	2.18	3.57
All India	4.13	4.00	4.27	6.66	5.71	7.61	4.14	3.72	4.59

Source: Computed from data provided in the CD form, *Census of India 2001*, D Series, Directorate of Census Operations, Arunachal Pradesh, Shillong.

Table 17: In Migration Rate 2001 (%)

	Total	*Male*	*Female*
Arunachal	15.54	17.62	13.22
Assam	1.94	2.10	1.76
Manipur	0.86	0.98	0.73
Meghalaya	3.97	4.40	3.53
Mizoram	4.34	5.50	3.10
Nagaland	4.30	5.14	3.37
Tripura	1.97	1.83	2.11

Source: Same as Table 16.

groups.This particular trend could be attributed to the high incidence of unemployment among the educated youth, low quality employment opportunities and low wage rate. The process was also further intensified by a negative industrial growth.

The inmigration rate (Table 17) in some of the states was also higher than the national average. The high rate in the states of Arunachal, Nagaland and Mizoram was because of large scale inmigration of casual workers, as the construction and low technology agriculture activities require a huge labour force. Hence, these states are characterized by both, high rate of in and out-migration. Thus the high rate of literacy and low wage rate have fuelled out-migration while low end manual jobs which the local educated youths did not find attractive lured large-scale migrant workers to meet the shortage of low skilled manpower required for agricultural and construction works.

To sum up, several development outcomes such as incidence of calorie deficient households, inequality in per capita consumption expenditure, employment, wage and per capita SDP performed poorly in the North Eastern states compared to the national level. Private investment in the North Eastern states was meagre. In fact, the total investment in the region was only 2.56 per cent of the total investment of India as in October 2004. Low private investment and slow technological adoption in agriculture led to a pressure on the government to create more jobs and consequent overstaffing and bulging of non-development expenditure squeezing capital expenditure for adding to productive capacity of the state economies. At another level, lack of employment opportunities in the private sector particularly in the states like Manipur, Nagaland, Mizoram and Tripura with high literacy spurred high out-migration.

SECTION III: IMPEDIMENTS TO GROWTH

To understand the persistent underdevelopment of the North Eastern states as shown above, it is important to identify and examine the working of the major variables such as land availability, water resources, government support to farmers, infrastructure, and investment that have acted as impediments to growth in the North Eastern region.

Land Availability

Most of the North Eastern states are land-scarce economies, though the total geographical area is large. The density of population ranges from 13 (Arunachal) to 340 (Assam). The density of population in North Eastern states except for Assam is less than the national average. Yet in states like Arunachal Pradesh, Manipur, Meghalaya, Mizoram and Nagaland, the hilly terrain constitutes more than 90 per cent of the total geographical area and thus the plain land available for cultivation is only 5 per cent. Table 18 shows that except for Manipur, none of the North Eastern states has Net

Irrigated Area as percentage of Net Sown Area above the national average in 2000-01. This indicates that the spread of modern farming was highly limited and to that extent the marketable surplus was small.

Table 18: Land Availability in the North East

State	*Population*	*Net Sown Area (NSA) (In thousand hectares)*	*Net Irrigated Area (NIA) (In thousand hectares)*	*NIA as % of NSA*
1	*2*	*3*	*4*	*5*
Arunachal	1091117	185	36	12.6
Assam	26638407	2701	572	21.2
Manipur	2388634	140	65	46.4
Meghalaya	2306069	221	48	21.7
Mizoram	891058	109	9	08.3
Nagaland	1988636	261	63	24.1
Tripura	3191168	277	35	12.6
All-India	1027015247	142598	57055	40.0

Source: Column 2, *Economic Survey 2001-02*; Columns 3 & 4, *Annual Report 2002-03*, Ministry of Water Resources, GOI (Reproduced in *Economic and Political Weekly*, October 4, 2003); Column 5 is computed.

Due to high population growth in the 1990s, landless population increased considerably in the North Eastern states except for Meghalaya and Manipur while it declined for the country as a whole (Table 19). Landlessness is quite acute in states like Tripura and Assam, where 34.59 and 35.58 per cent of households respectively did not possess any cultivable land in 1999-2000.

Table 19: Households with No Cultivable Land (%)

States	*1993-94*	*1999-2000*
Arunachal	22.81	25.38
Assam	34.55	35.58
Manipur	24.74	16.18
Meghalaya	17.87	12.42
Mizoram	10.25	14.43
Nagaland	6.35	10.54
Tripura	33.10	34.59
All-India	41.36	40.80

Source: Amaresh Dubey and Others.[10]

Water Scarcity

The North Eastern region is widely perceived as a region rich in water resources. Surface water irrigation potential of this region is 3.04 per cent of the total potential of India. In terms of utilization of water resources the region lags far behind the national average. Table-20 shows that, in all the states (except Nagaland), the Net Irrigated Area to Irrigation potential is very low compared to the national average. Thus there exists a huge gap in the utilization of irrigation potential in the North East region.

In terms of ground water development also the region is much behind the national average. The utilizable ground water potential is one percentage point above the national average but the level of development of ground water is very low to negligible.

Table 20: Water Resource in North East

States	*Irrigation Potentials (thousand hectares)*	*Net Irrigated Area (NIA) (thousand hectares)*	*NIA as a% of Potentials*	*NIA as a% of NSA*	*Utilizable Ground Water Potential to Total Potential*	*Level of Ground Water Development (%)*
	1	2	3	4	5	6
Arunachal	168	36	21.42	19.46	76.50	NA
Assam	2870	572	19.93	21.18	76.07	7.46
Manipur	604	65	10.76	46.43	76.50	Negligible
Meghalaya	168	48	28.57	21.72	76.48	Negligible
Mizoram	70	9	12.85	8.26	NA	NA
Nagaland	85	63	74.12	24.14	76.45	Negligible
Tripura	281	35	12.46	12.64	76.49	33.43
All India	139893	57055	40.78	40.01	75.21	37.24

Source: Annual Report 2002-03, Ministry of Water Resources, GOI, (Reproduced in *Economic and Political Weekly*, October 4, 2003); Columns 5 & 6 are computed.

Inequality in Technology Adoption

Poor utilization of irrigation potentials has led to non-adoption of modern technology. This coupled with high population growth resulted in a decline in per capita food grain production over the years. For example, in Assam the per capita food grain production was 178.15 kgs in 1951-52 which came down to 159.60 kgs in 1997-

98 (Assam HDR 2003). Fertilizer consumption per hectare of Gross Cropped area taken as a proxy measure of adoption of modern technology clearly brings out the fact of low adoption of new technology. All the states of the North Eastern region except for Manipur were far behind the national average consumption of fertilizer (Table 21) and thus in adoption of modern technology. Manipur performed better in adoption of modern technology as suggested by more than national average (1990-91) fertilizer consumption. This was possible because of its relatively better irrigation facilities. Perhaps for this reason, a reverse shift in occupation was taking place in Manipur from the tertiary to primary sector in the 1990s.

Table 21

States	*Fertilizer Use Per Hectare of Gross Cropped Area*		
	1990-91	*1998-99*	*% change*
Arunachal	2.42	2.82	16.40
Assam	8.97	19.82	121.05
Manipur	42.81	79.21	85.01
Meghalaya	11.03	13.99	26.82
Mizoram	10.31	9.84	-4.51
Nagaland	5.39	2.32	-56.98
Tripura	20.58	20.00	-2.81
North East	10.64	19.55	83.74
All-India	67.55	87.03	29.28

Source: For North East and Different States, NEDFi[11], For all-India, computed from RBI.[12]

While fertilizer consumption was low and even declined over 1990-91 in three states, government support in the form of fertilizer subsidy in Assam, for example, was less than one-third of the national average (Table 22) or even lower than the backward states like Orissa. It can be argued, therefore, that in a flood-prone state like Assam where farm risk is high, only strong government support could have helped the dissemination of modern technology.

Table 22: Statewise Fertilizer Subsidy

State	*Subsidy Per Hectare (Rupees)*	*As a Percentage of all India Average*	*Subsidy Per Hectare (Rupees)*	*As a Percentage of All India Average*
	1990-91	*1990-91*	*1999-00*	*1999-00*
Andhra Pradesh	304.1	180.2	652.6	164.7
Assam	20.9	12.4	103.6	26.1
Haryana	251.3	148.9	609.7	153.9
Punjab	412.2	244.2	740.5	186.9
Orissa	51.8	30.7	145.3	36.7
Bihar	148.7	88.1	411.5	103.9
West Bengal	211.4	125	549.00	138.6
All-India	168.8	100	396.2	100

Source: Singh (ibid), p. 298.

Investment

Table 23 gives the trend in total investment in the North Eastern region and India from the period October 2000 to October 2004.

Table 23: Trend in Total Investment (Rs Crore)

States	*As on Oct. 2004*	*As on Oct. 2003*	*As on Oct. 2002*	*As on Oct. 2001*	*As on Oct. 2000*	*As a% of NE as on Oct.2004*
Arunachal	11339	2839	2852	4134	4078	24.71
Assam	16812	11971	14012	12313	11151	36.63
Manipur	5591	5610	9970	1207	1108	12.18
Meghalaya	910	737	748	697	728	1.98
Mizoram	2552	2633	1939	1196	1053	5.56
Nagaland	312	303	436	275	928	0.68
Tripura	8376	4585	5465	5609	3446	18.25
North East	45892	28678	35422	25431	22492	100.00
All-India	1793979	1413698	1499670	1543378	1397639	

Source: Cap. Ex. (2004), CMIE (as reported in *Economic and Political Weekly*, December 4, 2004).

Table 23 reveals that as in October 2004, the North East region received 45892 crore of investment which was only 2.56 per cent of the total investment in India.This was disproportionately low compared to its population share. Of the total investment in the region, the major share went to Assam (36.63%). The second, third and fourth recipients of the investment were Arunachal (24.71%), Tripura (18.25%). and Manipur (12.18%), respectively. Meghalaya, Mizoram and Nagaland together got a share of 8.22 per cent. Thus, the North East region received a very small fraction of the total investment in the country and what is more, investment flows were unequally spread across the states.

Infrastructure

Empirical evidences worldwide suggest that the level and quality of infrastructure attract investment to a region. In this regard, too, the North East states lagged behind the national level. The infrastructure indices of the North Eastern states are given below.[13]

Table 24: Infrastructure Index

States	*Infrastructure Index (1977-78)*	*Rank in India*	*Distance from National Average (%)*	*Infrastructure Index (2000)*	*Rank in India*	*Distance from National Average (%)*
Arunachal	n.a	-	-	69.71	25	66.18
Assam	85	12	85	77.72	17	73.79
Manipur	52	20	52	75.39	22	71.58
Meghalaya	49	21	49	75.49	21	71.67
Mizoram	n.a	-	-	82.13	14	77.97
Nagaland	75	15	75	76.14	19	72.29
Tripura	53	19	53	74.87	23	71.08
All-India average	100		100	105.33		100.00

Source: For 1977-78 Planning Commission 1978, as reported in Krishna Raj (1981), "The Centre and the Periphery: Interstate Disparities in Economic Development", *Social Action*, January-March, pp. 1-34. For 2000 figures, Eleventh Finance Commission as reported in Government of India (2002), *Tenth Five Year Plan 2002-2007*, Vol. III, p. 70.

Table 24 shows that between 1977-78 and 2000 the distance from the national average infrastructure index increased in two states, Assam and Nagaland. In Manipur, Meghalaya and Tripura improved substantially the value of their respective indices. Even so, in 2000, all the North Eastern states other than Mizoram and Assam ranked at the lower end of the infrastructures index. Though the state of Mizoram came close to Orissa and Himachal Pradesh in ranks, the quantum of investment flow to Mizoram accounted for only 5.93 per cent of the total flow to the North East region. Though Mizoram was ranked above Madhya Pradesh and Rajasthan in the infrastructure index, it received less investment than these mainland states.[14] Similarly, even with substantial improvement in infrastructure availability in some of the states[15] of the region over time, investment inflow was very low compared to other mainland states.This suggests that higher level of infrastructure alone was not sufficient to attract larger investment. There must be other forces[16] responsible for the persistent underdevelopment of the region. In another essay[17] in this volume, we have discussed in detail the constraints that are binding on the development process of the North Eastern states. These are briefly indicated in the concluding section.

Section IV: Concluding Observations: Explanatory Hypothesis

To conclude, there are five major impediments to the economic development of the North Eastern states. These are: 1. initial conditions such as (i) disruption of traditional trade and transport links; (ii) population influx; (iii) unharnessed resource endowments; (iv) enclave economy and (v) monopolistic operations of deeply entrenched trading interests, 2. Infrastructure deficits, 3. Insurgency, 4. Imperfection/distortion in factor and product markets and 5. Poor governance. They still stand even at the end of more than five decades of planning as binding constraints on the economic development of the North Eastern region.

We submit two paradigms. One relates to overstress on security/strategic consideration rather than development efforts in a well-thought out development framework. The other relates to the minimum intervention in the traditional systems and institutions of the hill economy, which is what has led to their non-compatibility while market integration is at work at least to an extent.

These paradigms continued to impact the thinking and action of the Government of India. Since the mid-1990s, the North Eastern economic development began to find a place in the mainstream collective psyche as reflected in the growing national level debate deliberations and discourse as well as announcement of special economic packages for the North East economic development. With the articulation of 'Look East Policy' in the early 1990s, a new vision in development perspective as a gateway to dynamic East Asian economies was shaped.

An attempt followed to revamp the NEC recognizing explicitly the economic interdependence of the constituents of the North East. Only in February 2005, the NEC had been restructured more as a regional planning mechanism than an administrative one with the overtone of strategic consideration.

With the emergence of an economic perspective, a shift in policy thrust on the part of GoI, was clearly visible. Attention is being directed towards road connectivity between the North Eastern states[18], connectivity and communication between the region and the rest of the country, other infrastructure, harnessing the resources of the region, development of potential areas such as tourism and paving the way for large trade with the East and South East Asian countries and flow of funds with specified objectives indicating initiatives in a development perspective. Development activism in civil society also played an important role.

It is not to argue, however, that the binding constraints discussed earlier have all been and adequately addressed. There are several areas of concern: such as governance, sensitive issues like influx of people from across the border and burgeoning mass of unemployed youths who are attracted by numerous militant groups. As the situation stands now, one can only wonder whether it is the beginning of the end of the long and dark tunnel.

NOTES

1. This article has dealt with the North East region in its initial demarcation comprising seven states.
2. A high level Commission, "Transforming the North East" was constituted under the Chairmanship of Shri S.P. Shukla following the Prime Minister's announcement of 'New Initiatives for the North Eastern Region' on October 27, 1996 and the Report was submitted in March 1997. Prior to that, the Planning Commission constituted a Working Group on the Development of the North Eastern Region during the Seventh Five Year Plan, 1985-90 under the Chairmanship

of P.H. Trivedi, Secretary, NEC. Also, the Planning Commission at the instance of the Union Home Ministry constituted a Committee under the Chairmanship of L.C. Jain, then Member, Planning Commission to look into the question of economic development of Assam under Clause Seven of the Assam Accord and the Report was submitted in April 1990.

3. Gross State Domestic Product (GSDP) is used to compute the growth rate. Two different sources of data are used. The data for the period 1980-81 to 1992-93 is taken from the Economic and Political Weekly Research Foundation (EPW 2003) and data for the period 1993-94 to 1998-99 (series 1993) and 1999-2000 to 2005-06 (1999 series) is taken from the CSO website. Since EPWRF data is based on CSO data, for computing growth between the 1980s and 90s there is no serious mistake involved. In the CSO website time series SDP data of Mizoram at constant prices for the period 1993-98 is not available. In order to find the figures at the constant price, the paper has used the Nagaland price deflator, because both the states are more or less similar in topography.
4. For all states GSDP data are not available for 1999-07. Therefore, for Assam, Manipur and Meghalaya the post-liberalization period phase-II covers the time 1999-2007 while for Arunachal and Tripura it is 1999 to 2005-06, for Mizoram it is 1999-2008.
5. Dubey, A. and V. Pala (2008), "Poverty, Hunger and Calorie Deficiency in Arunachal Pradesh", background paper prepared for the *Arunachal Development Report*, Rajiv Gandhi University, 2008.
6. Change in sectoral share in GSDP is computed from the triennium average of the periods 1993-94, 1994-95 and 1995-96 and 1999-00, 2000-01 and 2001-02; change in sectoral share in employment is computed between the period 1993-94 and 1999-2000. NSSO data on distribution of employment on principal and subsidiary status is available for rural and urban areas. To get the distribution of employment of all the areas we have taken the weighted average of rural and urban area's distribution pattern, where the weight is the share of rural and urban population in total population.
7. Revised Report No. 406, *Key Results on Employment and Unemployment*, NSS 50th Round (July 1993-June 1994), July 1996 and *Employment and Unemployment Situation in India*, Part I, NSS 55th Round (July 1999-June 2000), May 2001, NSSO, Department of Statistics, Government of India.
8. NSSO (2005): *Employment and Unemployment Situation in India, January-June 2004,* Ministry of Statistics and Programme Implementation, Government of India.

9. The out-migration rate is computed from the data available in each and every state and union territories of India. People migrating to a state from other states is available. So from the destination people migrated from the North Eastern states is computed. Then the migrated population is added to the respective state's population and the migration rate is computed from that population in percentage terms.The in-migration rate is computed taking the population not born inside the state as a percentage of the total population.
10. Amaresh Dubey and Others (2004): "Poverty in the Hill Economy of North Eastern States", Paper presented at the Seminar on Transforming the Hill Economies, held at Itanagar, November, organized by the Institute of Human Development and Arunachal University.
11. NEDFi (2005), *Data Bank Quarterly*, Vol. 4, Issue 1, January.
12. RBI, (2005), *Handbook of Statistics on the Indian Economy, 2004-05*, Reserve Bank of India.
13. It must be kept in mind that the two infrastructure indices of the year 1977-78 and 2000 are not strictly comparable but they reflect some proxy trend over the period of time.
14. CMIE, op. cit.
15. The recently published ranking of Indian States by *India Today* (September 12, 2008) has put Assam as the 15th in the ranking of 17 states in India in terms of the Infrastructure Acceleration Index.
16. The chapter, Why North East States Continue to Decelerate discusses in detail the binding constraints.
17. Why North Eastern States Continue to Decelerate.
18. The GoI has recently cleared a multilane North East Express Highway linking all the capitals of North Eastern states spanning 6,907 kms towards connectivity within and between different units of the region, infrastructure development (4,464 kms of national highways, 2,050 kms of newly declared highways and 393 kms of NEC roads).

6

Industrialization in the North Eastern and Eastern Zone*

Introduction

Viewed in the context of the rest of the country, the North Eastern states have two important similarities. With the exception of (undivided) Bihar, all the states within the zone are characterized by the preponderance of SC and ST population. As compared to the all-India share of 22.80 per cent, SC and ST population ranged from 27.6 per cent in West Bengal to 93.1 per cent in Mizoram. The other striking similarity is that despite a higher level of per capita income in four extremely small states, viz. Nagaland, Mizoram, Arunachal Pradesh (AP) and Sikkim each of the states in the zone are far behind the rest of the country in terms of administrative, social and economic infrastructures, be it per capita power consumption, credit-deposit ratios, road and railway transport network. Yet another similarity among the states as compared to the rest of the country is that most of the units in the zone recorded high decadal population growth even during 1981-91.

But the states within the zone are dissimilar in many more ways. They are dissimilar in terms of population size. The population size varies from 0.4 million in Sikkim to 86.3 million in (undivided) Bihar. Population density ranges from 8 per sq. km. (Arunachal Pradesh) to 766 per sq. km. (West Bengal) which is the highest among the states in the country. They are also dissimilar in terms of urbanization rate, literacy rates and other demographic characteristics, physical features, stages of economic development

---

* Jointly with Amarendra Sahoo, Indian Statistical Institute, Delhi Centre, Sansanwal Marg, New Delhi 110 016.

etc., leaving aside the socio-cultural differences. Such dissimilarities coupled with the fact that seven out of eleven states constituting the zone are hill states, present a serious problem in attempting a rigorous analysis of industrialization of the states at the zonal level; more so in making any meaningful policy prescriptions. What is more, the Annual Survey of Industries does not still extend to several units of the zone, viz. Arunachal Pradesh, Mizoram, Nagaland, and Sikkim, thus inhibiting any disaggregated analysis of industries in these states. Even the Basic Statistics of the North Eastern Region published by the North Eastern Council Secretariat is not much helpful in this regard. Keeping these facts in view, we have made an attempt to understand the role of the industrial sector in the state economy within the region; the structure of the industrial sector, the extent of industrial diversification, broad linkages of the lead industries of each region and finally, to reflect on the constraints and prospects of industrialization.

Structure of State Economy and Role of Manufacturing

State economics within the zone do not reflect in several respects the general development pattern of the country as observed during the period 1980-89. For example, compared to the all-India average, contribution of agriculture to the NSDP was considerably higher in most of the states in 1980-81 and remained so even at the end of 1988-89. Interestingly, the role of agriculture in income generation was considerably low in a couple of hill states such as Nagaland and Mizoram, in 1980-81 and further declined in the subsequent years. Again, in contrast to the general pattern, the share of agriculture in NSDP remained almost steady or increased over the years in a few states such as Tripura, Mizoram and West Bengal. Further, the contribution of Banking and Insurance to NSDP was substantially lower than the all-India average in 1980-81.

Even with some increase over the years, the relative position did not alter substantially. The structure of state income varied from state to state within the zone. States like Assam, Meghalaya, Mizoram, (undivided) Bihar and Orissa derived a considerably larger proportion of income from mining and quarrying ranging from 2.017 per cent in Mizoram to 6.20 per cent in (undivided)

Bihar as against 23 per cent for the aggregate at the all-India level in 1989. This clearly indicates rich endowment of mining resources in these states. Similarly, the contribution of construction was higher. It was higher than the all-India average in all the states except for Assam and West Bengal. A much higher than all-India average share in total income was also derived from real estate, ownership of dwelling, business service by the states other than Orissa. Further, public administration contributed a much larger share to NSDP in all the states except for (undivided) Bihar and Orissa. It is important to note that trade, hotels, restaurants generated a considerable income even in the hill states though the sector's share tended to decline over the years in most of the states.

The manufacturing sector, in contrast, contributed far less share to NSDP in the states except for West Bengal. The share of this sector to NSDP ranged from 1.9 per cent in Arunachal Pradesh to 23.2 per cent in West Bengal as against the all-India average of 19.6 per cent in 1988-89. Its share declined from 3.17 per cent in 1980-81 to 2.17 per cent in Nagaland and from 24.77 per cent to 23.2 per cent in West Bengal. Although the registered manufacturing sector's share in NSDP showed an increase in the states other than Nagaland and West Bengal, its contribution was far less than the all-India average in all the units except for West Bengal. Even in regard to the unregistered manufacturing sector, its share in NSDP was much lower than the all-India average level. Two important points may be made in this regard. First, the importance of unregistered manufacturing for income generation was overwhelmingly higher compared to the registered sector in all the hill states except for Sikkim. Second, in contrast to the rising share of the unregistered sector of the country as a whole, the sector's share in NSDP remained steady or declined over the years in the states other than Manipur and Mizoram. Thus it emerges that the only state which reflects the all-India level or even higher level of industrialization is West Bengal. Even this state deteriorated compared to its earlier level between 1980-81 and 1988-89. The other states within the zone were far lagging behind the all-India average level of industrialization as reflected in the manufacturing sector's contribution to NSDP.

Industrial Base and Diversification

Having examined the size of the manufacturing sector in the state economics within the zone, it will be useful to identify the sectors which play an important role in the respective state economies. For this purpose we have worked out location quotients and specialization coefficients. It compares an industry's share of local employment with its share of national employment. It is a very quick and useful tool in determining a region's key industries.

By using the same notation the location quotient is formulated as:

$$LQ = (E_{ir} / E_r) / (E_{in} / E_n)$$

where i=industry, r= state, n= national, e=employment

The location quotient (LQ) simply gives a measure of the share of the industry in employment in the state over the industry's share of national employment. If LQ=1, then the industry's share in the state's employment is the same as the industry's share nationally. A LQ>1 implies that the industry employs a greater share of the state's workforce than it does nationally, which also implies that the industry is producing more goods and services than are consumed within the state and hence the industry is exporting the goods or services and which generates income for the state economy and helps the state economy to grow. If location quotients are computed using value added, E is replaced by V.

The specialization coefficient S_i measures the degree of specialization or diversification. If S_i=0, the state is as diversified as the national economy while if S_i=1, the state specializes entirely in one industrial sector.

$$Si = E_{ij} / E_i$$

where i=state, j= industry, E=employment and j=1,2,3,.......m and the summation is carried through either for positive or negative values and m is the number of industries.

The location quotients (LQ) computed both in terms of employment and net value added of the factory sector indicate the industrial base of the states. However, due to non-availability of the data for the states of Arunachal Pradesh, Mizoram, Nagaland and Sikkim the LQ could not be estimated and therefore, no attempt had been made to indentify the industrial base of these states. It is conceivable, however, that the industrial base of these small hill states is extremely narrow at least at the factory level.

The industrial base of Assam (in 1980-81) was constituted of manufacture of food products and sugar (20-21), wood and wood products (27), gas and steam (41) and repair services (97). Over the years i.e. in 1988-89, two additional sectors, viz. manufacture of rubber, plastic, petroleum and coal products (30) and manufacture of non-metallic mineral products (32) were added to the industrial base of the state. But repair services lost its importance over the years. The industrial base of Manipur in 1980-81 comprised manufacture of food products (20-21), wood and wood products (27), paper and paper products (28) and repair services (97). By 1987 the only industrial sector that emerged was 'other manufacturing' (38) while food products gradually lost its significance. In Meghalaya wood and wood products (27), paper and paper products (28), non-metallic mineral products (32) and repair services (97) made up the industrial base. One other industry, i.e. other manufacturing (38) was added to the industrial base by 1987-88 while the iron and metallic mineral sector (32) lost its significance. Tripura had six important factory level industries, viz. beverages, tobacco or tobacco products (22) wood and wood products (27) non-metallic mineral products (32), metal products and parts except machinery and transport equipments (34), water works and supply (42) and repair services (97). By 1987-88 jute textiles (25) and other manufacturing (38) emerged while beverages (22) wood products (27) and metal products (34) became insignificant.

Considering the four North Eastern states together, the following broad observations can be made. First, the industrial base comprising of significant factory level industries is very narrow. Second, the industrial sectors mainly consist of first stage processing industries such as grain mills, wood and wood products based on local resources and demand induced industry like repair services. Third, the few modern industries such as non-metallic mineral products and gas and steam that have come up in certain parts of the region are also resource based. Finally, except for the growth of some miscellaneous type of industries, the factory level industrial had not been much altered even in 1987-88.

Now the industrial base of the three Eastern states viz.

(undivided) Bihar, Orissa and West Bengal may be taken up for discussion. Bihar (undivided) had nine significant factory level industrial sectors in 1980-81. They were food products (20-21), beverages, tobacco and tobacco products (22); rubber, plastic petroleum and coal products (30); chemical and chemical products (36); non-metallic mineral products (32), basic metals (33), electricity (40); storage and warehousing (74) and repairing services (97). By 1987-88 three more, viz. transport equipment and parts (37), gas and steam (41); and water works and supply (42) emerged as important sectors while food products (20-21) and beverages (27) lost their importance. Orissa's industrial base was provided by only six industrial sectors, viz. wood and wood products (27); paper and paper products (28); non-metallic mineral products (32); basic metal and alloys industries (33); metal products and parts (34) and electricity; (40). Over the years, i.e. in 1987-88 only gas and steam (41) emerged as a significant sector. The industrial base of West Bengal in 1980-81 was constituted of eight factory level industrial sectors. They were jute textiles (25); leather products (29); rubber, plastic, petroleum and coal products (30); basic metal and alloys (33); transport equipment and parts (37) other manufacturing industries (38), water works and supply (42) and storage and warehousing (74). The industrial sectors that assumed significant importance by 1987-88 were metal products and parts (34) electrical machinery (36) and gas and steam (42). But the important point to note is that the most important sector of West Bengal vis-a-vis the national economy which is jute textiles in 1980-81 lost its significance totally by 1987-88.

The identification of the industrial bases of the states would be useful to examine the extent to which each of the state economies is industrially diversified. As indicated earlier, the extent of industrial diversification or concentration has been evaluated using specialization coefficients which measure the deviation of the industrial structure of a state economy from that of the national economy. It may also be pointed out that specialization coefficients have been worked out using both employment and net value added of different industrial sectors in 1980-81 and 1987-88. A few observations that emerged from the examination of specialization coefficients may be highlighted.

The economies of the four North Eastern states were far removed from the general industrialization process of the national economy in 1980-81. In other words, the industrial activities in these states were concentrated in a fewer number of sectors. This inference further strengthened when the concentration of industrial activities was examined on the basis of specialization coefficients, which had been worked out using net value-added. More importantly, the industrial diversity had further narrowed down over the years, i.e. in 1987-88.

Second, among the eastern states within the zone (undivided), Bihar or West Bengal, depending on whether it is evaluated in terms of employment or value-added, the results show s greater closeness to the national industrial pattern. Also, the extent of industrial diversity of all the three states was found to have narrowed down in 1987-88, when it was evaluated in terms of value-added. When industrial diversity in these states is measured in employment, the results showed that the diversity in Orissa and West Bengal improved while it worsened in (undivided) Bihar. Such divergence in findings depending on employment or value-added probably reflects technological change of industrial activities over the years.

The results obtained for the states of Eastern and North East India indicate that while the general industrial pattern in the three Eastern states showed a similar trend with the national economy, the economies of the North Eastern states became more clustered in conformity with their geographical isolation.

Production Linkages

It is possible to argue that the lead industries identified in respect of each state economy would suggest the type of industries that can be developed on the basis of production linkages, backward and forward. State economies being highly open, this approach to industrialization is subject to severe limitations. Nevertheless, an attempt has been made to suggest in an illustrative manner, the industrial sector that can be developed on the basis of backward and forward linkages of the lead sectors indicated earlier. It should be pointed out that these linkages have been worked out using national reference technology. To the extent the technology at the level of state economy is different from the national technology;

the measure of linkage will be biased. Of the four lead sectors in the Assam economy only two, viz. manufacture of food products and manufacture of wood and wood products, furniture and fixtures reveal high backward employment linkages, the linkage estimates are 1.11 for the former and 1.29 for the latter. This suggests that an increase in output of these two sectors would lead to employment generation in the industries supplying inputs to them. But only one of the lead industries which happens to be wood and wooden products, has a high forward employment linkages (1.56). In Manipur and Meghalaya also the wood and wood products sector shows high backward and forward linkages. In both these economies this is the only sector which has high linkages. Tripura has one sector, viz. jute textiles which has high forward and backward employment linkages, but this sector came up in the state after 1980-81. While none of the lead industries in (undivided) Bihar showed backward or forward employment linkages higher than unity, manufacture of wood and wood products in Orissa generates fairly limited backward and forward employment linkages. In West Bengal it is only leather products among ten important industrial sectors which have shown backward employment linkages higher than unity, but the estimated results do not show any forward employment linkages. This discussion on production linkages should he qualified. As mentioned earlier, production linkages based on national reference technology may not be necessarily relevant to a state economy, at least not to the same extent to all state economies. Secondly, it is possible that there are industries other than the revealed lead industries, which may have higher backward and forward linkages but we have not considered them in our analysis.

Finally, as discussed in the preceding section, backward and forward linkages indicate only the direction of demand. But supply factors may be far more critical for industrial development.

Some Reflections on Constraints and Prospects

There are many factors which facilitate or inhibit the industrial development of a state. These factors can be classified into two broad sets: one of these relates to supply side factors while the other relates to the demand side factors. Resource endowments, infrastructural support, evolution of the right type of institutions, access to market, availability of human capital in the form of entrepreneurship and skilled labour, credit availability, etc. are undoubtedly, important determinants affecting supply side. Production, consumption and investment multipliers act on the demand side of industrialization by way of inducing demand in an economy. Both these sets of factors need not be binding for the industrial development of a state which has a highly open economy. However, the working of the national economy over the past years has been favourable to the growth of some of the state economies while it has been differentiating against the economies of many other states. In the process of evolution of the national economy, the product and money/credit market got integrated faster with the national market while the labour market got associated with many rigidities emerging especially from labour surplus situations.

When supply side factors are not equally conducive to all states, an integrated product and credit market unaccompanied by the similarly integrated labour market is bound to lead to a reverse flow of resources from the less developed to the more developed state economics. This has been the experience of growth and development across the states in India in the post-independence period. More importantly, such asymmetry results in adverse effects on local industries by way of introducing competition from technologically superior industries from other regions or states. This process has been eminently visible in the context of the entire Eastern and North Eastern zone and it is particularly true in the case of all the states of North East India, all of which are in a disadvantageous position to a varying level because of the supply side constraints. A submission of this type raises the obvious question: Why is it that West Bengal with its initial advantages has failed to keep up with its industrial growth? Some of the more important reasons why some states have developed comparatively faster than others can be broadly explained as follows.

First, there were differences in the initial level of capital accumulation, human capital and infrastructure in some states. Second, and more importantly, some states succeeded in identifying clear priorities and developing a mechanism for better participation of people particularly in the prioritized sectors. This probably had helped developing a higher level infrastructure and also a system with accountability that led to their more efficient utilization of resources. This is particularly important in a mixed economy framework where the public sector takes a lead role in directing the limited resources for providing infrastructures while the private sector use the facilities for investing in industrial development. To illustrate the point, Punjab and Haryana accorded consistently high priorities to the agricultural development. When the growth takes place in the prioritized areas and gets trickled down to the primary stakeholders (farmers in this case), they create pressures for releasing the operational constraints faced by them. Industrial development in Gujarat and Maharashtra, and the high level of social services and their efficient delivery in Kerala can similarly be attributed to clear prioritization and the development of a mechanism that ensured synergized mutual interaction between the decision-makers and the people. The failure of West Bengal to take advantage of the initial advantage for industrial development can probably be attributed to mutually inconsistent and diluted signals that were given by the government to various economic actors in the economy.

This obviously raises the question as to why some of the states succeeded while others failed in determining their clear priorities for economic development of the states. The answer possibly can be found in the diverse socio-economic factors prevailing in these states and the accompanying policy interventions made within the broad polity that prevailed in those states. Besides the general approach to development, it would also be worthwhile to refer to certain other factors that are inherent in the economic systems or in the past growth processes of some of the states in the zone. A few illustrations are given below:

The economic base of North Eastern Hill states and Sikkim is very narrow. More importantly, they are characterized by activities which are carried on with primitive technology. This presents two-fold problems. On the one hand, the administrative, social and economic infrastructure as also human capital need to be developed. On the other hand, the narrow economic base stands as a great handicap in mobilizing the resources for developing the required infrastructures. There is also some ambiguity in the perception of needs and goals of economic development in a hill state predominantly inhabited by tribal population. It is argued that tribal identities need to be retained in the development process. But because of the presence of a relatively large public sector in those states as pointed out earlier, there is a perceptible change in the level and composition of consumption baskets of at least some segments of the population directly and indirectly associated with government operations. Demonstration effects might have resulted in introducing the new products into the consumption basket of the traditional hill people of this remotely located region. It should be recognized that the activities carried on with primitive technology cannot enable the people to sustain a higher level of consumption. Therefore, there is a need for reorganization of economic activities with .better technology and higher productivity, which will inevitably lead to changes in people's lifestyles. There is a perceptible fear that if rapid economic development of these hill states has to be ensured, the so-called 'tribal ethnic identity' is bound to be influenced and cannot be retained in its pristine form. The narrow economic base and limited use of tax instruments for resource mobilization in hill states have also imposed restrictions on Assam in its efforts at resource mobilization. Assam which is a valley state is surrounded by hill states, the nature of economic concessions (like income tax exemption, low sales tax, etc.) granted to the state are far less than those granted to the hill states of the region. This often acts as a deterrent and the state is forced to keep its taxation level at low margins lest there is a flight of economic activities to the neighbouring states. The major industrial activities that have come up in Assam (undivided), Bihar and Orissa are essentially resource-based: it is oil and plantation in Assam, coal and steel in (undivided) Bihar and aluminium and other mineral-based industries in Orissa. The backward linkages of these industries are rather limited, while their forward linkages are with the industries located in the big metropolises elsewhere. The result has been the emergence of an enclave economy, i.e. a few modern industries in the midst of traditional industries having minimal or no interactions between the two. As mentioned earlier, with the increasingly greater degree of integration of the product market, the development of traditional industries which essentially make up the industrial profile of most of the states in the zone is no longer feasible; more so, in the context of the present liberalized framework. These state economies can be developed only if the productivity levels can be raised using higher technology.

The observations cited above have been made with a view to highlight the nature of constraints and challenges to industrialization of most of the units of the zone. They also suggest the need for more effective public intervention in creating the required infrastructure including the development of human capital and also in removing the constraints on their utilization. There are at least two important areas in which zonal level planning can contribute to the higher industrialization of these small state units. This zone is endowed with rich water resources. Zonal level planning for generating hydel power may be useful in providing one of the most critical inputs for industrialization. The other is that this zone has got all the important requirements for becoming an attractive tourist destination, e.g. hill resorts, water, natural game sanctuary, archaeological sites, etc. which together provide an excellent potential for an important tourist belt. A zonal level planning may go a long way not only in developing a tourist belt, but also in providing a foundation for rapid industrialization in other directions.

7

Globalization and Higher Education: With Special Reference to the North Eastern States*

A few developments that have taken place in the recent past both at the global and domestic levels have huge implications on the education sector in general and higher education in particular. This paper attempts to discuss some of these major developments and bring out their implications on the level and structure of manpower demand and consequent challenges and opportunities in the higher education of the country. It also considers the Indian realities and options with special reference to the North Eastern states.

WTO and Education

The General Agreement on Trade in Services (GATS) is one of the agreements of the World Trade Organization (WTO). GATS that also covers education came into force in the beginning of 1995. GATS aims at deregulating international markets in services through successive rounds of negotiations. 'Most favoured nations' and 'national treatment' are two underlying principles of GATS. 'Most favoured nations' treatment requires that all countries be treated equally regarding import or export and 'national treatment' requires countries to treat foreign companies at par with their national counterparts. The idea behind these principles is the creation of an open, global market for services, like education.

GATS recognizes four different modes of supplying services. In the case of education, these would be: (1) Cross-border supply,

---

* The revised and enlarged version of the article published under the title, "Threats and Opportunities in Higher Education" in *Arunachal University Research Journal* (2004), Vol. 7, No. 1.

such as distance education; (2) Consumption abroad, such as travelling abroad to study; (3) Commercial presence, such as University branch campuses or partnership agreements and (4) Presence of natural persons, such as teachers and professors.

Globalization of education has some important implications. Without going into all of them, I will highlight one or two important implications for institutions of higher education in the country. It is that higher education institutions in the country today are in competition with each other, with their own respective past and above all with the best foreign institutions providing opportunities for diverse skill generation as well as promoting excellence. This means that our universities/institutions have to benchmark themselves with the best in the world.

At another level, internationalization of education leading to its 'commodification' and homogenization tends to undermine diversity in contexts, age-old values and traditional knowledge that our communities have bequeathed. This situation is indicative of the nature and character of threats and challenges as well as opportunities that our higher education institutions today have encountered.

Service as Key Driver of Global Growth and Trade: Indian Presence

The second development is that world trade in services has emerged as the key driver in the structural change in the world economy.[1] The total world export of services rose eleven times from US $ 396 billion in 1980 to US $ 1.6 trillion in 2002 to $ 4.4 trillion in 2012. Service exports' share in total global trade grew from 16.7% to 19.6% in the corresponding years[2]. Industrialized countries dominate the trade in services and earn a surplus in their balance of trade in service vis-à-vis the emerging economies and the least developing countries. Some of the emerging economies led by India have, however, witnessed an increasing role in international trade in services.

The emergence of India as one of the fastest growing economies in the world since the 1990s is to a significant extent due to rapid growth of its service sector. In the last two decades the service sector grew at an average annual rate of 9% accounting for close to 60% of the overall growth of the economy. India's service exports recorded a growth of over 17% and grew two and a half times faster than the domestically traded part of the service sector. India now claims 3.2% of the global exports in services as compared to a mere 1.4% in goods.

The most dominant growth in services in India relates to information technology and business process outsourcing services. In fact, Indian software exports shot up from USD 40.3 billion in 2007-08 to over USD 65.9 billion in 2012-13 (based on balance of payment data), at an average annual increase of USD 5.12 billion(at annual growth or 10.3 per cent) per year, and now account for almost 60.8 per cent of miscellaneous business, professional, financial and technical services. Its share in India's total service exports declined, to an extent from 46.2 per cent to 43.7 per cent in the respective years, due to global slowdown. However, the NASSCOM (National Association of Software and Service Companies) has projected an export target of $ 175 billion by 2020 from the current level of $ 47 billion. It has also projected that the present level (2013) of employment at 3 million is expected to increase ten times to 30 million (direct and indirect) by 2020[3]. The IT and IT services would require 3.8 million new entrants per annum. The export component of the Indian industry is expected to expand three-fold and reach USD 175 billion in revenues by 2020. Focused initiatives and innovation-led growth can lead to additional revenues of up to USD 135 billion by 2020. The domestic component will grow to USD 50 billion, equal to today's exports revenues. Focused initiatives can drive an additional USD 15 billion in revenues by 2020.

Other sectors such as telecommunications, financial services, community services and hotels and restaurants have also surpassed the growth of GDP.

Structural change in the Indian economy as well as its comparative advantage in services in world trade suggests a change in the structure of demand for skills. This means that skill requirement has to be in tune with the country's fastest growing service sector.

Demographic Trend and Manpower Demand

The third development relates to the changing demographic

profiles of the developed countries and, to an extent, in countries like ours, that would have important implications on the job market.

The economic success of the Western industrialized countries has impacted the choice and attitude of the households with rising demand for labour, wages and employment opportunities. At the same time, labour-saving gadgets have made household chores simpler, easier and less time-consuming, This has made possible for women to have wider choices for engagement outside the home. The process has progressed the furthest in the advanced countries leading to increasing independence of women, the breakdown of the traditional division of labour between sexes and disintegration of the nuclear family. This process is visible even in countries such as ours in the form of dissolution of the extended/joint family system.[4]

As more and more women have taken up jobs while the traditional support structure for child-bearing and rearing has crumbled, birth rates in rich countries have slumped as is happening in the better off segment of urban India. In a very few advanced industrial countries today, the total fertility rate, i.e. the number of children born to an average woman during her reproductive age span is above the replacement level of 2. In the US the total fertility rate hovers around the replacement level of 2 (1.9 in the last two years) due to very high Latino fertility rate of 3 and a black fertility rate of 2.4. But in countries like Japan and Italy it has averaged at 1.4 in the past five years. In the high-income countries as a group, the total fertility rate has plunged to 1.7 during the same period from 2.25 a quarter century ago (1970-75).[5] Even in India it has fallen to 2.6 in 2011 from 5.3 in 1971.

Increasing longevity accompanied by falling births has drastically altered the age structure. In high income countries together, the population over 65 years is projected to rise to 17.7% in 2015 from 14.6% in 2002 while that below 15 years is expected to fall to 16.6% of the total population from 18.3% in respective years[6].

In India the population over 65 years will be relatively low at 6.3% (4.8% in 2011) in 2015 though rising from 5.1% in 2002 while 27.7% (32.9% in 2011) of the total population will still be under 15 years. This demographic trend in India vis-à-vis high income countries' highlights the fact that the advanced countries are aging fast while India is young with more than two-thirds (68.0%) is below the age of 35 in 2011.

The aging population in the West means the growing burden of old age support. A declining working population will have to provide for the growing size of retirees. But the elderly has claim on current output through social security and pensions as well as through their ownership of the largest part of the nation's wealth. While they would have adequate rent income and social security and pension provisions, they would demand various types of services that the shrinking working population will not be adequate to supply. The West will thus have to look to the young nations not only to provide the support service of the aging population of the West but also to sustain the present level of activities.

This demographic trend clearly indicates the nature and types of manpower that will be in greater demand globally in future.

Emerging Role of Knowledge Intensive Activities

It is widely perceived that knowledge has emerged as a source of societal transformation and wealth creation. India has the second largest pool of English-speaking manpower in the world and the third with respect to scientific and technical manpower. Information Technology (IT) and IT Enabled Services (ITES) employed 2.5 million professionals directly and 8.3 million additional employment indirectly till 2012 as per NASSCOM estimates. The number of technical personnel at all levels is growing at a fast pace. They have made notable achievements in fields like agricultural science, space, oceanography and technologies. India has vast biodiversity capable of supporting rapid advances in the highly promising field of Biotechnology. To leverage on all this, the Planning Commission constituted a task force in 2000 "to prepare a road map that would make India a major knowledge power within this decade."[7]

The Task Force aided by a Steering Committee under the chairmanship of the former President of India, Dr. A.P.J. Abdul Kalam and distinguished scientists like Dr. R.A. Mashelkar notes: The 21st century will be the century of knowledge. It states the characteristics of a knowledge society as follows:

i) It uses knowledge through all its constituents and

endeavours to empower and enrich its people.

ii) It uses knowledge as a powerful tool to drive societal transformation.

iii) It is a learning society committed to innovation.

iv) It has the capacity to generate, absorb, disseminate and protect knowledge and also use it to create economic wealth and social good for all its constituents.

v) It enlightens its people to take an integrated view of life as a fusion of mind, body and spirit."[8]

The Task Force has identified three key drivers of a knowledge society. They are: one, societal transformation for a just and equitable society by focusing on education, health care, agriculture and governance; two, wealth creation by focusing on technology-related areas such as IT and Communication, Biotechnology, Space Technology, Materials Technology and Oceanography and on service areas such as disaster mitigation, weather modification, telemedicine, tele-education, native knowledge products, information, infotainment, conventional and non-conventional energy and environment and ecology and three, protection of knowledge, "not only the one generated in research laboratories but also its traditional knowledge generated by our communities over centuries in laboratories of life."[9]

The thrust articulated by the Task Force underscores the kind of skills that would have growing demand. Recognizing this trend, a large number of institutions have come up in the recent years largely at the private initiative to generate skills that are growing in demand. Government regulated universities and institutions, have also opened up new avenues of skill generation. A vast majority of them, however, largely for lack of either resources or initiatives or both, have not yet been able to gear themselves to the emerging trends.

Indian Realities and Options

Globalization that has swept the entire world particularly since the last decade of the 20th century has thrown up great challenges to higher education in India. For one thing, there were inadequacies in the coverage and content of higher education during the colonial period. Added to it, was the fast growing aspiration for higher education in the development process in the post-independence era. For the other, the integration of the Indian economy with the rest of the world has spurred the demand for a wide variety of skills that the erstwhile institutions of higher education did not envisage to impart.

Despite the Indian higher education system being one of the largest in the world, it is grossly inadequate to educate all the youths numbering 121.2 millions or 15 per cent of the population in the age group of 17-24. This could cover only 25.9 millions or 17.9 per cent of 121.2 million youths in the age group of 18-22 in 2011-12. It is remarkable that China could extend higher education to 29.3% of its population in the same age group in 2009.

One projection estimated that India would need by 2011, 344 conventional universities as against the existing 178 in 1997 or 256 in 2001, 12,695 Arts and Science colleges as against 6759, 778 Engineering colleges against 418, 1231 Medical colleges against 655, and 1375 Technical training colleges as against 697.[10] However, India already had 620 universities in 2012 which include 298 state universities, 130 deemed, 44 central and 148 private universities.

While the need is so large, public expenditure on education, though rose from 1.2% of gross domestic product in 1950-51, was barely 3.31% of the country in 2012-13 (BE) as against the recommended 6% by the Education Commission way back in 1964-66. Even with 12.2%[11] of the total expenditure under education being allocated for higher education—down from 50% in British India—public investment on higher education would fall short of the rising needs. On the other hand, student fees that contribute less than 5% of the total expenditure on higher education do not supplement the needs significantly.[12]

In the recent years primary education has rightly received greater attention of the government and higher education has been treated as non-merit goods. Two important findings have led to treating higher education as non-merit goods. First, the rate of return to investment in primary education (estimated for the period 1974-1982) is found to be much higher (20%) than that in higher education (at only 11%).[13] Again, both social and private rates of return to investment in primary education as worked out for Asia are almost double those in higher education.[14] This has motivated the government to withdraw subsidies slowly for higher education.

The other is that higher education particularly those relating to growth oriented institutions such as IITs and IIMs benefited more the smaller segment from the higher income groups who have affordability.

Such perceptions coupled with the shift in the economic policy to a market-driven system has tilted the focus of government to primary education thus leading to its less involvement in higher education. At the same time the massive expansion of higher education institutions in the post-independence period even if it falls far short of the required level, is of the order that the public sector cannot provide adequate resources.

On the other hand, the shift to the market-driven system and to the integration of the Indian economy with the global system calls for continuous modernization and upgradation of technology for competitive development, which in turn demands a vast educated, and skilled workforce within a minimal time frame. Globalization through cultural integration has also facilitated newer choices in numerous spheres that require products of education and training of a high order in diverse spheres ranging from leisure industries, fashion industries to various luxury products and their servicing.

It follows that demands on higher education that technology, market economy and globalization have put, are far beyond the resources of the public exchequer. What is more, the rigid rule and regulation based higher education system under the public sector that has existed, cannot cope with the pace and diversity in manpower demand. The considerations such as above provide the basic rationale for the private sector to play a greater role in higher education

Viewed even in the context of India's constitutional and policy framework, the private sector has a role to play in higher education. The Indian Constitution promises school education to all children up to the age of 14 and opportunities of further education even beyond. Till 1976 education was the exclusive responsibility of the states while the union government was concerned with areas such as coordination and standards in technical and higher education. In 1976 it was included in the concurrent list through the 42nd amendment to the Constitution. As a result, education came to be the joint responsibility of both the centre and the states. The National Policy on Education, 1986 and the Programme of Action, 1992 also envisage free and compulsory education for all children up to the age of 14. Thus it appears that school education but not higher education has been envisaged as the exclusive responsibility of the state.

However, the Indian Constitution incorporated social and economic equality in the Directive Principles of State as one of the goals of independent India. This has clearly a bearing on the state's responsibility since access to higher education impacts income distribution.

To meet the ever growing needs for diverse higher education, the government has indeed allowed the entry of private trusts, corporate houses, and individuals to set up self-financing institutions to provide education as also qualified manpower. The government has also attempted to recover partly or fully cost from the students.

There could be two broad types of private participation in higher education: government aided institutions and self-financed ones. The former adopting usually conventional pedagogy does not have the flexibility and dynamism to meet global standards in providing skills, self-confidence and communicative competence. On the other hand, some of the self-financing institutions with financial and administrative autonomy have proved to be capable of providing globally comparable academic and human resource support. Many of them have demonstrated their capability for academic innovations by way of offering enrichment courses, part-time courses, modular inputs, industry linking and several other things that lead to successful skill generating activities in tune with demand.

But the danger inherent in the self–financing institutions is the commercialization/ commodification of education, that is profit being the sole driver. This is not compatible with the core of National Policy on Education that seeks equity and social justice within the framework of our secular and social Constitution. There is also the danger of mushrooming private institutions without adequate infrastructure and teaching staff and capability.

To avert such consequences, appropriate regulatory

mechanism has to be put in place to ensure adequate infrastructure and teaching staff for quality education. At the same time, a creative public- private partnership in higher education has to be forged to ensure dynamism of the private sector, on the one hand and non-exclusivity of the public sector, on the other. This, however, is easier said than done. In fact, this is one of the major challenges to higher education.

North East India: Realities and Options

Having highlighted a few emerging global as well as domestic forces impacting the direction, diversity and quality of manpower needs, I would like to flag a few points in regard to the North East situation.

North East India has more than 30 million people below the age of 35[15]. The region together has a considerably high literacy rate, the region's average literacy being 75.51% as against the national average of 74.04% in 2011. The size of young people conversant with the English language is significantly high. The people of the North East region have strong motivation to educate their children. Information and communication technology have provided a unique opportunity to neutralize at least, to an extent, some of the disabilities arising from remoteness and physical isolation. The region is recognized as one of the major hotspots of biodiversity in the country and is the world's fifth hotspot in terms of endemic species. Taking cognizance of the comparative advantages that the region has, institutions of higher education have to gear themselves to tapping the potential in some of the areas of a knowledge society as the Task Force has suggested.

The North East has 36 universities 9 of which are centrally funded, one IIT and four other engineering colleges including NERIST, one regional medical college and three other medical colleges and a host of degree colleges in science, arts and commerce. Yet a sizeable number of young bright students go to different parts of the country annually in pursuit of higher education. This causes an enormous outflow of the region's income for the pursuit of education elsewhere.

Why is there such a large out-migration for higher education? Is it because institutions of higher education in the region lack the range of avenues of education that the young people seek? Or in their perceptions are these institutions not adequately equipped to provide an environment conducive to learning and preparing them for the job market? Or is it because the conventional system of higher education is not flexible to redesign their programmes relevant to the changing demand structure and quality level of a dynamic job market? There could be several other reasons. But the point is that all stakeholders have to give serious thought as to how the institutions of higher education in the region could meet the aspirations of the young people by creating a dynamic learning environment.

It is true that uninterrupted disturbed situations in large parts of the region over a long period of time have made the whole environment inhospitable for any drastic reforms in the education system or for serious pursuit of education. On the other hand, educational institutions particularly in the state sector have been facing an acute resource crunch leaving very little to strengthen educational infrastructure such as libraries and laboratories or to add new faculty for diverse programmes. While state governments find it difficult to provide larger funds for higher education, any attempt to raise fees from students meets with resistance.

At the same time many institutions in the form of franchise or in distance mode or even entirely private venture promising skill enhancing programmes in diverse areas ranging from computer education to air hostess training have mushroomed in small, medium and big towns and even in semi-urban and more advanced villages in the North East. One is not sure how well equipped these educational shops/joints are and what kind of quality in education they provide. But the fact is young people in hordes join these programmes and pay substantial amounts.

Here is a paradoxical situation. Young people resist any enhancement of fees in conventional institutions of learning while they willingly pay in private-run joints providing training of uncertain or indifferent quality. Is it because conventional education is perceived as less relevant to market situations? Or is it because the credibility and stature of the university system as a bastion of knowledge and wisdom have vastly eroded due to its inability to cope with the newer challenges? I do not have an answer. I am just doing some loud thinking. But the point is that such phenomena have to be understood and appropriately addressed.

What do we learn from this widely visible phenomenon? We learn two things. One, young people are desperately looking for some skill that will enhance their employability and/or opportunities for self-employment. Two, given a free choice and perceived relevance, they are willing to pay for acquiring skills that will offer wider job opportunities.

Is there any way out for the universities, especially the state-funded ones which have found themselves highly stretched due to fund constraints to meet the challenges that the globalization process and market forces have thrown up? My own humble submission in this regard is as follows:

First, all universities and institutions of the North East should network with one another and share their expertise and resources.

Two, they should collaborate with one another to design new educational programmes that have a growing demand. They should consider introducing joint programmes pooling their respective expertise and experience.

They could even consider campus-hopping programmes. I would like to elaborate what I mean by campus-hopping programmes. Suppose we pool the best regional resource persons in one campus to give exposure to all PhD scholars of a subject, say Physics of the region for a fortnight in a workshop mode. At some interval the same group of students could be exposed to the nation's best experts for a specified period in another campus. Again, at another time the group could be exposed to some of the internationally renowned scholars in the subject in yet another campus. This three-level exposure would widen the horizon of their knowledge in the specified subject and go a long way in improving the quality of their own research. They will gain in confidence, too. There will be some other benefits in terms of peer group interactions and understanding as well as appreciation of academic environments in different universities. This is just an illustration. The exact modality could be worked out.

Similarly, conventional universities can team up with specialized universities/institutions such as agricultural universities, IIT, IIIT, engineering colleges and even medical colleges to design some training/educational programmes as add on skills to students of conventional courses with a view to improving their employability. For example, it is possible in collaboration with engineering colleges to design and run, for example, a diploma course in computer repairing, maintenance and assembling for the students of conventional courses thereby giving skills for being self-employed. Such teaming up is possible even with private industries/ and financial institutions in certain areas, entrepreneurship development programmes, for example.

With these illustrative examples I am trying to make two points. First, such teaming up does not require institutionalization of a department adding long-term financial commitment and yet makes it possible to run a large number of skill enhancing programmes parallel to conventional courses outside the normal teaching hours. This would give wider options to students for acquiring skills they value. Second, those who value such skills would be willing to pay to meet the required cost of running the programmes. After all, they would get a formal certificate from a university that ensures quality and adequacy of content of the programme. It is a far superior choice than what is offered in a market place.

At another level, there is enormous scope for inter-university collaboration in a wide variety of research programmes in areas such as biodiversity, indigenous knowledge and herbal medicines, biotechnology, energy, ecology and environment.

Recent developments in information and communication technology have made all such collaborative programmes easier.

The short point is that: being faced with various challenges arising from different sources together with growing unemployment and frustration of the youths of the region, financially stressed institutions of higher education will have to move out of the traditional bounds and pioneer initiatives that would offer wider choices for learning while enriching the intellectual environment. After all, churning out unemployable and unemployed degree holders would only add to the stock of potential insurgents in the region.

Concluding Remarks

In wrapping up the discussion, I should submit that I have

addressed the issues of higher education within a narrow canvas. I have not addressed the issues from the angle of basic objectives of higher education. What I have kept in mind are expectations from investment in higher education such as accessibility, adequacy of manpower needs of development and remaining in the forefront of knowledge. What have also been kept in view is the declaration of UNESCO in the World Conference on Higher Education on the theme of Higher Education in the Twenty-First Century: Vision and Action[16]: "The conference was unanimous in considering that renewal of higher education is essential for the whole society to be able to face the challenges of the twenty-first century, to ensure its intellectual independence, to create and advance knowledge and to educate and train responsible, enlightened citizens and qualified specialists without whom no nation can progress economically, socially, culturally and politically."

"...Since society is increasingly knowledge-based, higher education and research now act as essential components of cultural, socio-economic and environmentally sustainable development of individuals, communities and nations. The development of higher education must, therefore, feature among the highest national priorities."

It is in this background that I have dealt with the pressing demands on higher education arising from some significant global and domestic developments.

These developments have widened the contour of higher education and stressed the thrust on excellence. The rapidly growing service sector, particularly IT and ITES and India's prominence in the global trade has impacted the pattern of manpower needs while increasing integration with the global economy has led to the demand for diverse skills. The rising importance of the service sector has enhanced demand for manpower trained in newer disciplines with focus on relevant skill generation.

At the same time there is a growing need to enlarge accessibility of higher education to cover the increasingly larger number of youths in the country. But the resources available for higher education are not expanding at the required pace. In a situation such as this, there is a wide scope for private participation in higher education. In fact, it is growing at a fast pace.

In view of the growing number of private institutions of unknown and uncertain quality, there is an urgent need for putting in place an appropriate regulatory mechanism to ensure quality education and skill generation.

Rules and regulations governed and resource stressed universities especially in the state sector lack both flexibility as well as means to cope with the growing demand for a variety of skills and quality manpower.

The problem is more serious in the North East being in the whirlpool of insurgency and acute unemployment both of which feed on each other. This has resulted in a massive outflow of the youths for higher education to different destinations.

In such a situation universities of the North East are required to pioneer schemes such as resource sharing, and collaborative teaching and research programmes. These should leverage on the region's potential and promote industry university partnership for skill generation to meet the challenges of today and prepare the youths to make best use of a wide range of opportunities for jobs and self- employment. A wide variety of skill enhancing options would spur the imagination of the youths and impart dynamism in the campus environment.

NOTES

1. For further details see, Pritam Banerjee, "Negotiating on Services: An Appropriate Approach for India", Presented at Outreach Seminar on WTO and India: Issues and Negotiating Strategies, Department of Economics, Cotton College, Guwahati, August 11-12, 2004.
2. UNCTAD (United Nations Conference on Trade and Development Database).
3. NASSCOM (2013) 'Perspective 2020: Transform Business, Transform India'. This outlines the roadmap for the Indian Technology and Business Services Industry and the Report is based on the research conducted by McKinsey & Company.
4. For a detailed discussion of the point, see Ashok Guha, "The WTO and Our Role in the World Economy of the Future", Outreach Seminar: WTO and India: Issues and Negotiating Strategies, Department of Economics, Cotton College, Guwahati, August 11-12, 2004.
5. UNDP, *Human Development Report 2004-5, Demographic Trends,* pp. 152-155.

6. Ibid.
7. Government of India, Planning Commission (2001), *India as Knowledge Superpower: Strategy for Transformation*, New Delhi.
8. Op. cit., p. 1.
9. Ibid.
10. Op. cit., p. 11.
11. Analysis of budget expenditure on education 2009-10 to 2011-12.
12. Ibid.
13. The World Bank, Priorities and Strategies for Education: A World Bank Review 1995.
14. The social rate of return to investment in primary education in Asia is worked out at 19.9% while the private rate of return is 39%. The corresponding rates of return to investment in higher education are 11.7% and 19.9%. Priorities and Strategies for Education: A World Bank Review 1995.
15. Arunachal Pradesh, Assam, Manipur, Meghalaya, Mizoram, Nagaland and Tripura.
16. October 5-8, 1998, Para 12 of the declaration.

8

WTO and India: Issues and Negotiating Strategies—Special Reference to North East India*

The World Trade Organization is an organization that deals with the rules of trade between nations. There are many facets of the WTO but it would be more pertinent to briefly deal with four broad questions by way of providing the background for contextualizing the issues in WTO which would be relevant for the region. The four broad questions that would be taken up for discussion in the subsequent sections are as follows:

- How has the WTO evolved and what is it?
- What are the basic principles on which the WTO is anchored?
- What are some of the important aspects that the WTO covers?
- How does the WTO concern the North East region?

Let Us Begin with the First Question—How Has the WTO Evolved?

To understand the genesis of the WTO it would be necessary to go back to its history that spans from its hesitant start in 1948 in Havana (Cuba) via Annecy (France), Torquay (UK), Tokyo (Japan), Punta del Easte (Uruguay), Montreal (Canada), Brussels (Belgium) and finally culminating at Marrakesh (Morocco) in 1994. The WTO was born on January 1, 1995 in the shadow of the failed attempt in 1948 to create an International Trade Organization. After the failure to create an international trading organization (ITO) with the two 'Bretton Woods' institutions, viz. the World Bank and IMF, 23 out

* Keynote address delivered at outreach seminar on WTO and India: Issues and Negotiating Strategies with Special Reference to the North East at Cotton College, Guwahati, August 11-12, 2004.

of 50 original participant nations agreed to accept some of the trade rules and concessions of the draft ITO Charter. These agreed clauses were modified in the form of the General Agreement on Tariffs and Trade (GATT) to provide the rules for world trade. The GATT remained only a provisional instrument governing international trade from 1948 till the creation of WTO in 1995.

Over the eight rounds of GATT trade negotiations, the member countries expanded from 23 to 123. The first five trade rounds concentrated on reduction of tariffs. During the fifth round of negotiations in the mid-sixties new rules on GATT Anti-Dumping Agreement and a section on development was incorporated. The eighth, the Uruguay round of 1986-94 was the last and most extensive negotiations covering tariffs, non-tariff measures, rules, services, intellectual property, dispute settlements, textiles, agriculture and more importantly the culmination of discussions for creating the WTO. The WTO is the culmination of the 1986-94 negotiations called Uruguay Round and earlier negotiations under the GATT.

The Second Question is—What is WTO?

An interesting anecdote from someone participating in a discussion on the WTO sums up what WTO is all about. In the discussion on diverse ideas relating to What the WTO should do someone said, "Wait a minute. The WTO is a table. People sit round the table and negotiate—what do you expect the table to do?" The WTO is a forum for national governments to engage in negotiations on trade liberalization agreements, to settle disputes and operate a system of rules for trade that binds governments to keep their trade policies within agreed limits.

The Third Question Relates to—What is the Coverage Under WTO?

The WTO agreements are legal texts and cover many areas: these deal with agriculture, textiles and clothing, banking, telecommunication, government purchases, industrial standards and product safeguards, food sanitation regulations, intellectual properties, etc. There are certain fundamental principles which run through these agreements and the principles are the foundation of the multilateral trading system.

The Fourth Issue is—What are These Principles on Which the Multilateral Trading System is Evolved?

The principles on which the multilateral trading system evolved include-

Without discrimination—a country should not discriminate between their trading partners. If a nation grants a lower tariff rate for one of its products to one trading partner, the same has to be extended to all other WTO members—in technical jargon it is known as most favoured nation (MFN).

Freer trade—Lowering trade barriers by way of bringing down tariffs and progressive liberalization.

Predictability—There are times when promising not to raise tariffs is as important as lowering tariff because the promise gives the foreign companies, investors and governments a clear view of the future opportunities. The system offers an environment to make the business environment stable.

Fair competition—The rules of MFN and national treatment discourage 'unfair' practices such as export subsidies and dumping products at below cost to gain market share and ensure free and undistorted trade environment among the nations.

Encourage development and economic reform—The WTO arrangements contribute towards development. The developing countries need greater flexibility in time to adjust to the clauses of the WTO system with special assistance and trade concessions.

The case for an open trading system among nations is based on experience of world trade and economic growth since the Second World War.

What is the Basic Perception Behind the Multilateral Trading System?

Trade barriers such as customs duties and measures like import bans or quotas restrict quantities selectively and thus discourage trade. Lowering such trade barriers encourage trade. Liberal trade policies allow for competition, motivate innovation and breed success.

The theoretical underpinning of this is comparative advantage. This reminds me of an interesting intellectual challenge.

Mathematician Stanislaw Ulam once challenged Nobel laureate

in Economics, Paul Samuelson: 'Name me one proposition in all the social sciences which is both true and non-trivial." Paul Samuelson after pondering for a long time found the answer in comparative advantage. He explained, "That it is logically true need not be argued before a mathematician; that it is non-trivial is attested by the thousands of important and intelligent men who have never been able to grasp the doctrine for themselves or to believe it after it was explained to them."

Comparative advantage does provide the single most powerful insights into economics. The basic intuition of the doctrine of comparative advantage can be illustrated with a simple example of a two country model. If country A is better than country B at making cars and country B is better than A at making bread – both countries obviously gain if A specializes making cars and B bread – case of absolute advantage. Even if country A is better than B at making both, both can still benefit if each of them specializes at making the one it does best. The experience of world trade and economic growth since the Second World War shows that tariffs on industrial products have fallen steeply and now average below 5 per cent in industrial countries. During the first 25 years after the war, world economic growth was about 5 per cent per year, a high rate that was partly the result of lower trade barriers. World trade grew even faster at 8 per cent on an average during the period. However, individual countries' commitments to open markets in specific sectors and how far those markets will be open are the outcome of negotiations.

How Could the Agreements at the WTO Impact the North East Region?

Coming to the fourth and the final question, I would like to mention some of the challenges and opportunities specially in four areas that concern the NER very significantly in terms of income and employment generation. The areas are:

Agriculture, plantation, weaving and bio-diversity

As noted earlier, the WTO provides a forum for negotiation among the current 147 members and for arriving at agreements.

The agreement on agriculture—AoA is the name given to this

agreement reached at the end of the negotiations on trade in agriculture under the Uruguay round of the erstwhile GATT. The AoA demands that countries open up their economies to agricultural products. The idea is to establish a fair and market-oriented trading system by way of correcting and preventing restrictions and distortions in the world agricultural markets. Commitments under the AoA relate to market access, export competition and domestic support. All the members are required to make commitments in each of these areas though the extent of commitments may vary.

Market Access Conditions

Under the market access condition both developed and developing countries were to convert all non-tariff barriers into tariffs. Each country had to commit itself to ceiling on its tariffs. While developed countries had to reduce import tariffs by 36 per cent across the board over a six-year period and ensure a minimum tariff reduction of 15 per cent on any product, the developing countries had lighter commitments—a 24 per cent cut across the board with a minimum of 10 per cent reduction on individual products.

Export Competition

Under the export competition commitments, developed countries were to reduce the value and volume of export subsidies by 36 per cent and 24 per cent respectively over a six-year period using 1986-1990 as the base period. The developing countries were to reciprocate the process by reducing the value and volume of export subsidies by 24 per cent and 10 per cent respectively.

Domestic Support

The Uruguay Round has fundamentally changed the way domestic support in favour of agricultural producers was treated under the GATT 1947. A key objective has been to reduce domestic support while at the same time leaving enough scope for governments to design domestic agricultural policies in the face of, and in response to, the wide variety of the specific circumstances in individual countries and individual agricultural sectors. The WTO classified different kinds of subsidies to agriculture into amber box, blue and green box subsidies depending on their trade destroying implication. For example, Amber Box subsidies constitute all form of domestic support deemed to be trade destroying, primarily by encouraging excessive production while domestic support with no, or minimal, distortive effect on trade on the other hand is referred to as Green Box measures. The commitments made under AoA were restricted to Amber Box subsidies alone. Developed countries were to cut these by 20 per cent from the basis of 1986-1990 over six years starting from 1995 and the developing countries were to achieve a cut by 13 per cent over 10 years.

However, the problem lay in the fact that developed countries extended subsidies to their farmers to the tune of $ 300 billion yearly— six times bigger than the development assistance flowing from these countries to all developing countries together. The subsidy offered by EU and US taken together stands at almost $ 1 billion a day.

The implication is that production subsidies concentrated in developed countries impedes the export possibilities of developing countries. Besides, with newer and better technology and inputs, access to better transportation and other services and more credit these countries are able to produce more and export the surpluses abroad at cheaper subsidized prices. The developing countries (with bulk of its population dependent on agriculture for survival) are far less advantageously placed even to compete in their home markets in the face of cheaper imports from developed countries. This has made the developing countries hesitant in opening their markets or easing their own trade barriers, which could in the long run reduce import prices, increase productivity and help expand exports. The hesitation and reluctance on the part of the developing countries resulted in the near collapse of the Cancun Round of WTO in September 2003.

The Geneva talks that were concluded on July 31, 2004 led to the approval of the framework in which the rich nations agreed to withdraw their subsidy support and import tariff and the developing countries to open up their markets. The agreement, if leads to withdrawing the high rates of subsidies and support to agriculture by the developed countries, Indian farmers in general and farmers from North East India in particular would find newer opportunities for engaging in the global market. The opportunities are not without challenges. The challenges that stand in the way are the various impediments in the form of poor infrastructure such as irrigation, roads, power and storage facilities that hinder productivity. The opportunities that open up through engagement in the emerging international market environment rest on the fact that there would be no barriers with access to a wider market in the world.

The important question here is whether farmers from North East India would be able to take advantage of the new opportunities? A lot would depend on the removal of various impediments that hinder productivity gain in agriculture as well as their profit maximizing behaviour.

One sector that holds prominence is the tea plantation. India is the largest producer of tea in the world. The tea industry provides direct employment for one million workers and more than two million persons in ancillary activities associated with production, value addition and marketing of tea. In Assam the tea plantation directly employed 5.89 lakh workers in 1998. The removal of quantitative restrictions from April 1, 2001 should have offered much greater opportunities for exports. In reality, India's share in world export slumped from 16 per cent in 1998 to 13.09 per cent in 2001; tea dusts from 13 countries started to flood the domestic market. As is widely perceived, the tea industry in Assam has faced a crisis. The Committee under the chairmanship of Dr. Jayanta Madhab which submitted its report have examined the causes of the crisis and recommended remedial measures. One can only hope that the tea industry in Assam would come out of the woods and take full advantage of the opportunities that the removal of QRs has offered for larger market access.

Textiles is another sector which holds large prospects of gain under the WTO. The textile sector can broadly be classified, into power loom, handloom and weaving. It is one of the important sectors in the country accounting for close to 20 per cent of the industrial labour and the same proportion of the total industrial production. The textile exports constitute one of the four largest categories of the Indian exports. Opportunities existing for the sector particularly the handloom sector are highly significant for the states of North East India. Indian exports had been subjected to quota limit under the voluntary restriction scheme (the Multi-Fibre Agreement). The textile agreement under the Uruguay Round in the mid-nineties has succeeded in reducing the incidence of this non-tariff barrier and would eventually lead to the abolition of the Multi-Fibre Agreement by January 1, 2005. This would provide much greater access to the world market as well as tougher competition. Indian exports could take advantage of the larger market access if they had a competitive edge by way of adopting better technology leading to productivity gains. This is equally true in the case of the handloom sector in the North East.

The fourth area where the North Eastern states have opportunities to gain is biodiversity. India is the world's fifth hot spot in terms of endemic species. The North East is recognized as one of the major hotspots of biodiversity. The year 2000 was the deadline for developing countries to bring their national laws into compliance with the trade-related intellectual property rights (TRIPS) agreement under the WTO. India had already passed the Patents (Amendment) Act, 2002 and the Patent Rules, 2003. One could argue that extending intellectual private property rights to plants and indigenous knowledge system in particular threatens bio diversity.

The important issue is whether the North East has the means to protect itself and its environment from exploitation by the countries with superior resources, technology and skill.

Economic theory suggests a chain of causality: human development is enhanced through income growth; income growth is greater with trade; and trade is increased through lesser trade barriers. Such reasoning lies behind the efforts to develop an integrated, more viable and reasonable multilateral trading system earlier by GATT that subsequently culminated in the form of WTO. The progress towards this goal has to be attempted in an unequal global trading system. On one extreme, there are developed countries with much higher income level, technological capability and even greater negotiating skill. On the other extreme there remain the developing countries which are less endowed in any of these areas mentioned.

Starting off from such unequal situations, the strategy of

collective negotiation by developing countries seems the best bet as has been evidenced in the Cancun Round. Agriculture, plantation, textiles and biodiversity in particular that have come under multilateral agreements are important areas for the economies of the states of North East India in terms of their importance in income and employment generation. The strategy to deal with the challenges that have been thrown up and its success will determine the extent of benefits that the region would enjoy within an integrated global system.

9

Financial Inclusion and Inclusive Growth: With Special Reference to the North Eastern Region*

Inclusive development is a broad concept. It extends beyond the narrow confines of economic goals and encompasses within it social and cultural dimensions of development as well. Different institutions such as state, market and civil society organizations and their arena of activities expand or restrict the bounds of inclusion/exclusion of people within the development process of a country. Similarly religion and philosophy, cultural beliefs and practices, social norms also contribute to the process inclusion/exclusion of communities and people from the development process. Inclusive development transcends the bounds of economic criterion even though people often continue to identify inclusive growth as an outcome of economic intervention. Growth prospects of a country are primarily shaped by the natural endowments but the process of growth is shaped by the social, cultural, philosophical, political contexts which have their influence on the economics of resource behaviour of the country and hence inclusive/exclusive growth continue to be perceived as a process of economic behaviour.

The concept of inclusive growth is not new either in the context of India or for the world. Inclusive approach was embedded in India's development perspectives even before independence. There

* Keynote Address delivered on October 25, 2013 at the National Seminar on Financial Inclusion and Inclusive Growth organized by the Department of Business Administration, Tezpur University (October 25-26, 2013).

were four well-known documents on the thinking and strategy of economic development that independent India could pursue. All four documents represented different perspectives but what was common in all of them was inclusive approach. To be more specific, the Report of the National Planning Committee set up by the Indian National Congress Committee in 1938 declared its aim as "to ensure an adequate standard of living for the masses". The Bombay Plan prepared by leading industrialists in the country and published in 1945 also identified elimination of poverty as the central objective of development. The third document, "Reconstructing India" published by the famous engineer, M. Visvesvaraya in 1920 and the fourth document which is the People's Plan by the Indian Federation of Labour in 1944 laid emphasis on removal of poverty and the importance of the role of government in economic development[1]. The prime objective of the development strategy adopted by India since independence has been to establish a socialistic pattern of society through economic growth based on self-reliance, social justice and alleviation of poverty. Notwithstanding the far-reaching shift in policy regime from 'physical control' regime to a market-driven one in 1991, the emphasis on inclusive approach has not withered away. One can, say that India pursued inclusive growth even if with limited success.

The experience at the global level shows that different countries have adopted and pursued different development policies as deemed fit to achieve growth and equity. Sen and Dreze (1995) observed: "More successful countries, which have left India behind, have pursued very diverse economic policies, from market-oriented capitalism (South Korea, Taiwan, Thailand) to communist party led socialism (Cuba, Vietnam, pro-reform China) and also various mixed systems (Costa Rica, Vietnam, Jamaica and Sri Lanka)."[2] Their growth performance varied but all of them could reduce poverty and improve human development.

The immediate context in which inclusive growth has received renewed thrust in India is the growing perception that the liberalization policies with heavy reliance on market forces pursued since 1991 have excluded large sections of population. In response to such a disturbing perception, the UPA government which came to power in 2004 gave more thrust *inter alia* on agriculture, rural development, employment and other social concerns with a view to moving towards faster and more inclusive growth. Accordingly, the Eleventh Five Year Plan (2007-12) made 'Inclusive Growth" as the subtitle. The Twelfth Five Year Plan (2012-17) further emphasized it giving a subtitle to the Plan as "Faster, more inclusive and sustainable growth." The notion of inclusive growth thus finds an overt expression in the Plan document itself. The idea of inclusive growth is to "increase the social opportunity function, which depends on two factors: (i) average opportunities available to the population, and (ii) how opportunities are shared among the population."[3] The 'inclusive growth' as a strategy aims at ensuring equal access to all by creating productive opportunities for the poor and the vulnerable. The questions that intrigue are:

Is There Any Causal Relation Between Finance and Growth?

The role of finance in growth had been recognized for long. Hicks (1969)[4] argued that finance played a critical part in ushering in industrialization in England by facilitating capital mobilization. In more recent years, the endogenous growth theories argue that with positive marginal productivity of capital, development of the financial market spurs growth, both in the short and long run.[5] Empirical studies (e.g. Bell and Rousseau: 2001) have shown in the Indian context that financial intermediation is one of the major determinants of economic performance in terms of promoting aggregate investment and output and thereby industrialization.[6] Several other studies both at the theoretical and empirical levels have investigated the relationship between finance and growth and have found that financial intermediation indeed plays an important role in the process of economic growth.[7] Financial intermediation is, therefore, one of the important determinants of economic growth.

Recognizing the importance of financial intermediation in the process of economic growth, the RBI Committee on Financial Sector Plan for North Eastern States (2006) observed: "Strengthening financial institutions, increasing their outreach, and ensuring efficient payment and settlement systems covering the maximum number of population in a region, can provide impetus to growth."[8] Thus "a well-functioning financial system", as the Rangarajan

Committee (2008) puts it, "empowers individuals, facilitates better integration with the economy, actively contributes to development and affords protection against economic shocks"[9]. Incidentally, financial services broadly refer to savings, credit, insurance, remittance facilities, etc. Greater financial inclusion through secure savings, properly priced credit and insurance products and payment services helps weaker sections such as low income groups and disadvantaged segments to increase income, acquire capital, manage risk and move out of poverty. The Rangarajan Committee (2008) defined financial inclusion as the process of ensuring access to financial services and timely and adequate credit needed by the vulnerable groups, such as the weaker sections and low income groups, at an affordable cost. Thus financial inclusion comprising the delivery of basic banking services to all sections of the society at an affordable cost, in a country like India is essential not only for the reason of social inclusion but also for economic reasons as revealed from theoretical and empirical research.[10]

What Hinders Financial Inclusion?

Both supply and demand factors are responsible for financial exclusion. On the supply side, lack of formal financial institutions, low network of branches and hence limited outreach, lack of simple customized and flexible financial products supplied by formal financial institutions to suit the needs of the local population and cumbersome and "unfriendly" procedures and lack of awareness of banking services act as barriers to financial inclusion. Financial inclusion can be improved by expanding financial institutions and by putting in place better delivery of financial services. In the context of demand, it is important to recognize that there are regions, sections of population and sub-sectors of the economy with weak demand for financial services. The underlying differences in these areas arise from factors like "topography of the region, infrastructural bottlenecks such as transport, communication and power, low level of commercialization, lack of entrepreneurship, law and order situations in some parts of the NER, land tenure system especially in hilly areas, development strategy based on grants rather than loans"[11] as also sparse settlements of population particularly in the hilly areas and traditional ethnic tribal culture where the need for savings and credit is limited.

Where Does North East India Stand in Matters of Financial Inclusion?

It is widely recognized that the availability of and access to financial services in the North Eastern states in India as indicated by the relevant parameters are way behind the all-India level. For example, the percentage of indebted farm households to total rural households from all sources was only 23.3 per cent compared to the all-India level of 49 per cent in 2005[12]. What is more, the extent of indebtedness of farm households varied widely across the states from 4 per cent in Meghalaya to 49 per cent in Tripura. Even this low level of debt was mainly from the informal sources in the NER: 84 per cent of the indebted farm households borrowed from informal sources. In fact, the loan from the formal source was as low as 2.00 per cent in Meghalaya and highest at 46 per cent in Tripura.

The share of population of North Eastern states in all India population is 3.7 per cent and its share of bank branches is 2.50. The share in deposit is 1.60 per cent of the all-India total while the credit share is still lower at 1.50 per cent. The C-D ratio which broadly indicates the contribution of the banking system to the economic development stood at only 47.8 in 2007 for North Eastern states as against 72.4 for the country as a whole. What is noteworthy is that while the all-India C-D ratio rose to 72.4 in 2007 from 63.0 in 1985, it increased by less than 1 from 46.9 almost over two decades. In 2005 only 59.3 per cent of the Indian adult population had bank accounts, savings and/or current which is very low as compared to the developed countries. The performance of North Eastern states was even lower at 37.3 per cent. What is worse, between 1991 and 2005 bank account holders declined in the NER, even if marginally. The decline was much sharper in urban areas of North Eastern states -the number of bank accounts per 100 urban adult population in the region went down to 124.4 in 2005 from 134.6 in 2001 while it increased for the country as a whole. Though one may argue that the increase in both deposits and credit per 100 adult populations between 2001 and 2006 for the region was almost at par with the all-India rate, the volume of deposits or credit was less than half of the all-India level in either case. There are several other parameters such as Kisan Credit Cards (KCC) and bank loan to SHGs to gauge the degree of financial inclusion. Even the more comprehensive examination of the other parameters does not alter the broad message: the access to financial services in the North Eastern states is very low.

What is more disturbing is the change in the distribution of bank credit by Scheduled Commercial Banks over the years in the North Eastern states. Over a period of ten years between 1997 and 2007, the share of core sectors of the economy like agriculture, industry, transport services and even trade in the number of accounts as also the amount outstanding declined to a varying degree; only the personal loans rose sharply over time. For example, the share of agriculture in the number of loan accounts and the amount outstanding slumped. The share of the number of accounts came down to 28.7 per cent in 2007 from 33.2 per cent in 1997 and the share of outstanding credit decreased to 9.18 per cent in 2007 from 16.9 per cent in 1997. On the other hand, the share of personal loan in the number of accounts and the amount outstanding increased rapidly during the period: the share in the number of accounts rose to 44.6 per cent from a mere 13.2 per cent and the share of personal loans in total credit to 41.4 from 13.2 per cent in the corresponding years. This clearly suggests that financial intermediation of this type could have only a limited impact on growth in the region.

What Attempts Have Been Made to Improve Financial Inclusion?

Recognizing the need for financial inclusion in pursuance of the 'Inclusive growth' objective, the Government of India set up a Committee on Financial Inclusion in 2008. Even earlier the Reserve Bank of India had constituted a Committee on the Financial Sector Plan for the North Eastern Region in 2006. In the light of the recommendations of these Committees, the RBI took up proactive measures like no frill account, simplified Know Your Customer (KYC), introduced general credit card system, one-time settlement for overdue loans up to Rs. 25,000, business facilitators and correspondence model, IT solution for financial education, etc.[13] to improve the financial infrastructure in the region and be more inclusive in its service coverage. The pertinent question is whether such steps have led to financial inclusion in the NER in the face of various impediments. As the RBI Committee (2006) rightly noted that the region has serious impediments to the development of banking and financial services. These are mainly attributable to topography of the region, low population density, infrastructure bottlenecks (transport, communication and power), low level of commercialization, lack of entrepreneurship, pockets with law and order problems, system of clan or community based land tenure, exposure to grant-based development approach, low network bank branches, lack of simple customized and flexible financial products to suit services and inadequate payment settlement systems. These Committees have made many useful recommendations. It will be worthwhile to examine to what extent these recommendations have been translated into policy actions and to what extent such policy actions have led to financial inclusion in the region. I believe that most of the recommendations made by the Thorat and Rangarajan Committees are very perceptive and relevant and the issues identified in these reports require empirical insights.

Why is It That the Region Does Not Seem to Have Significant Improvement on Financial Inclusion?

The objective conditions such as the ones highlighted by the Thorat Committee[14] as noted above are undoubtedly crucial for the region. Taking these constraints as data, one has to seek out remedies that are flexible to suit the local conditions. 'One size fits all' approach in the macro policy framework will not deliver the requisite change in the region. Perhaps a community-based initiative such as the 'communitization' experiment for different government programmes in Nagaland could be a way forward. Another variant of community-based approach could be a buy back approach linked to the product for which credit is extended. In the hilly mountainous terrains of the region with sparse population settlements and community ownership of land, it would be prudent to organize producers/farmers' groups and recognize these groups as the units for credit disbursal linking such disbursal with buy back agreement with the marketing/processing units of the concerned products. The linkage would have two-fold advantages. One, group lending against potential marketable surplus that would be disposed of under the buy back arrangement would obviate the need for land as collateral. Second, it would minimize default in repayment. Incidentally, introduction of the buy back arrangement in sparsely populated regions could be more creatively designed for productivity enhancement as well as for elimination of intermediaries in the marketing network ensuring retention of the profits with the producers. The access to the full share of profit from production will incentivize the group members while at the same time promoting greater equity and inclusiveness.

India is a country with large regional diversities in terms of geographical features, population density, dispersion of human settlements with varying customary systems, income and its distribution, standard of physical infrastructure as well as social fabric. Any attempt to expedite the process of financial inclusion would call for appropriate design of instruments taking into account objective realities such as those mentioned in the previous section. Needless to add, financial inclusion and economic growth feed on each other.

NOTES

1. For further details, see, Dev, Mahendra S. (2006), *Inclusive Growth in India*, Oxford University Press, New Delhi, pp. 8-10.
2. Dreze, J. and A. Sen (1995), *India: Economic Development and Social Opportunity*, New Delhi and Oxford: Oxford University Press, p. 2.
3. Ali, Ifzal and Hyun Hwa Son (2007), *Asian Development Review*, Vol. 24, No. 1, p. 1.
4. Hicks, John (1969), *A Theory of Economic History*, Oxford: Clarendon Press.
5. Bencivenga, V. and D.B. Smith (1991), 'Financial Intermediation and Endogenous Growth', *Review of Economic Studies*, Vol. 58 (2), April, pp. 195-209.
6. Bell, Clive and Peter L. Rousseau (2001), 'Post-Independence India: A Case of Finance-led Industrialization?' *Journal of Development Economics*, Vol. 65, No. 1, pp. 153-175
7. For further discussion, see, Kodan, A.S., N.K. Garg and S. Kaidan, 'Financial Inclusion: Status, Issues, Challenges and Policy in North Eastern Region', *IUP Journal of Financial Economics*, Vol. IX, No. 2, 2011, p. 28.
8. RBI (2006), Report of Committee on Financial Sector Plan for North Eastern States.
9. GoI, Report of the Committee on Financial Inclusion (January 2008), p. 28.

10. See for example, R. Levine, Norman Loayza and Thorstenbeck (1999), 'Financial Intermediation and Growth, Causality and Causes', The World Bank, Country Economic Department Papers 2059, Washington DC, 1999; G. Shaw (1973) *Financial Deepening in Economic Development*, New York, Oxford University Press, 1973.
11. RBI (2006), Report of the Committee on Financial Sector Plan for North Eastern States, p. 14.
12. Statistics are used from the study of Kodan et al., op. cit.
13. For comprehensive listing, see, Kodan et al., op. cit., pp. 37-38.
14. Report of the Committee on Financial Sector Plan for the North East Region, 2006, Chairperson Usha Thorat.

10

Globalization and Challenges to Natural Resource Management: With Special Reference to Arunachal Pradesh*

North East India as a region and Arunachal Pradesh in particular is highly endowed with natural resources like water, forest, oil and gas, mines and minerals although the Geological Survey of India has not yet surveyed its large part. The region has 30% of the national water resources and 41% of the country's hydropower potential while the region accounts for 3.8% of the country's population and 7.8% of the geographical area. The forest cover in the North Eastern states ranges from 30.2% (Assam) to 87% (Mizoram), 85.4% (Naga) and 82.2% (ARP) against the all-India average of 19.4%.

Among the North Eastern states, Arunachal Pradesh is one of the richest in biodiversity, ethnic and cultural diversity. The state accounts for 30% of landmass and 3% of North East population. Being part of the Himalayan range, Arunachal Pradesh has great variations in physiography and climate with floral, faunal, ethnic and cultural diversity. The state has all types of vegetation: tropical, sub-tropical, temperate and alpine; it has one third of the country's known 15,000 seed plants; and it has 500 exotic orchids.

Arunachal Pradesh is the habitat of 96 terrestrial mammals, eight out of 16 India's primates, 233 species of birds, 76 species of fishes, 23 species of amphibians apart from numerous reptiles, butterflies and other insects. Globally six species get lost per hour.

* Revised version of the Keynote Address at the National Seminar on National Resources and Tribal Communities of North East India held at J.N. College, Pasighat.

Since they are renewable, awareness and concerted efforts matter a good deal in preserving them.

Twenty-six major tribes inhabit Arunachal Pradesh and bring in huge cultural diversity which is discernible in their cuisine, customs, cultural practices, religious and belief systems and handicrafts. The ethnic and cultural diversity together with rich biodiversity has contributed to the richness of the indigenous knowledge system of the state.

The dependence of the indigenous population on natural resources is very high. More than 50 per cent of their requirements in terms of food, water and other basic necessities used to be met from the natural resources such as forests, streams birds and animals. One Chief of the Adi tribe has explained how his functionally efficient and reasonably comfortable traditional dwelling has been built without much cash transactions. As he explained, he obtained the materials such as wood, bamboos and thatch without any financial cost from the forest for the construction of his thatched house. His relatives and neighbours provided free labour. All he had to do was to give a feast. Even here he arranged most of the ingredients from the forest: he hunted birds and animals in the forest for meat, collected firewood and vegetables, too, from the forest and rice from his granary. Only edible oil and salt had to be bought from the market. The market valuation of the dwelling that the Chief had would cost anywhere between 5 and 6 lakhd at 2004-05 prices. This illustration shows the extent to which the tribal population depended on natural resources. However, with change in lifestyle and the penetration of modern ways of living, the dependence on nature as was in the primitive tribal society has declined drastically particularly in urban and semi-urban areas.

The tribal society in the North East has evolved traditional methods of resource management to maintain and preserve an ecological balance. They could do so, because biological, ethnic and cultural resources are mutually supportive. The tribal community generally treats the natural resources as common property. They have also evolved certain practices of resource renewals. For example, the Apatani tribe in Zero areas not only treat natural resources as common property but also puts in place the practice of renewal of resources by way of planting a certain number of trees if someone wants to fell trees for his domestic use.

But such age-old practices of maintaining the ecological and environmental balance have been greatly eroded over time and that has led to deforestation, land degradation, etc. Several factors have contributed to such developments. One of them is population explosion. In Arunachal Pradesh the population in 1951 was only 2.68 lakhs which rose to 10.91 lakhs in 2001; its percentage share in the country's population increased accordingly from 0.08% to 0.11%. With increase in population the Jhum cycle has declined to only 5 years or even less.

Another factor relates to the shift from self-sufficiency to market economy following the process of integration of the regional to the national market. In that process the dependence of the people on forest products has declined but the commercialization of forest products has increased; similarly, there has been a growing substitution of local products with the entry of modern industrial products which has led to larger cash needs. The penetration of the market economy into the economy characterized by the barter system and self-sufficiency has resulted in the popularity of private ownership rather than community ownership of property such as land and other natural resources. The process has got a boost in the process of globalization that had accelerated since the 1990s. What is globalization?

In a lighter vein, the truest definition of globalization could be appreciated in terms of Princess Diana's death as somebody puts it: "An English princess with an Egyptian boyfriend crashes in a French tunnel, driving a German car with a Dutch engine, driven by a Belgian who was drunk on Scottish whisky, followed closely by Italian paparazzi, on Japanese motorcycles, treated by an American doctor, using Brazilian medicines."

There are several consequences of globalization. For example, globalization leads to homogenization of consumption baskets, production process and even to cultural practices. For example, McDonald, Domino Pizza, Kentucky Chicken and branded products replace the traditional basket of consumption. Such a homogenization process leads to a loss of cultural diversity.

Again, intellectual property rights which have come into force in the wake of the WTO regime act as a threat to the indigenous knowledge system evolved through ages from ethnic and biodiversity. At another level, the use of modern technology for natural resource utilization has environmental consequences. Arunachal Pradesh has enormous hydro-power potential, to the tune of 56,000 Megawatts according to an estimate. Mega hydropower projects for harnessing power threaten the environment and ecology and even the loss of biodiversity. The modern method of production has adverse impacts on air, environment and ecology unless proper measures are taken. There are also threats to biodiversity inherent in its physiographic and climatic variations. These could be in the form of floods and erosion and landslides as also earthquakes since the North East is situated in a very high earthquake-prone zone.

In this context, the most pertinent question that arises is: if the globalization process or harnessing natural resources result in adverse impacts on environment and ecology and biodiversity, what should be the approach of a resource rich tribal state for improving levels of living or economic well-being? In choosing the path for improving levels of living/economic well-being while conserving and preserving biodiversity, ethnic and cultural diversity, the following cautions should be taken.

One can choose economic activities that are in harmony with natural resource conservation. Activities such as eco-tourism, cultural and ethnic tourism horticulture, farm forestry and fisheries are good examples. The word, ecotourism was coined by H.C. Lascurian in 1983 to describe nature-based travel to relatively undisturbed areas. With proper education it is conformable with sustainable tourism.

There should be investment in research and development for identifying and developing appropriate technology for harnessing natural resources for development while preserving ecology and rich biodiversity in a hill state like Arunachal Pradesh.

Initiatives towards enhancing awareness of the value and the responsibility of the present generation to preserve the rich biodiversity for posterity would be steps in the right direction. Similarly, a community-based approach to resource sharing and utilization is quite in keeping with the tradition and heritage of a tribal society. What is important to emphasize is that the need-based approach rather than consumerism is compatible with the preservation of a environment, ecology and biodiversity. Finally, there should be focused attention to discovering and documenting more and more of the diversity of the region as also documenting and validating indigenous knowledge scientifically as a step against the threat of intellectual property rights. Arunachal Pradesh with huge geographical diversity and rich natural resource endowments should focus on Geographical Information System (GIS), disaster management programmes, and environment assessment and impact analysis. The short point is that the present generation has the responsibility to protect and preserve the rich biodiversity, ethnic and cultural diversity as also human heritage while at the same time harnessing its natural resources such as water, forest, mines and minerals for economic well-being minimizing adverse impacts on biodiversity, ecology and environment.

11

Small Enterprises/Informal Sector in the North Eastern States*

This chapter attempts to (a) identify the major categories of informal/small enterprises that have come into existence in the North Eastern region; (b) review the role of institutions/agencies as promoter and as facilitator of informal enterprises; and (c) finally suggest an action plan.

I. SMALL/INFORMAL/UNORGANIZED ENTERPRISES

To start with, the role of non-agriculture sectors as a source of livelihood is significantly smaller in the North Eastern states other than in Tripura and Assam. In the other six states secondary and tertiary sectors provide employment to 14 to 29 per cent of the workers. In Assam and Tripura their contribution is 39 and 62 per cent respectively (Table 1). This means that even with the declining share of the primary sector as elsewhere, agriculture remains the primary source of livelihood in most of the North Eastern states.

Nevertheless, if the unregistered sector in the Gross State Domestic Product is interpreted as the informal sector, this sector is quite significant both for income and employment generation in the manufacturing sector in most of the North Eastern states. Apart from Assam, the unregistered/informal manufacturing sector accounted for 45 per cent (Meghalaya) to 100 per cent (Arunachal Pradesh) of the income generated in the manufacturing sector in 2002-03 (Table 2). In Assam this sector contributed only 21 per cent of the income generated in the manufacturing sector as a whole.

Non-farm informal enterprises in the secondary and tertiary sectors generated employment in the range of 19.06 per cent in Arunachal Pradesh to 61.87 per cent of the total workers engaged

---

* This was prepared jointly with Biswajit Saikia who is no more.

in the unorganized sector inclusive of those engaged in the primary sector as well.

Composition

Industrial development in the North Eastern states is sturdy. Though the region has various mineral resources that could be used for diversified industrial growth, industrial diversification has not taken place. The industries that have come into existence are largely confined to resource-based industries such as tea, jute, oil and natural gas. Tea factories alone account for more than 50 per cent of the net output from manufacturing industries of the region. Interestingly, backward and forward linkage-based industries even of the oldest industries like oil and tea have not come up in the large or small sectors.

The informal sector plays a significant role in income generation. In the extreme case of Arunachal Pradesh, large industries are non-existent and the entire income generation in the manufacturing sector in 2002-03 originated in the unregistered sector which can be considered as the informal sector. Even in Manipur and Mizoram the unregistered sector contributed respectively 98.1 per cent and 80.7 per cent of the income in the manufacturing sector. In the other North Eastern states, the unregistered sector contributed in the range of 63.3 per cent (Tripura) to 44.3 per cent (Assam).

Registered Small-Scale Industry

Small-scale industry in the North Eastern states (NES) broadly cover handloom, bell-metal, match, handmade paper, soap, candles, straw, fruit processing, leather goods, chemicals, garments, bread, biscuits, pencils, ropes, steel trunks, exercise books, surgical bandages, plug pins, plug sockets, tyres and tubes, cement pipes, garments, spices, furniture and fixtures, jewellery, etc. Broadly speaking, small-scale industries that have come up in the region can be classified under (i) Forest-based; (ii) Mineral-based; (iii) Petro-chemicals-based, (iv) Agro and food processing-based and Textiles-related industries. This suggests that only resource and agro-based small-scale industries play a prominent role in the region.

There were 69,377 registered small industries in the NER with a cumulative investment of Rs. 1,098.7 crores (excluding Sikkim) in 2000-01. These units provided employment of 30,512,214. Of these 65.1 per cent was in Assam, 8.4 per cent in Manipur, 6.9 per cent in Arunachal Pradesh, 6.7 per cent in Mizoram, 6.6 per cent in Meghalaya, 4.2% in Tripura and 1.6 per cent in Nagaland (North Eastern Council, *Basic Statistics of North Eastern Region*, 2002, p. 211).

In Arunachal Pradesh the number of SSI registered were 4,750 with investment in plant and machinery of Rs. 74.1 crore and employment of 20,660 persons up to 2000-01. The predominant small-scale industries relate to tea-processing, wood and wooden furniture, handloom textiles, carpets, handicrafts and services. A few distilleries and bottling plants have also been set up recently in the state.

At the end of December 2002, Assam had a cumulative total of 45,193 registered small-scale units providing about 2 lakh employment and an investment of Rs. 297.7 crores in plant and machinery. Tea-processing, food products, plastic products and fabrication and wire products, printing and stationery are the dominant groups. Following the implementation of the North East Industrial Policy (NEIP) industries such as cosmetics, consumer non-durables, paan masala, gutka, pharmaceuticals, white goods such as ACs, refrigerators, etc. were established.

In Manipur registered small-scale units cumulated at 5,779 units with an investment of Rs. 38.8 crore and employment of 26,702 at the end of 2002-03. Handloom textiles, wood furniture and repairing services other than capital goods were the most prominent ones.

Industrially, Meghalaya is the second most advanced state after Assam in North East India. The number of SSI units registered in the state added up to 4,599 with an investment of Rs. 38.8 crores in plant and machinery at the end of 2002-03. These units employ 26,702 persons. The predominant industries in the state are basic metal units such as ferro alloys, secondary steel products, food products, handicrafts, etc. Following NEIP 1997 a few cosmetic manufacturing units were established.

Mizoram has 4,668 units of registered small-scale industry as on March 31, 2001 with an investment of Rs. 58.0 crore. They provide employment to 23,460 persons. Prominent among these units are those relating to handloom textiles, handicrafts, fruit processing and steel fabrication.

In Nagaland there are 1,119 registered SSI units as on March 31, 2001. The total employment in these units were 3,900 persons. These industries relate to handloom textiles, handicrafts, metal products and fruit processing.

SSIs registered in Sikkim added up to 385 with an investment of Rs. 16.1 crores at the end of 2001-02. These units employed 2,900 persons. The predominant industries were handicrafts, repairing services except capital goods, distilleries and food processing.

Tripura had 2,884 registered SSI units with an investment of Rs. 14.5 crores in plant and machinery till 2000-01. These units gave employment to 9,110 persons. Handicrafts, bamboo products and repairing services other than capital goods are the major sectors in SSI units that were set up.

Unregistered Enterprises

The registered sector does not give the total coverage of the informal sector that has a large spread in the region. The share of unorganized workers (83.44 per cent) in the workforce of NES is overwhelmingly large. The state-wise details are given in Table-. The share of unorganized workers in the total workforce ranged from 73.7 per cent (Nagaland) to 92.4 per cent (Meghalaya) among the North Eastern states in 1999-2000. But this also includes very large farm sector employment. Even non-farm unorganized workers accounted for in the range of 51.0 per cent (Arunachal Pradesh) to 77.9 per cent (Assam) of the total unorganized workers in the region.

Having indicated the preponderance of unorganized non-farm workers, their broad activity-wise distribution would suggest the structure of the state economies of the region. Therefore a brief discussion is attempted by states.

Arunachal Pradesh

Arunachal Pradesh had the total unorganized workforce of 281,858 of which 53,730 or 80.9 per cent were in the non-farm sector. The most prominent sectors in the non-farm sector are public administration (38.0 per cent), construction (21.4 per cent), retail trade (14.5 per cent), education (2.7 per cent) and other service activities (2.3 per cent). These service categories absorbed about four-fifth (78.9 per cent) of the total the non-farm workers. The manufacturing activities provided employment to 12.5 per cent of the non-farm workers. This pattern indicated limited diversity of the state economy. This might have prompted NABARD to identify non-farm activities such as fish rearing and processing, rural retail trade, sericulture and silk textile fibre products, construction, small plantation products, handloom, handicrafts, products of cane, bamboo and wood.

Similarly, the Arunachal Pradesh Industrial Development and Financial Corporation (APIDFC) which was set up in 1978 for promotion of industries in the state identified the following thrust areas for industrial development: Agro and horticulture-based units; Mining and mineral-based units; Plantation crop-based units, Cottage industry product units and Adventure tourism.

Table 1 shows percentage distribution of informal sector employment in the major categories of activities.

Assam

In Assam 24.74 lakh workers were engaged in unorganized non-farm enterprises in 1999-00. They constituted 38.77 per cent of the total farm and non-farm workforce. The largest segment of unorganized enterprises were operating in the service sectors such as retail trade 30.01 per cent of the total non-farm workers), land transport (8.42 per cent) and other services. Among the manufacturing enterprises that engaged a significant number of workers, textiles, wood and wood products, food products and beverages and furniture were the dominant ones.

Manipur

Of the total unorganized workers of 5.73 lakh, 1.56 lakh were non-farm workers accounting for slightly over one-fourth (27.19 per cent). In Manipur also unorganized enterprises were largely engaged in diverse service activities. Retail trade, construction, public administration and other services were the major activities for unorganized workers. Among the manufacturing sectors, textiles was the most prominent sector that engaged the largest segment of unorganized workers.

Meghalaya

In Meghalaya only 14 per cent of the total unorganized workers were engaged in non-farm activities while the rest were in the farm sector inclusive of forests, fishing and mining. Among non-farm activities various types of services provided employment in the state. Retail trade, land transport, hotels and restaurants and other services mostly provided employment to unorganized workers. While several manufacturing activities engaged workers, the most prominent manufacturing sector was wood and wood products.

Mizoram

Non-farm workers constituted 21.86 per cent of the total unorganized workers in Mizoram. As in other North Eastern states unorganized workers were found in various service activities. Retail trade, public administration, education and health and social work mostly provided employment to unorganized workers. Manufacture of wearing and apparel, dressing and dying and manufacture of furniture were the two most prominent manufacturing sectors for unorganized workers in Mizoram.

Nagaland

Slightly more than one-fifth (22.53 per cent) of unorganized workers in Nagaland were found in non-farm activities. They were mostly in retail trade, public administration, land transport, education and health and social work. The only significant manufacturing sectors were textiles and food products and beverages. Other less significant manufacturing activities for employment of unorganized workers were manufacture of wood and wood products and manufacture of furniture.

Sikkim

Non-farm unorganized workers accounted for almost a quarter (24.92 per cent) of the total unorganized workers in Sikkim. They were mostly engaged in service activities such as retail trade, land transport, hotels and restaurants and a significant percentage (11.58) with 'private households with employed persons'. There were only a very few manufacturing activities that engaged unorganized workers. The only prominent sector was manufacture of furniture that provided employment to 4.92 per cent of non-farm workers in Sikkim.

Tripura

Tripura's total working population increased from 31.1 per cent in 1991 to 36.2 per cent in 2001. About 51 per cent of the workers are engaged in the agriculture sector. West Tripura district has the largest percentage of other workers, indicating those engaged in trade and other non-agricultural activities. This is also attributed to the fact that West Tripura is most urbanized. Of the total workers 79 per cent of the workers are main workers, while the remaining 21 per cent are marginal workers. In Tripura 82.7 per cent workers were engaged in the unorganized sector and approximately 89 per cent were unorganized workers. Retail trade and manufacturing accounted for 63 per cent of non-agricultural establishments and 47 per cent of employment in Tripura's OAE's and establishments.

Summing Up

The above discussion broadly indicates the importance of unorganized enterprises as reflected in the distribution of unorganized workers across different activities in North Eastern states. Generally speaking, service enterprises are mostly dominant in North Eastern states. Even so, a few manufacturing enterprises

Table 1: Artisan Based Rural Clusters in North Eastern States

Serial No.	*State*	*No. of Clusters*
1	Arunachal Pradesh	11
2	Assam	20
3	Manipur	6
4	Meghalaya	Not available
5	Mizoram	6
6	Nagaland	8
7	Sikkim	2
8	Tripura	11
9	All North Eastern States	64

Source: General Review Study of Small and Medium Enterprise (SME) Clusters in India brought out by the Ministry of Small Scale Industries, Government of India.

have come into existence in all the states. In fact, a few artisan-based rural clusters have emerged as has been established by a study referred to in the paper on General Review Study of Small and Medium Enterprise (SME) Clusters in India brought out by the Ministry of Small Scale Industries, Government of India. It is shown that out of 917 clustera compiled, 64 clusters are located in North Eastern states as given table 1:

It is not known, however, the exact activities around which these clusters have come into existence. It is possible that the activities in which the dominant presence of unorganized workers has been noted in the respective states.

II. ROLE OF PROMOTIONAL INSTITUTIONS/AGENCIES

At the outset, it should be recognized that small industries fall in the State List of the Indian Constitution. States are, therefore, responsible for the promotion and development of small and medium-scale industries within the state jurisdictions. Recognizing the importance of small-scale industries for addressing the problems of poverty and unemployment in a labour-plenty but capital-scarce country like ours, the Government of India from the very beginning of planning particularly since the Industrial Policy of 1956 assigned high priority in development of small enterprises. Accordingly, it set up a wide range of agencies for the development and promotion of the SME sector in India. The agencies range from regulators and facilitators, advocacy, to specialized financing institutions. These agencies also perform the promotional role in the North Eastern states along with other states. This section therefore proposes to discuss briefly the role of these institutions with special reference to North Eastern states.

The institutions/agencies that are engaged in promoting small enterprises in the North Eastern Region exist at three levels: national, regional and state. The national level agencies established by the Government of India have countrywide jurisdiction. Regional level institutions such as the North Eastern Council and North East Development and Financial Corporation (NEDFi) pursue policies for the North Eastern Region as a whole while the state government and its instrumentalities design and implement state-specific policies. In addition, there are NGOs which work for development of small enterprises. We will therefore briefly discuss the role of institutions at four levels: National, Regional, State and NGO.

A. Central Level Institutions/Agencies Engaged in Promoting Small Enterprises

The Ministry of Small Scale Industries of the Government of India implements its policies and programmes for providing infrastructure support services to small enterprises through its instrumentalities, namely the Small Industries Development Organization (SIDO), statutory bodies like Khadi and Village Industries Commission (KVIC) and Coir Board and organizations/ institutions like National Small Industries Corporation (NSIC) and three training institutes: National Institute of Small Industry Extension Training (NISIET), Hyderabad, National Institute for Entrepreneurship and Small Business Development (NIESBUD), New Delhi and Indian Institute for Entrepreneurship (IIE), Guwahati.

The Small Scale Industries (SSI) Board is the apex advisory body that renders advice to the government on all issues pertaining to the small-scale sector.

The agencies which have been set up for the promotion of the SME sector in India are briefly dealt with one by one below.

(a) Small Industries Development Organization (SIDO): SIDO set up in 1954 along the SME Development Agency established in many countries of the world, functions as the nodal Development Agency to coordinate and oversee all government interventions relating to this sector. Over the years it has evolved itself as an agency for advocacy, handholding and facilitation of the small- scale sector. SIDO has over 60 offices and 21 autonomous bodies such as Tool Rooms, Training Institutions and Project-cum-Process Development Centres under its management. SIDO provides a wide range of services such as facilities for testing, training for entrepreneurship development, preparation of project profiles and assistance for exports to the small industries sector. The field offices additionally function as effective links between the central and the state governments. In the context of globalization SIDO sees its role as a catalyst of growth of small enterprises in the country. It is

giving a thrust on providing support in the fields of credit, marketing, technology and infrastructure to SSIs.

The central government directly and through its instrumentalities have put in place a number of schemes such as the following for the SSI sector.

1. Credit Linked Capital Subsidy Scheme for technology upgradation (CLCSS): Capital subsidy @ 12 per cent upto Rs. 4.8 lakhs on loans taken for technology upgradation for individual SSIs.
2. Credit Guarantee Fund Scheme for Small Industries (CGFSI): collateral free loans up to a limit of Rs. 25 lakhs for individual SSIs. To begin with, CGFSI was to be operational for a period of one year on pilot basis.
3. ISO 9000/ISO 14000 Certification Reimbursement Scheme: Reimbursement of expenses was provided for acquiring Quality Management System (QMS) ISO 9000 certifcation/ environment management (EMS) ISO 14001 certification to the extent of 75 per cent of the expenditure subject to the maximum of Rs. 75,000 in each case. This facility was available for individual permanent registered Small Scale, ancilliary, tiny or Small Scale Service Enterprises (SSBE) units till March 31, 2007.
4. Participation in International Fairs: With a view to encouraging participation by SSI units in international fairs, full subsidy was given on space rent, handling, clearing charges, insurance and shipment charges of their exhibits in international exhibitions.
5. Purchase and Price Preference Policy: Under this scheme 358 items are reserved for exclusive purchase from SSI by the central government. In addition, other facilities available include tender documents free of cost, exemption from earnest money and security deposit and 15 per cent price preference in central government purchases for individual SSIs. This policy of reservation of items for exclusive purchase has been in operation since the late 1960s. This Policy aims at providing market support to the SSI sector.
6. Prime Minister's Rozgar Yojana (PMRY) (Scheme of Ministry of ARI): Under this scheme which has been in

operation since 1993, subsidy and margin money upto 20 per cent of project and the balance as loan are extended for projects not exceeding Rs. 1 lakh and Rs. 2 lakhs for other activities. The upper age limit of the beneficiary has been relaxed by 10 years beyond 35 years for SC/ST and women as also the educational qualification from matric to 8th passed. The scope of the PMRY scheme is also expanded to cover all economically viable activities including agriculture and allied activities but excluding direct agricultural operations like raising crops, purchase of manure, etc.

7. As for the North Eastern region, certain relaxations of norms in the PMRY scheme since its inception have been given. For example, the scope of the PMRY has been widened to cover areas of horticulture, piggery, poultry, fishing, small tea gardens, etc. so as to include all economically viable activities. Again, the upper age limit was fixed at 40 years and family income ceiling at Rs. 40,000. Further, no collateral will be insisted for projects costing upto Rs. 1 lakh. Furthermore, group financing upto Rs. 5 lakhs is also eligible with a subsidy component @ 15 per cent subject to the maximum of Rs. 15,000 and margin money varying from 5 per cent to 12.5 per cent of the project cost both adding upto 20 per cent of the project cost.
8. Integrated Technology Upgradation Management Programme (UPTECH): This scheme was introduced in 1998 to address concerns like product quality, productivity, energy and environmental issues relating to SSIs. The scheme applies to a cluster of industries that have commonality in production method, quality control and testing, energy conservation, pollution control among the units of the cluster. The scheme aims at addressing the issues of modernization and the technological needs of the cluster.
9. Integrated Infrastructure Development (IID): This scheme was launched in 1994 to develop infrastructure for facilitating location of small-scale industry in rural/ backward areas which were not covered under the Growth Centre Scheme. It aims at promoting stronger linkage between agriculture and industry for employment

generation. Operationally, under this scheme assistance upto 40 per cent or Rs. 2 crores are available to state government/ industry associations/NGOs for setting up industrial estates in rural/backward areas. For the North Eastern region assistance to the extent of 80 per cent or Rs. 4 crores has been provided.

The cost to set up an IID Centre is worked out at Rs. 5 crores. This cost is shared by the Government of India and Small Industries Development Bank of India in the ratio of 2:3. The former contributes in the form of grants whle the latter as loan. Any excess over the estimated cost of Rs.5 crores is borne by the respective state/UT government/ implementing agencies.

With a view to giving a fillip to growth of small-scale industries in the North Eastern Region, the government has recently relaxed the funding pattern by way of the Government of India providing a grant in the ratio of 4:1-Government of India's grant would be Rs. 4 crores while State/SIDBI loan Rs. 1 crore. The High Powered Committee constituted under the scheme sanctioned 53 IID projects till March 2000.

10. Mini Tool Rooms: The Government of India established a few Tool Rooms for the benefit of industries in the SSI sector at an estimated cost of over Rs. 50 crores each to provide facilities for design and manufacturing toolings as also for training to improve the skills of tool makers. In order to meet the growing need of the SSI sector, the Government of India has indrouced a scheme to assist the state government for setting up Mini Tool Room and Training Centres woking out the cost of a typical Centre at Rs. 15 crores-Rs. 10 crores towards machinery/equipment. Accordingly, the central assistance would be in the form of one-time grant-in-aid equal to 90 per cent of the estimated cost of machinery/ equipment or Rs. 9 crores in the case of a new Mini Tool Room and 75 per cent or Rs. 7.5 crores for upgradation of the existing ones.Under this scheme assistance to the maximum of 50 per cent or Rs. 50 lakhs is available for industry associations to set up Testing Centres.

11. Sub-contracting exchanges: Industry associations are given a one time grant for procurement of hardware and thereafter matching grant on a tapering basis at 50 per cent, 30 per cent and 10 per cent of running expenses not above Rs. 1.25 lakhs, Rs. 0.75 lakh respectively during the initial three years subject to a ceiling of Rs. 1.57 lakhs per exchange.
12. Scheme for Market Development Assistance for SSI Exporters (SSI-MDA): This scheme facilitates SSI Entrepreneurs' participation in overseas fairs/trade delegations by way of providing financial assistance to the extent of 90 per cent of to and fro air fare. The scheme also provides for 25 per cent of production costs of publicity materials, cost of sector-specific studies to the limit of Rs. 2 lakhs and 50 per cent or up to the maximum of Rs. 1 lakh for contesting anti-dumping cases by individuals or associations.
13. Assistance to Entrepreneurship Development Institutes. the Government of India provides assistance to state governments for strengthening training infrastructure in EDIs. The assistance could be to the maximum of 50 per cent of cost or Rs. 50 lakhs whichever is less

(b) Small Industries Development Bank of India (SIDBI): SIDBI, a subsidiary of IDBI, was established in 1990 under an act of Parliament. It is designed as the principal financial in stitution for the promotion, financing and development of industry in the SSI sector. It is also to coordinate the functions of the institutions engaged in the promotion and financing or developing industries in the small-scale sector. SIDBI schemes broadly relate to four categories. Refinance, Bills Finance, Project-related direct finance, Promotional and Developmental Schemes.

(c) National Small Industries Corporation (NSIC): The Government of India established the National Small Industries Corporation Ltd in 1955 to promote, aid and foster the growth of small industries in the country. NSIC remains at the forefront of industrial development with its wide variety of programmes and projects to assist the small-scale sector in the country. Its programmes include Composite Term Loan Scheme, Machinery and Equipment Hire

Purchase Scheme, Equipment Leasing and Working Capital Finance, Marketing Support Programmes, Tender Marketing, Publicity to Small Industries Products, Integrated Marketing Support, Government Stores Purchase Programme, Technology Upgradation, Technology Transfer Centres, Software Technology Parks, Exports, Special Export Programme-UN Supplies.

(d) Training: Under the Ministry of Small Scale Industries there exists a network of training institutes across the country that provides training and develop manpower specially suited to the SME sector. They are National Institute of Small Industry Extension Training (NISIET), Hyderabad, National Institute for Entrepreneurship and Small Business Development (NIESBUD), New Delhi, Integrated Training Centre (Industries), Nilokheri, Small Entrepreneurs Promotion and Training Institute (SEPTI), Tiruvalla and Indian Institute of Entrepreneurship (IIE), Guwahati.

(e) Khadi and Village Industries Commission: Khadi and Village Industries Commission (KVIC), established in 1957 as a statutory body under an Act of Parliament of 1956, is entrusted with the responsibility of planning, promoting, organizing and implementing programmes for the development of khadi and village industries in rural areas in coordination with other agencies engaged in rural development in the country. The main objective of KVIC is to generate employment opportunities in rural areas and to create self-reliance amongst the people. KVIC's activities include building up reserves of raw materials and implements for supply to producers, creation of common service facilities for processing of raw materials as semi-finished goods and provision of facilities for marketing of khadi and village industries products, apart from organizing training programmes for artisans engaged in these industries. To promote the sale and marketing of khadi, products of village industries and handicrafts, KVIC forges linkages with established marketing agencies. KVIC provides financial assistance to institutions and individuals for development of khadi and village industries and equips them through supply of designs, prototypes and other technical information. Besides loans, KVIC provides assistance in the form of margin money under its Rural Employment Generation Programme (REGP) for financing viable village industries projects.

B. Regional Level Institutions and Policy and Programmes

(a) North Eastern Region Specific Industrial Policy: Apart from the above types of general schemes that have been in operation for development of the SSI sector in the country, the Government of India introduced for the first time on December 24, 1997 an industrial policy known as the North East Industrial Policy (NEIP), 1997 as supplementary initiatives for industrial development of the North Eastern Region but exclusive of Sikkim. The salient features of the Policy are as follows:

i) Expenditure on Growth Centres subject to the maximum of Rs. 15 crores will be met through central assistance.
ii) Funding pattern Integrated Infrastructural Development for NER Government of India and SIDBI will be 4 :1 instead of 2:3 as applicable elsewhere. The Government of India contribution will be in the form of grants.
iii) Industries located in the Growth Centres will be given capital subsidy at the rate of 15 per cent on Plant and Machinery subject to the maximum of Rs. 30 lakhs.
iv) An interest subsidy of 3 per cent on the working capital will be provided for ten years from the date of commencement of production.
v) The transport subsidy scheme was extended till April 1, 2007. The subsidy will be disbursed through NEDFi.
vi) Growth Centres and IIDCs will be tax-income tax and excise duty- free zones for a period of ten years. Certain industries with high potentials will also enjoy tax free status irrespective of the location in the NER.
vii) Comprehensive Insurance Schemes will be available to cover new industrial units.

The Government of India approved a new policy known as North East Industrial and Investment Promotion Policy (NEIIPP), 2007 as replacement of NEIP with effect from April 1, 2007. This Policy also covered Sikkim within the ambit of NER. The major features of this Policy are as follows:

i) Incentives will be available to all industrial units, new and existing ones on their substantial expansion, located anywhere in the NER.
ii) 100 per cent Income Tax and Excise Duty exemption on

finished products as available under NEIP, 1997 will be continued.

iii) Capital Investment Subsidy is enhanced to 30 per cent from the earlier 15 per cent of the investment in plant and machinery subject to a ceiling of Rs. 1.5 crores under automatic approval and of Rs. 30 crores with approval of an Empowered Committee. Proposals beyond Rs. 30 crores will be possible with the approval of the Union Cabinet.

iv) Interest subsidy @ 3 per cent on working capital loan as was available earlier under NEIP, 1997.

v) New industrial units as well as the existing ones on their substantial expansion will be eligible for reimbursement of 100% insurance premium.

vi) Transport subsidy will continue as before subject to an early evaluation.

(b) The following industries will not be eligible for benefits under NEIIPP, 2007: (i) Tobacco and manufactured tobacco substitutes; (ii) Paan masala; (iii) Plastic carry bags; and (iv) Goods produced by petroleum oil or gas refiners

(c) Incentives under NEIPP will also be available to Service sector activities/industries: (i) Hotels (not below Two Star), adventure, leisure sports including ropeways; Medical and health services; and Vocational training institutes; (ii) Biotechnology industry and (iii) Power Generating industries will continue to get under Section 81 A of the Income tax Act up to 10 MW based on conventional and non-conventional sources will also be eligible for capital investment subsidy, interest subsidy and comprehensive insurance as applicable under NEIIPP, 2007.

1. North Eastern Council (NEC)

The North Eastern Council launched a "Scheme for Promotion of Industrialization in the North East" (SPINE). Under this scheme the NEC will provide subsidy to the extent of 25 per cent of the project cost including cost of land, building, plant and machinery and miscellaneous fixed assets subject to the maximum limit of Rs. 50 lakh. Only the enterprises with cost of plants and machinery not exceeding Rs. 5 crore and with accent on employment generation will be eligible for subsidy under this scheme.

Support to Entrepreneurship Development Programmes (EDPs)

NEC together with other funding agencies like IDBI, SIDBI, NSIC, etc. has been co-financing about 40 to 45 EDPs annually. During the Eighth Five Year Plan, 197 EDPs were conducted and about 4,500 people participated in these programmes. Keeping a target to produce about 1,000 entrepreneurs per year, NEC proposed to conduct 40 to 45 EDPs per year during the Ninth Five Year Plan. Amongst the 30 EDPs conducted, there were 14 General EDP, 9 Women and 7 Rural EDPs. Apart from these, NEC has funded a few product-specific EDPs and short duration training programmes for Final Year College and University students.

2. North Eastern Development Finance Corporation Ltd. (NEDFi)

North Eastern Development Finance Corporation Ltd. (NEDFi), promoted by all-India financial institutions and SBI, was incorporated in August 1995 under the Companies Act, 1956. Its objective was to provide long-term solutions to the industrial financing needs of the North East Region. It was also to guide entrepreneurs in identifying viable projects as also to equip them with the requisite skills and technical capabilities. NEDFi deals mainly with first-generation entrepreneurs, small-scale industries, new technologies and startup projects. Besides offering financial products like Working Capital Loans, Composite Loans, North East Equity Fund and Micro Finance, NEDFi extends assistance for development of market for products manufactured in the NER as also for preparation of techno-economic feasibility studies. NEDFi also acts as the nodal agency for disbursement of central capital investment subsidy, transport subsidy and working capital interest subsidy for the North Eastern states.

C. State Level Institutions and Programmes

(i) State Industrial Development Corporations: Each state government set up State Industrial Development Corporation (SIDC) under the Companies Act, 1956 as a wholly-owned undertaking with the specific objective of promoting and developing medium and large-scale industries. There are 28 SIDCs in the country. SIDCs in Andaman & Nicobar, Arunachal Pradesh, Daman & Diu and Dadra & Nagar Haveli, Goa, Manipur,

Meghalaya, Mizoram, Nagaland, Tripura, Pondicherry and Sikkim also play the role of State Financial Corporations (SFCs) in regard to promoting and providing assistance to small and medium enterprises.

The SIDCs extend financial assistance in the form of rupee loans, underwriting and direct subscription to shares/debentures, guarantees, inter-corporate deposits, structured finance and also open letters of credit on behalf of their borrowers. The SIDCs also undertake a range of promotional activities including preparation of feasibility reports, conducting industrial potential surveys, entrepreneurship development programmes and developing industrial areas/estates. The SIDCs, as nodal agencies of state governments, also manage and operate state incentive schemes. Further, some SIDCs act as nodal agencies for NRI investment and Foreign Direct Investment (FDI) in their respective states. With a view to sustaining their relevance and viability in the changing economic environment, SIDCs have initiated various measures to expand the scope of their business, including undertaking a variety of fee-based activities.

(ii) State Financial Corporations: The State Financial Corporations (SFCs) are state-level financial institutions which play a crucial role in the development of small and medium enterprises in their respective states in tandem with national priorities. Of the 18 SFCs in the country, 17 were set up under the SFCs Act, 1951. Tamil Nadu Industrial Investment Corporation Ltd., which was originally established as Madras Industrial Investment Corporation in 1949 under the Indian Companies Act, 1913, also functions as a SFC. The SFCs provide financial assistance by way of term loans, direct subscription to equity/debentures, guarantees, discounting of bills of exchange and seed/special capital. Besides, the SFCs operate a number of schemes of refinance and equity-type assistance on behalf of SIDBI, in addition to special schemes for artisans, and special target groups such as SC/ST, women, ex-servicemen and physically handicapped.

The SFCs (Amendment) Act 2000, which became effective from September 2000, *inter alia,* provides greater flexibility to the SFCs to cope with the challenges posed by the deregulated financial system. However, the Committee, constituted by the Government of India for looking into the functioning of SFCs and for making recommendations for their restructuring and revitalization, indicated in its Report that the future business prospects of SFCs are likely to be affected by stiff competition emerging in the financial system.

Further, in a "Report of the Working Group on Development Financial Institutions" brought out by RBI in May 2004, it is stated that, due to the combination of several factors, the SFCs' financial position has irretrievably deteriorated. Barring four, the remaining 14 SFCs in different states have significantly negative capital to risk adjusted asset ratio (CRAR) and average non-performing assets (NPAs) of 64 per cent. According to the RBI Report, the issue of restructuring of SFCs has been defying any solution, despite recommendations of an Expert Committee advocating infusion of a considerable amount of funds. Also, it is uncertain whether these SFCs would turn around even after such infusion of funds. In the final analysis, the Report advocates that the SFCs should be phased out within a definite timeframe, and the credit gap, if any, created by the exit of the SFCs from the market can be filled by banks and also by suitably repositioning SIDBI.

(iii) State Small Industries Development Corporations (SSIDCs): State Governments established SSIDCs under the Companies Act, 1956 as state government undertakings with the specific objective of promoting and developing small, tiny and village industries in the States/Union Territories. Over the years, the SSIDCs diversified the range of their activities and services to cater to the emerging needs of SSI units in the changed economic environment.

Some of the important functions/activities of SSIDCs include procurement and distribution of raw materials, supply of machinery on hire-purchase basis, assistance to SSI units for marketing their products, establishment of testing laboratories, construction/upgradation of basic infrastructure facilities in industrial estates/sheds, development of Industrial Parks, extending seed capital assistance on behalf of the respective state governments, organizing training programmes for unemployed youths, providing managerial assistance to production units and management of States' Emporia for providing sales windows for handlooms, handicrafts, and SSI items. Some of the SSIDCs also run manufacturing units.

(iv) Technical Consultancy Organizations: All-India financial institutions in collaboration with state-level financial/development institutions and commercial banks promoted Technical Consultancy Organizations (TCOs) in various states during the 1970s and 80s to cater to the consultancy needs of the small and medium enterprises and new entrepreneurs. In all, there are 18 TCOs in various states with some of them operating in more than one state. TCOs provide various types of consultancy services such as, preparation of feasibility studies and project reports/ profiles, identification of potential entrepreneurs, technical and management assistance to new entrepreneurs, product-specific market research/surveys, project supervision, energy audit and energy conservation assignments, consultancy assignments on a turn-key basis, export consultancy for export oriented projects, management consultancy services, especially for diagnostic study of sick units or improvement in the existing units and rehabilitation programmes, entrepreneurship development programmes/skill upgradation programmes and merchant banking services.

D. ROLE OF NGOs

Rashtriya Gramin Vikash Nidhi (RGVN)

It is increasingly realized that CBOs/NGOs (Community Based Organizations/Non Government Organizations) can play an important role in implementation of the community-related projects. For, it is not possible for the government to discharge all major social tasks due to constraints of high transaction cost, rigid and formal organization structures, etc. NGOs with its informal and flexible structure and its proximity to the people have the qualities needed to undertake social tasks.

It is in this context that the Rashtriya Gramin Vikas Nidhi was set up as an apex NGO that coordinates the activities of smaller NGOs and serve as the linkage between the government and the community in regard to implementation of development projects in the North Eastern and eastern region of the country. The RGVN in its decade old existence has evolved a strategy and mechanism, which ensures participation of all stakeholders at all levels of project implementation. It has collaborated with the Assam Rural Infrastructure and Agricultural Services Project (ARIASP) Society towards implementation of the ARIAS Project of the World Bank in Assam (2000-03). RGVN has acted as an extended arm of the Project Implementation Unit (PIU), Government of Assam to carry forward poverty alleviation interventions. RGVN's role as an Apex NGO was envisaged as follows:

1. To develop a strategy/mechanism to ensure active participation of the beneficiaries, NGOs, farmers' groups, water users' groups, women's groups in the project activities.
2. To motivate and sensitize the personnel of the project implementing agencies, NGOs and senior policy makers to grass root level issues/problems, participatory approach, gender issues, environmental impact of ARIASP activities.
3. To create a forum between the project staff and NGOs for effective and efficient participatory planning and implementation of the project activities.
4. To help the PIU in identifying and involving NGOs under ARIASP at different levels while implementing the activities.

The sectors covered under RGVN-ARIASP collaboration were irrigation, fisheries and veterinary. In the first year of its operation RGVN intervened in the irrigation sector only. In the second and the third year of its collaboration with ARIASP, RGVN spread its operational network to the fishery and the veterinary sector respectively.

The Deputy Commissioner, Kamrup (M), Assam requested RGVN to assist in the implementation of the Swarna Jayanti Sahari Rojgar Yojana (SJSRY), a welfare scheme that provides employment opportunities to the urban unemployed or underemployed poor living below the poverty line. The programme was carried out as a pilot project for the welfare of the urban poor in collaboration with the District Urban Development Agencies (DUDA).

(E) Self-Help Groups (SHG)

One recent development of great significance is the growth of SHGs in the NER like anywhere else in the country. Two factors have contributed to its growth. One, promoters' preference for SHGs rather than individuals in matters of extending various forms of support for small enterprises has led to formation of SHG on a massive scale. The other reason is that producers particularly in the hill states of NER cannot access credit from formal credit institutions, even if they are eligible. It is because land which is an important asset is owned by the community and not by individuals. Therefore people do not have individual land title that can be used as collateral for credit.

In view of the two reasons mentioned, there has been enormous growth of SHGs though we do not have any estimate of the number of SHGs that have come into existence in different states in the NER. Interestingly, the emergence of SHGs in a particular trade/ traditional craft has contributed to the evolution of clusters as in the case of the bell-metal industry in Hajo or weaving in Sawalkuchi in Assam.

III. TOWARDS ROBUST GROWTH AND PERFORMANCE

Learning from Case Studies

In order to get an idea of the nature of constraints and the performance of small enterprises, we have conducted six case studies of small enterprises in Assam. Ideally, such case studies should have been carried out in other states of NER. That would provide many useful insights into the working of small enterprises. But due to time constraints this exercise had to be restricted to Assam alone. However, it is conceivable that even the insights gained from this smaller number of case studies seem to have wider relevance.

The case studies that have been carried out are based on a priori information of their existence or emergence in certain areas. These cases: (i)Brass metal cluster at Hajo, (ii) Beekeeping and Honey processing plant at Charigaon, Jorhat, (iii) Chapma Silk Factory and weavers' SHGs, Sualkuchi, (iv) Saru Tezpur Bengapara weavers' SHGs, Rampur, (v) A.S. (blacksmith) SHG, Karanga in Jorhat district and (vi) Pottery SHG, Sanmagori village, near Baihata Charali-spread over different parts of Assam.

All these case studies relate to clusters of traditional and weaving enterprises at household level though individual entrepreneurship as in the case of the honey processing plant has played a role. Some of these cases such as the honey processing plant which has been organized along the Amul model and Chapma

Silk factory are more successful enterprises while others are not so. We will highlight the major findings below. Self-help groups have emerged as an important and acceptable form of small enterprise organization. SHGs at the level of the beekeeping and honey processing unit providing a market outlet for the former is a good example of reasonable success case though it could perform a lot better with better training in packaging and market linkage with large enterprises.

- All the cases lack technology linkage meaning their plant and machinery are old and require upgradation and modernization.
- Infrastructure inadequacy in terms of power supply, credit availability, etc. has hindered them in carrying out optimal-level operation.
- All of them lack market linkage in terms of information in regard to proper market outlet, product design, and consumer preferences or demand situations. Traders operating in a non-competitive manner buy their products at less than incentive prices.
- High cost and poor quality raw materials hurt most of them.
- All have felt the need for skill upgradation through proper training. Existing training institutes have not reached out to them. Even when they did, training has been inadequate or conditions prevailing in their environment stand in the way of making use of the new skills learned through training.

These observations made in regard to small enterprises operating in Assam which has several advantages over the other states in the NER can be expected to hold good to a much higher degree in the case of small enterprises operating in other states of the region.

Broadly speaking, weak technology linkage that hinders productivity gain, infrastructure bottlenecks that lead to cost disadvantage, market distortions due to dominance of deeply entrenched traders and middlemen at one level and weak market linkage at another level that prevent incentive price realization ail the operation and performance of small enterprises in the NER. As a result, even though clusters of enterprises have emerged in different parts of NER, they do not enjoy scale economies or a dynamic relation between agglomeration and infrastructure development that spurs growth through backward and forward 'linkages, spillover and labour-related effects'.

Where to Go from Here

To begin with, it should be recognized that despite all the disadvantages, North Eastern states have witnessed a spurt of activities in recent years. It is partly because of focused attention that the central and state governments have been paying for North East development particularly since 1997 when the then Prime Minister, H.D. Deve Gowda extended a special dispensation for NER development. It is also because increasingly higher numbers of educated unemployed youths facing a gloomy employment situation have begun to venture enterprises. It is a myth that NER lacks entrepreneurship. The fact is that entrepreneurs in NER are to function in a situation of high risk, low accumulation, poor infrastructure, weak market linkage due to remoteness and weak market compatible institutions like community land ownership in hill states.

Yet small enterprises have grown in number in the recent years. SHG has emerged as a popular form of business organization. Clusters of traditional crafts, handlooms, furniture, a variety of resource and local demand-based small enterprises have come into existence. Interestingly, as compared to goods producing enterprises, various types of service enterprises are more ubiquitous. But their performances seem to be far from optimal. Our small number of case studies have brought out and highlighted what generally ail small enterprises in the NER as discussed above. Keeping in view the major constraints faced by small enterprises in the NER, we propose the following model of development for small enterprises in the region. To start with, there should be an apex institution/organization of stakeholders for each industry wise cluster of enterprises in the NER. This institution/organization which should be modelled on federating basis should perform multiple functions: (i) create a data bank and kiosk for access of the enterprises in concerned trade/industry; (ii) establish linkage with suitable buyers for their products and make buy-back arrangement; (iii) establish linkage with technology providers and relevant R&D centres of the country and facilitate access to new technology; (iv) identify skill needs and organize training by appropriate training institutes; (vi) disseminate information on available support and assistance provided by government and various promotional agencies and assist enterprises in accessing them; and (v) create a market research centre for identification of suitable market, improvement of product design and packaging and dissemination of demand conditions such as prices, preferred design and quality for the benefit of enterprises and (vi) network with producers of similar products for information exchange.

An effective functioning of such an organization would contribute a good deal to the performance of enterprises by way of enhancing productivity through continual upgradation and modernization of technology, expanding market and realizing incentive prices. But clusters of enterprises, even if function more efficiently and profitably would not automatically enjoy benefits of agglomeration. This could be possible if growth poles could be developed to link several industry-wise clusters. The interdependence of these clusters of small enterprises would lead to "external economies from their simultaneous and complementary functioning. Such positive externalities can be derived from (a) forward and backward linkages in productive activities, such as units using each other's demands for inputs and production of output, both within and outside the area ; (b) use of common facilities for social overhead capital like roads, other forms of transport, communications and market connections, both within the country and for exports; (c) allowing inter-linkages of different services to develop a network with the clusters of activities."

The development of world class infrastructure covering the contiguous areas in which clusters of several industries already exist as well as potentials for further growth of enterprises would facilitate agglomeration and thus robust growth of small enterprises. Keeping this in view, we have compiled the available information on both revealed industrial hubs and potential enterprises in different states in NER and presented these in Tables- and respectively.

Broadly speaking, North Eastern states hold out a great promise for agro processing and handlooms and handicrafts, mineral-based, agro processing, forest-based, backward and forward linkage of plantations, tourism related, animal husbandry related, medicinal and aromatic, health care related and IT and electronic enterprises. North Eastern states have already set up industrial estates in their respective states. This information is available and shown in the Tables. But the information on cluster of enterprises in and around the industrial estates of different NER states is not available. One can argue that growth poles have generally to be considered in the neighbourhood of state capitals of North Eastern states. It is mainly because apart from Assam, air and rail connectivity is limited only to the state capital of NER states, if at all, while connectivity is an essential requirement for location of a growth pole.

On a priori basis, the following places can be suggested for location of a growth pole in respective states: Pasighat or Zero in Arunachal Pradesh, a couple of districts adjoining to Guwahati, districts adjoining to Imphal in Manipur, Barapani and Barnihat areas in Meghalaya, districts adjoining to Aizol, Dimapur and its adjoining areas in Nagaland and Agartala and its adjoining districts. These could be possible places for location of growth poles in different states in the NER. Feasibility studies should be conducted to identify the existing cluster of enterprises and potentials and ascertain the right location of growth poles.

NOTES

1. Planning Commission, GoI, (1997), High Level Commission, Transforming the North East-Tackling Backlogs in Basic Minimum Services and Infrastructural Needs, p. 1.
2. Planning Commission, GoI (1997), *Assam Development Report* (Draft), p. 6.
3. Planning Commission, GoI (1997), High Level Commission, Transforming the North East-Tackling Backlogs in Basic Minimum Services and Infrastructural Needs, p. 1.
4. The estimate of hydropower potential of the North East widely varies. For example, the Central Electricity Authority places the total hydropower potential of the region at 34,920 MW against the all-India potential of 84,044 MW (*The Times of India*, February 28, 2005). According to the Brahmaputra Board, the hydropower potential of the Brahmaputra alone is about 40,000 MW.
5. Assam is losing on an average 20 sq. kms every year due to erosion

by the Brahmaputra river. Other allied problems relate to severe drainage congestion, urban floods and devastation of agriculture, Nayan Sharma, an IIT, Roorkee-based scientist at a seminar on Problems and Prospects in Linking the Indian Rivers organized at Gauhati University on March 28, 2005, *The Sentinel*, Guwahati, March 29, 2005.

6. For further elaboration, See Report of The Task Force on Economic Development of Assam, Vol. 1, April 5, 1988, Para 3.5, p. 12.
7. Planning Commission, GoI, Economic Development of Assam: Report of the Committee on Clause Seven of Assam Accord, 1990, p. 2.
8. *India Today* (Special Issue), India's Best and Worst States, August 16, 2004. Also see, Ministry of Finance, Government of India, Report of the Eleventh Finance Commission (2000-05), June 2000, p. 218.
9. Worked out on the basis of data available in the *Human Development Report, Arunachal Pradesh*, 2003 (unpublished) prepared by Arunachal Uinversity, 2004.
10. More than a hundred groups are said to have been engaged in militant activities in the North East. Most of these are essentially ethnic in character. The genesis of insurgencies, however, cannot be traced to any single factor particularly because there are more than 100 militant groups operating in the region for different motivations under different objective conditions. For a useful discussion and many relevant references on around the issue, for detailed discussion, see H. Srikanth, Insurgency and Counter–Insurgency, Agenda for Peace in India's North East, in C.J. Thomas (ed.) (2005), *Polity and Economy-Agenda for Contemporary North East India*, Regency Publications, New Delhi, pp. 1-24.
11. Planning Commission, GoI (1997), *Assam Development Report* (Draft), p. 6.
12. North Eastern Development Finance Corporation Ltd.
13. Data relating to registered SSI sector have been taken from NEDFi *Databank Quarterly, Quarterly Journal on North Eastern States Economy* (SME Sector), Vol. 2, Issue III, June 2003.

12

Why Assam Fails to Take Off

The growth performance of the Assam economy was more or less comparable with all-India during 1951-79. Thereafter it lagged behind the rest of the country except for 1990-92. For example, Assam grew at the rate of 4.2 per cent and 3.0 per cent as against 5.4 per cent and 7.3 per cent for all-India between 1980-81 to 1990-91 and 1991-92 to 96-97 respectively. With high population growth, the gap in per capita income between Assam and the rest of the country widened sharply with every passing year. Assam's per capita income of Rs. 1,173 at 1980-81 prices stood above the national average by four per cent at the base year of economic planning in 1950-51. But it continuously fell behind the national average per capita income (GSDP) in the subsequent years: it constituted just 57.5 per cent of the national average per capita income (GDP) at 1993-04 prices in 2000-01 and further lower at 53.5 per cent in 2004-05.

This outcome followed from the fact that Assam's per capita income rose by 7.0 per cent as against 12.5 per cent for all-India between 1970-71 and 1980-81. The differential growth sharpened in subsequent decades particularly in the decade of economic reforms. Between 1995-96 and 2004-05 Assam's per capita grew at the rate of 1.68 per cent per annum as against the national average per capita income growth of 3.89 per cent. In short, Assam which was the fifth highest in per capita income terms at the beginning of the planning process has found itself among the three poorest states—Bihar, Orissa and Assam, in that order in 2003-04.

This happened despite the general awareness and interest in development on the part of different segments of Assam's population. As the Committee on Clause 7 of the Assam Accord

(1990) observed: "This magnitude of popular awareness and interest in development is a rare social force."[1] Great concerns for Assam's development can, in fact, be traced back to the late 1970s and early 1980s in various charters of demands by the Assam Students' Union (ASU) at different times. For example, the Assam Accord (signed on August 15, 1985) contained a Clause (7) for all round development of the state. And the Assam government formed by student leaders constituted a Task Force on Economic Development of Assam (May 20, 1987) to suggest measures for the economic development of the state.

The central government also on its part took a number of major initiatives particularly in the 1990s. Having recognized the slow progress of the measures for speedy all round development of the state under Clause 7 of the Assam Accord, the Planning Commission constituted a Committee (under the chairmanship of L.C. Jain, Member Planning Commission) in February 1990. Further in November 1996, the Planning Commission in pursuance of the Prime Minister's announcement of 'New Initiatives for the North Eastern Region' constituted a High Level Commission[2] to critically examine the backlog in basic services and gaps in important infrastructures and to suggest policies, programmes and the requirement of funds for their removal. The important point to flag here is that all different state and the Centre Level Committees/ Commission in addition to many academic studies clearly brought out the constraints on the development of the North East in general and Assam in particular.

As part of its new initiatives, the central government took several important steps in the 1990s. The state was included among the special category states that get plan assistance on the basis of 90 per cent grant and 10 per cent loan. The North Eastern Development Finance Corporation (NEDFi) with authorized share capital of Rs. 500 crores was set up in 1995. The economic package of Rs. 6,100 crores for specific projects in North Eastern states as announced in October 1996 by the then Prime Minister, H.D. Deve Gowda included fourth rail-cum-road bridge over the Brahmaputra at Bogibeel, upgradation of Guwahati airports and a few industrial growth centres in addition to some road projects, drinking water supply schemes and health care programmes. He also introduced North East sub plans in all central ministries for which 10 per cent of their budgets would be earmarked.

I.K. Gujaral who followed H.D. Deve Gowda as Prime Minister also assured the implementation of the package in toto. In January 2000, Prime Minister, Atal Bihari Vajpayee further announced a Rs. 10,271.66 crore package for the region.[3]

On top of it all, the central plan assistance to Assam is quite high. For example, the per capita assistance to Assam (Rs. 3,161) was almost three times the all-India average (Rs. 1,080) taking the entire Eighth Plan period. Similarly, industrial licensing, concessional finance and investment subsidy, tax holidays, growth centres and freight equalization of some major industrial inputs have been used as instruments to induce economic development in the region.

What Ails the Assam Economy?

All this leads to a very basic question: Why is it that with all the popular awareness and interest in social development as well as special concerns and dispensation of the central government in recent years Assam continues to decelerate?

The answer to this question will be clear in the course of making a case that Assam failed to stir growth on a sustained basis essentially for lack of an appropriate policy frame keeping in view its constraints and strengths.

The problems impeding the economic development of the state were always fairly well known. We have already discussed at great length[4] five types of constraints while addressing the question why the North Eastern states continue to decelerate in Chapter 1. Those binding constraints that hindered the pace of development in the region are more appropriately applicable to Assam. It is because the North Eastern states are economically interdependent while Assam serves as a gateway; with close to 70 per cent of NER population as also being the early starter on the path of modern development, Assam played a dominant role in the overall performance of the region. Similarly, the argument made in that chapter to the effect that the development of the region requires an appropriate development framework explicitly recognizing and addressing the binding constraints holds for the state in a greater measure.

To avoid repetition, this chapter has refrained from an elaborate discussion on the constraints as well as the required framework once again. We would only reiterate the five constraints, viz. 1. initial conditions such as (i) disruption of traditional trade and transport links following partition (ii) population influx (iii) colonial pattern of harnessing its natural resources leading to an enclave economy and (iv) monopolistic operation of deeply entrenched trading interests; 2. Infrastructure; 3. Insurgency; 4. Imperfection/distortion in factor and product markets; and 5. Indifferent governance—which continue to impede the economic development of the state as also of the region. We would elaborate more on those constraints as also a few other impediments which have special implications for Assam.

Population Influx

In view of its special implications on the polity and the economy of Assam, we may discuss further the problem of population influx particularly from across the border. It is because the inability to effectively deal with this problem by the student leaders when they came to power after a protracted movement against this issue only highlights the extent of complexity of the issue.

This problem should be clearly understood, and its realistic solution must be found. Without going into details of the migrant population from across borders, the following points can be flagged. First, the flow of illegal migrants, which continued much beyond the aftermath of partition, has presumably been induced by economic considerations. This means that most of these immigrants have moved out of their hearth and home in search of better means of living, which sparsely populated North Eastern states, might offer. Second, these immigrants who are uneducated and unskilled, sought to be absorbed in agriculture and related sectors. These sectors being of an informal nature, they were not very visible till the growing mass started having an impact on the polity of the states. The extreme example of their presence was felt in Tripura where the migrant population marginalized the local inhabitants in power sharing. Third, complete uprooting of the vast immigrant population is not feasible as the student leaders of Assam realized while in power for almost two terms of five years each.

Having noted the above points, one should seek a solution to the problem of population influx in the following perspective. The problem of immigrants should first be bifurcated between the existing stock and the future flow. The existing stock reckoning from the cut off date of 1971 should be given the status of economic migrants. This status would entitle them to earn their living but not to property acquisition and political rights.

In order to arrest the future flow, a strategy with a longer time perspective needs to be adopted. This strategy should clearly recognize that fencing the vast border is neither easy nor is foolproof vigilance practicable. Even developed countries found it difficult to stop illegal migrants. It should also recognize that there exists an element of schizophrenic attitude among local inhabitants: In private they prefer cheap and pliant immigrants as farm or household labour while in public they discard them. This makes the problem more complex.

Therefore, a longer term strategy should aim at altering the objective conditions. There should be a well-designed attractive scheme of settling landless local inhabitants along the borders. They would greatly reinforce the existing vigilant force. Such a scheme at the same time would provide a viable means of sustenance to the landless poor. The other part of the strategy should be to upgrade technology in farms and other sectors. Such technology upgradation would necessitate higher skill, which immigrants do not have. A simultaneous effort to impart the required skill at the local level would meet the new demand while at the same time minimizing the opportunities for unskilled immigrant labour. With the expansion of the modern organized sector, the scope for absorption of immigrant labour will be shrunk. More so, when the land providing job avenues for immigrants as was the case before, does not exist any more. Thus a strategy of introducing new technology simultaneous with generating the required skill at the local level would provide the longer term solution to the much vexed problem of population influx. The success of the Bangladeshi mass literacy and other development programmes with rising employment opportunities at home would dampen the need for crossing the border for livelihood.

Infrastructure Lags[5]

As indicated earlier, transport linkage with the rest of the country was the most serious handicap that the partition inflicted on Assam, the gateway to the other North East Indian states. It remained so even after a half a century of planning. Other basic physical, social and administrative infrastructures for unleashing growth dynamics are also highly deficient. Physical infrastructures such as power, communications, transport, irrigation, market access, etc., are grossly inadequate to generate a dynamic growth process. Inadequacy of all this is reflected in poor market incentives and thus in low productivity and growth in different sectors of the economy.

However, the CMIE infrastructure development index for Assam (with weights given to transport 26 per cent, energy 24 per cent, irrigation 20 per cent, banking 12 per cent, communication 6 per cent, education 6 per cent and health 6 per cent moved up 4 points above the all-India average of 100 in 2000 from 93 in 1992-93).[6] Greater attention of the central government to the problems of development of the North Eastern region in the recent past might have contributed to this improvement at least in Assam. No study, however, has been carried out to evaluate the actual implementation of various packages announced in the 1990s. Given the critical role of Assam in the development of North Eastern India, the creation of some of the crucial infrastructures has two important dimensions. First, because of interdependence of the economic systems of the North East, it is essential to develop a good network of inter-state transport and communication in addition to developing intra-state market and basic service accessibility. The remoteness and hilly terrain involves larger unit cost as well as maintenance cost. Again, for longer run connectivity and effective trade links, it is necessary to develop border road and water transport network in liaison with the neighbouring countries like Myanmar, South East Asia, Bangladesh and South China, which are very close to the region.

Second, the full utilization of the power potentials of the region or effective flood controls in Assam not only requires heavy lump sum investment but also mutual understanding and cooperation of the individual units of the North East.

As for social infrastructure, it should be noted that several of the major changes collapse of the socialist world in the 1990s and the emergence of a unipolar world order and globalization are all essentially technology-driven. The thrust on continuous skill upgradation, which will facilitate technology assimilation, absorption and innovation, would, therefore, be the best survival strategy for a developing country like India. This is all the more important for the North East region with its unique features and problems requiring appropriate technological solutions and with rich resources needing their economic utilization.

By now Assam has established many educational and skill-generating institutions. At one level, these institutions should be strengthened in terms of equipping them adequately with advanced training facilities and teaching aids. At another level, there should be networking with similar institutions of excellence located elsewhere. Administrative infrastructure will be taken up later with the issue of governance.

Floods

Floods have been another exogenous source of impediment to the development of Assam. Floods in the Brahmaputra and Barak valleys of Assam cause "serious erosion, loss of life and livestock and heavy damage to infrastructure and property retarding agriculural productivity on account of risk avoidance and sandcasting, disrupting communications and education and posing health hazards. Majuli island is threatened.......The floods damage to crops, cattle, houses and utilities in Assam alone between 1953 and 1995 is estimated at Rs. 4,400 crores with a peak of Rs. 664 crores in a single bad year."[7]

The assessed flood-prone area in the state is estimated at 3.15 m ha or 92.6 per cent of the cultivated land as in 1992-93 almost half of which (1.63 m ha) do not have any flood management structures. Even these limited flood management structures are poorly maintained. The master plan prepared by the Brahmaputra Board involves Rs. 1,848 crores at 1995 prices for short-term measures and Rs. 50,000 crores for long-term measures up to 2050. In the meantime the state governments continue with fire fighting operations and provide flood/natural calamity relief causing a heavy drain on their otherwise meagre resources.

Floods impeded the technological transformation of agriculture in Assam. Farmers are reluctant to make farm investment for the fear of its being washed away by impending floods while the rest of the country perceive this reluctance as the manifestation of their indolence. On the other hand, R&D efforts are not adequate to find a high yielding variety of crops that suit the agro-climatic conditions of the state.

Unharnessed Resource Endowments

It is widely recognized that Assam is a highly resource endowed state. Undoubtedly, the state is endowed with mines and minerals, water and forest resources, fertile soil, etc. In fact, crude oil production and its refining as well as tea plantation and plywood industry are the few resource-based modern industries in the state. But both oil and tea industries, which have existed for more than a century and a half, have not induced the industries that could have been developed on the basis of their backward and forward linkages. For example, tea plantation requires a wide variety of inputs such as fertilizers, chappals, umbrellas, small tools, etc. None of these backward linkage-based industries, though economically viable, were set up in the state. Instead, the industry depended on supplies from outside the state. This long dependence on trading has given rise to well-entrenched vested interests, which work against the emergence of local entrepreneurship.

Similarly, the oil industry had been hesitant for long to develop refineries, and petrochemical complex, which could have led to developing many downstream industries in the region. On the other hand, the surplus that accrued in these industries year after year was siphoned off to investment activities elsewhere.

This has led to an 'enclave economy' in which these few modern industries exist without having any linkage with the stagnant traditional activities. For reasons such as these, the resource-based extractive industries have come to be perceived as the symbol of exploitation.

There are several other types of resource potentials, which are still to be realized. Water resources and natural gas deserve special mention. Hydel power potential of the North East is estimated at 50,000 MW plus or more than one-third of the country's hydel potential. Natural gas-based industries are also feasible.

But harnessing water for irrigation and hydel power generation as also economic utilization of natural gas and other resources involves a large investment, which the state with its stagnant or decelerating economy and narrow revenue tax base cannot provide. The resources available for state plans in terms of plan assistance can hardly be earmarked for such projects, as this type of investment cannot be made on an incremental basis. Nor are these projects finding a place in the Central Plan till recently. As a result, water resources, which could have been the source of a vibrant economy, have remained largely as a source of uncertainty, human suffering and property loss.

Neglected Agriculture

Agriculture and allied activities (fishing, forestry and logging) have overriding importance as a source of livelihood to the people of Assam. It still contributes close to one-third (32.4 per cent on an average during 2000-01 to 2004-05) of its GSDP as against the all-India average of 22.1 per cent and engages 52.2 per cent (40.2 per cent as cultivators and 12.0 per cent as agricultural labourers) of the total workers in 2001. But the average operational holding size is small at 1.31 ha as compared to 1.57 ha for all-India. On top of it, 92.6 per cent of the cultivated land is flood-prone.

Given the overwhelming importance of agriculture in Assam, its development should have received a very high priority in the planning process. But at the end of fifty years of planning, the net irrigated area as percentage of the net sown area was only 20.6 per cent in 1995-96 and 21.16 even after more than five years. The asset creation in agriculture and allied activities stood at only one per cent of the total capital outlay of the Assam government in 1998-99.

Good road network, in general, and farm to market roads, in particular, as well as marketing infrastructure such as cold storage, which provide market access and remunerative price to farmers and thereby induce them to increase market surplus are grossly inadequate in the state. Only 20 per cent of the total roads in Assam are paved as against 44 per cent for all-India and nearly 100 per cent in Gujarat and Punjab. Even then, the state has used only Rs. 60 crores upto February 2000 out of Rs. 10,000 crores RDIF I-IV fund.

The credit flow to agriculture is also very meagre. As in

December 2000 Kisan cards to the entire North Eastern states was only 2590 and crop loan was Rs. 2.70 crores.

It is no wonder, therefore, that only 39.7 per cent of the cultivated land was brought under high yielding variety in 1994-95. The fertilizer consumption (NPK) per hectare was just 12.8 kg against 74.8 kg for all-India in 1995-96. Only 2.3 per cent of the total electricity consumption took place in the agriculture sector against 28.2 per cent for the rest of the country in 1991-92. In a state of affairs such as this, it can only be expected that the crop productivity in the state was very low. For example, the productivity (kg per hectare) of its main crop, rice was only 71.7 per cent of the all-India average in 1997-98. Similarly, wheat productivity was only 52.6 per cent of the all-India average.

All this clearly brings out the stark neglect of agriculture. Its consequences on an economy with 89 per cent rural population are overwhelming. This is reflected in a much higher level of the people below the poverty line (36.09 per cent against 26.10 per cent for all-India).

Minor Role of Manufacturing

The secondary sector in Assam contributed 11.9 per cent of its NSDP as against the all-India average of 27.7 per cent NDP in 1996-97. Within it, the manufacturing sector claimed only 5.4 per cent in Assam as against 21.8 per cent for the country as whole. But construction had a much larger share (6.2 per cent) in that than (4.6 per cent) for the rest of the country in 1996-97. It is noteworthy that in the 1990s the share of the secondary sector in the state's income was fluctuating around 10-12 per cent, the manufacturing steadily declined from 6.5 in 1990-91 to 5.4 per cent in 1997-98. The number of factories also declined to 1514 in 1994-95 from 1548 in 1990-91. The contribution of the registered sector to the income generation fell continuously from 4.8 per cent in 1990-91 to 3.6 per cent in 1997-98.

Even in regard to the unregistered manufacturing sector, its share in NSDP (1.6 per cent) was much lower than the all-India average level (8.2 per cent) in 1996-97. What is more, in contrast to the rising share of the unregistered sector of the country as a whole, its role in Assam tended to decline over 1990-91. The point is that the manufacturing sector, which is already small, further decelerated in the 1990s.

The industrial sectors mainly consist of tea manufacturing, petroleum industry, first stage processing industries such as grain mills, wood and wood products based on local resources and demand induced industry like repair services. The few modern industries such as non-metallic mineral products and gas and steam that have come up in the state are also resource-based. What is more, except for the growth of some miscellaneous type of industries, the factory level industrial base had not been significantly altered even in 1997-88.

Distorted Growth of the Tertiary Sector

While both agriculture and secondary sectors were losing their relative shares in the state income, the tertiary sector gained in importance over time. Its contribution to the state NSDP rose to 46.7 per cent as against 43.6 per cent for the rest of the country in 1996-97 from 44.4 per cent (39.3 per cent for all-India) in 1990-91. Its growth is distortionary. It is reflected in the fact that the components of the tertiary sector that relate to infrastructural services not only claimed a smaller share but also their role increased slowly. For example, transport, storage and communication rose to 3.2 per cent of NSDP in 1997-98 from 2.8 per cent in 1990-91 while public administration did so to 7.0 per cent from 4.9 per cent in the corresponding years.

To sum up, all this eventually means that the economy does not stir up and fail to meet the growing aspirations of the people, particularly the younger generation. This, in turn, provides a fertile ground for grooming various militant groups or a spurt of popular uprisings. In some sense, lack of growth and disturbed environment feed on each other. This is exactly what is happening in most of the North Eastern states.

Unaccountable Governance

While public administration gained in importance, the governance in the state was remarkably poor. Responsive and accountable governance has enormous consequences on the pace and quality of growth in an economy.

It can be hypothesized that consistent pursuit of clearly defined priorities over a long period percolates down to the economic agents, who start demanding the state machinery to address their problems faster and thus leads to a better delivery system. In the process both the political masters and correspondingly bureaucrats become accountable to the economic agents for better delivery, which eventually induces growth.

Lack of accountable and responsive governance has manifested itself in many different ways in Assam. We may indicate a few, just to illustrate the point.

i. Apart from its planning efforts being constrained by a narrow tax base, Assam's approach to development was perfunctory without a clear set of priorities in an well-articulated perspective. As a result, its development efforts remained diffused without resolving any of its major constraints or achieving success in the areas of its strength.
ii. A large gap in whatever plan programmes formulated and their implementation led to many incomplete projects in several sectors such as irrigation and power.
iii. While government expenditure increased leaps and bound with bulging central assistance, the development efforts and the delivery system weakened. As a result, the capital development expenditure fell with every passing year: it dipped to 1.5 per cent of its NSDP in 1997-98 from 3.0 per cent in 1980-81.
iv. What is worse, in the absence of adequate job opportunities elsewhere, the Assam government opened its coffers widely for creating more and more government employees: more than nine-tenth (90.9 per cent) of its tax and non-tax revenue inclusive of share in central taxes and non-plan grants went for maintaining government servants, past and present, i.e. wage and salary and pension bill in 1997-98.[8]
v. Finally, at one level, widespread cynicism of the bureaucracy has become both cause and effect of a nonchalant approach to development. At another, the widely perceived phenomenon of growing leakage in government-funded programmes (corruption) has greatly eroded the credibility of the government system.

Understanding the Assam Economy

A 64 X 64-sector input-output table with 16 primary sectors, 39 secondary sectors and 9 tertiary sectors constructed for 1982-83 brings out a few important features of the state economy.[9]

i. The inter-sectoral interdependence of the Assam economy is low, about 70 per cent of the cells being empty. Agriculture, petroleum and tea industry, in that order, are the three most dominant sectors in the Assam economy.
ii. The inter-sectoral production linkage is very weak, intermediate consumption being only 35 per cent of the gross value of output.
iii. Except for 17 commodities/sectors such as other cereals, sugarcane, jute, other crops, crude oil, tea, petroleum products, plywood, silk textiles, refractories, and non-metallic mineral products, Assam is heavily dependent on net imports for meeting its internal demand.
iv. The fixed capital formation (inclusive of change in stock) in the state is as low as 6.5 per cent of the gross value of output.
v. The prime exports mostly consist of primary resource-based products such as tea, plywood, crude oil and petroleum products.

One way of taking a view of the development of an economy could be in terms of its sectoral contributions towards generation of income, output, employment and creation of impulses in other sectors through intersectional linkages. This could be evaluated on the basis of sectoral linkages, output and income multipliers based on the input-output table.

An exercise[10] made taking the structure of the Assam economy for 1982-83 identified top five sectors on the basis of backward linkages as: non-ferrous metal products, leather and leather products, non-metallic mineral products, electrical equipment and tea machinery and on the basis of forward linkages as iron and steel, Trade, storage and warehousing, crude oil and natural gas, animal husbandry and petroleum refining.

The first five sectors on the basis of output multipliers came out to be: non-ferrous metal products, non-metallic mineral products, electrical equipment, tea machinery and printing and publishing. In aggregate, the secondary sector has the highest output multipliers followed by the tertiary sector and then by the primary sector. This suggests that the growth of the manufacturing sector drive the gross domestic product.

Similarly, the top five sectors on the basis of high income effect (both direct and indirect) are: grain mill products, edible oil, sugar, non-ferrous metal products and jute textiles. This suggests that agro-based industries in the secondary sector have higher impact on income growth. In aggregate, however, it is the primary sector that has the highest income effect followed by the tertiary sector and then the secondary sector.

The results presented above are undoubtedly based on an exercise that is dated. But the basic insights that it has provided are still relevant partly because the structure of the Assam economy has not drastically altered. It also provides important clues to the basic question that this chapter has addressed.

What Do All the Above Add Up To?

Essentially, exogenous constraints as well as faulty planning priorities or lack of any, impeded the growth process in Assam. Snapping of traditional trade and transport links, population influx and geographical and economic isolation, all in the aftermath of partition acted as major binding constraints on Assam's development. The announcement but indifferent implementation of several packages by four successive Prime Ministers—basically recycled the components from one package into another—since the mid-80s has not done much yet to neutralize to any significant extent, the handicaps that the partition inflicted on the state economy.[11] The Shukla Commission recommendations on backlogs in infrastructure found only a peripheral place in the package announced subsequently.

Floods that the mighty Brahmaputra and its tributaries cause year after year still act as a severe deterrent to the technological transformation of Assam's agriculture that support more than two-thirds of its population. Effective flood controls or management involve a large investment that is far beyond the means of the state government.

Harnessing its enormous hydel power or oil and natural gas

similarly necessitates a large sum of investment. Non-availability of investible resources of that order led to a huge delay or non-realization of its potentials.

In all fairness, it should also be recognized that the state government's compulsion to deal with various protracted movements by its different parts for autonomous units/states was a distraction away from economic development in the first quarter century since independence (till 1972) when Meghalaya was carved out of Assam. Even later, the movement for Bodo land and insurgency continued to demand engagement of resources and attention.

Apart from these exogenous handicaps, the state government failed to formulate a set of priorities in the context of its objective realities. Its planning efforts were faulty and diffused in several ways. For example, given its importance in the state economy, the investment on irrigation, flood control, rural roads, marketing infrastructure, etc should have received a major thrust in its investment plan consistently over a long period. Given the potential as also market demand, other allied activities such as horticulture, fisheries and forestry deserved a far larger investment priority.

Faulty strategy was also reflected in the wrong type of capital investment, declining capital investment, inadequate and low quality infrastructure such as power, roads and other rural infrastructures. On the other hand, the state government failed to create a favourable environment for private investment to supplement its efforts.

It is true, however, that low fiscal capacity has always been a great handicap to make best use of even available central assistance. For example, the Assam government lost Rs. 650 crore central fund meant for rural development during the last four years for failing to pay the 'matching share of 25 per cent of the total allocation'.[12]

To sum up, Assam's economic development can be viewed in a more general framework. Many factors facilitate or inhibit economic development of a state. These factors can be classified into two sub-sets: One relates to supply side while the other to demand side. Resource endowment, infrastructure support, evolution of the right type of institutions, access to market, availability of human capital in the form of entrepreneurship and skilled labour, credit availability, etc are all important determinants affecting supply side. The income level and its distribution are amongst the important factors operating on the demand side. Both sets of factors need not really be binding for the development of a state, which is a highly open economy.

However, the working of the national economy over the past 50 years favoured some and differentiated against several other state economies. In the process of evolution of the national economy, product and money/credit market got integrated faster with the national market while labour market integration was hindered by several rigidities emerging especially from labour surplus situations.

When supply side factors are not equally conducive to all states, integrated product and credit market unaccompanied by similarly integrated labour market has led to a larger inflow of goods into and outflow of savings from a state-kind of reverse flow of resources from the less developed to the more developed state economies. More important, such asymmetry results in an adverse effect on local industries by way of introducing competition from technologically superior counterparts. This process is eminently discernible in the context of the entire North Eastern states.

It is in this general framework that the slow growth or the deceleration process in Assam has to be understood. As detailed earlier, the state is hugely deficient in administrative, social and economic infrastructure, as also human capital, all supply side factors. This coupled with the poor and uncertain law and order situation does not make Assam a favoured destination for private investment even with tax holidays or freight subsidy as has been extended. On the contrary, there are reports of flight of capital from the state to Siliguri.

Even the few modern industries that exist in the state operate in an enclave type of economy with minimal or no linkage at all with its traditional industries. What is worse, the investible surplus generated in these industries is not ploughed back in themselves or in those industries that are viable on the strength of their backward and forward linkages.

On the demand side, rising income, even if at a slow pace and in favour of a smaller segment of population has induced demand effect that is not supported by the state's production base or lacks any linkage with it. The Jain Committee (1990) estimated an annual outflow of the state at Rs. 700 crores in terms of the procurement of foodgrains, fish, edible oils and other food items alone to other states.[13]

Thus neither demand nor supply side factors are favourable for higher growth in the state. On the other hand, the state interventions in the planning process failed to make much difference to the situation for the reasons discussed earlier.

Reflecting on How to Go Ahead

The development strategy for Assam has to be based on the explicit recognition of the following:

(i) First and foremost, development initiatives have to be in many directions all at the same time within a clearly articulated framework. These have to be of such vast coverage though not necessarily in cost terms that people in general and the younger generation in particular perceives an economic stir all around and promises for them. It is important in a state that has witnessed massive unemployment among the educated youths: they constitute 70 per cent of the total unemployed (10 per cent of its population).

(ii) The development strategy should accept some of the existing constraints as given in the short to medium term and aim at maximizing the gains within them. The IT revolution if properly taken advantage of, could more than neutralize some of the existing disadvantages. It could also contribute towards more responsive and accountable governance as also facilitating upgradation of skill and technology through networking with national/international R&D institutions. Its potential in fact is immense.

(iii) The seven states that comprise the region are essentially interdependent sub systems both in terms of historical background and geographical location. This calls for an integrated approach to development for the entire region. The North Eastern Council if restructured appropriately and NEDFi can play an important part in this regard.

(iv) The unique features of most of these economies make it difficult to adopt a development strategy entirely based on the experiences of the rest of the country. It is, therefore, important to evolve an appropriate development strategy taking into account some of the state's strengths particularly in terms of social capital: the tradition of self-governance, liberal social outlook, greater women's participation in economic activities and popular awareness and interest in economic development, on the one hand and learning from the small successes (tea growers' association, for example) on the other.

(v) Concerted efforts are required to equip adequately the existing educational and technical institutions and build new institutions for generating marketable skills, on the one hand and to build the capability to adopt and absorb new technologies on the other. Equally important is to evolve the existing economic institutions and agents to make them technology friendly.

(vi) Transfer of all functions and revenue sources with local base to the panchayats will go a long way in improving the delivery system and enlisting local participation.

(vii) Hydel power potentials, if realized even partially, could be a source of attraction for power intensive but cleaner industries or at least a source of revenue from power export.

(viii) This region has all the important attractions such as hill resorts, pollution free environment, water, natural game sanctuary, etc which, together provide an excellent potential for an important tourist belt. Tourism, if developed linking East Asian countries will contribute to income and employment generation directly in tourism-related sectors and indirectly in the well developed labour-intensive handloom and handicrafts. NEDFi can take the initiative of preparing a master plan for tourism development in the North East.

(ix) The present mercantile capital should be encouraged to invest on linkage-based industries and on those whose products have markets in the neighbouring countries such as Bangladesh, Bhutan and South East Asian countries.

(x) Having lagged behind in terms of the level and quality of administrative, social and economic infrastructures, Assam and other North Eastern states will not attract much private investment flows immediately. In the immediate future, therefore, the public sector has to play a much greater role particularly in the infrastructure sector.

(xi) At the sectoral level, thrust on agriculture, fisheries, animal husbandry, horticulture, bio-diversity, and forestry including farm forestry in the primary sector will be appropriate both on the considerations of excess demand and supply potentials. In the secondary sector, the thrust should be generally on environment-friendly industries. Industries based on forward and backward linkage of tea and petrochemical industry and processing industry of horticultural products have very good chances to succeed. In the tertiary sector, tourism-related activities, road and marketing infrastructure, communication and skill generation and upgradation in general and for IT in particular and R&D, to indicate a few, should be high on the agenda.

(xii) Finally, the need for hydel and coal and gas-based power generation, flood control and irrigation, strengthening road and communication connectivity between the North Eastern states and with the rest of the country and promotion of border trade can hardly be overemphasized.

Overall, all the above should be weaved around in a development framework emanating from the new development paradigm according to which the North East economy should get integrated with the dynamic South East Asian economies.

NOTES

1. Planning Commission, GoI (April 1990), Report of the Committee of Clause Seven of Assam, p. 1.
2. The Commission in its report made the following major recommendations for Assam:
   - Full funding of Bogibeel bridge over the river Brahmaputra.
   - Construction of Pagladia dam (flood control).
   - Railway gauge conversion; New Bangaigaon-Siliguri (280 kms).
   - Two stretches of road–Doboka-Lanka-Halflong-Silchar (290)kms and north-Guwahati-north Salmara 9120 kms)- To be declared as National Highways and upgraded suitably.
   - Guwahati airport to be made an international airport as well as a

regional hub.

- Priority to irrigation development.
- Priority to inland water transport for transit/transhipment facilities with Bangladesh.

3. The breakdown of the funding patterns: Central Plan including funds from financial institutions/multi-lateral funding agencies: Rs. 7,663.42; Central non-plan: Rs. 1,800 crores; North Eastern Council: Rs. 258.24 crores and Banks (NABARDS?NEDFI: 550.00 crores).

   Proposal included were:

• Provision for Rural Infrastructure Development Fund	Rs. 550 crores (NABARD)
• NEDFi's disbursement	Rs. 50 crores
• Setting up Export Development Fund	Rs. 5 crores (Central Fund)
• Development of four border townships	Rs. 20 crores (Central Plan)
• Upgradation of NEIGRIHMS	Rs. 422.60 crores (Central Plan)
• Setting up of Mizoram University	Rs. 25 crores (Central Plan)
• Doubling of it is	Rs. 101.39 crores (Central Plan)
• Modernization of police force	Rs. 40 crores (Central Plan)
• Sanction of three Reserve Battalion	Rs. 40 crores
• Peace Bonus	Rs. 230 crores (Central non-Plan/Plan)
• Fencing of Indo-Bangladesh border	Rs. 1,335 crores (Central non-Plan)
• Yearly allocation from central non-lapsable pool	Rs. 500 crores (Central Plan)
• Loktak downstream project	Rs. 578 crores (Central Plan+FIs)
• Teesta hydro-electric power project	Rs. 2,198.04 crores (Central Plan+FIs)
• Subansiri lower project	Rs. 3,000 crores (Central Plan)
• Rural electrification	Rs. 30 crores (Central Plan)
• Add assistance for critical/subcritical transmission system	Rs. 239.92 crores
• Eight road/bridge project	Rs. 258.24 crores (NEC)

- Development of 12 new national highways Rs. 100 crores (Central Plan)
- Computer Information Centres (447 blocks) Rs. 220 crores (Central Plan)
- Excise concessiion to Numaligarh Refinery Rs. 200 crores (Central non-Plan)
- Technolgy Mission for Horticulture Rs. 262.50 crores (Central Plan)
- Development of Bodo Autonomous Council Rs. 90 crores (Central Plan)

4. Planning Commission, GOI, (1997), High Level Commission, Transforming the North East—Tackling Backlogs in Basic Minimum Services and Infrastctural Needs, p. 1.
5. The Shukla Committee has estimated an indicative requirement of investment for development of various infrastructural requirement for the North East as a whole–power, roads, railways, irrigation, flood control (short-term measures only), inland water transport and miscellaneous at Rs. 93,619 crores in addition to Rs. 17,995 crores for the Ninth Plan.
6. Weights given by the CMIE for 1992-93 infrastructure indices are different from those for its 2000 indices. They are: power 20 per cent, irrigation 20 per cent, roads, 15 per cent, railways 20 per cent, post offices 5 per cent, education 10 per cent, health 4 per cent and banking 6 per cent.
7. Shukla Commission, op. cit., p. 33.
8. Computed on the basis of estimates available in NIPFP (1998), State Fiscal Studies: Assam, p. 40.
9. Department of Economics, Gauhati Universiity and Indian Statstical Institute, Delhi Centre (1987-88), The Structure of the Assam Economy (1982-83) and A Perspective Plan of Assam upto 2000 AD.
10. For greater details, see Department of Economics, Gauhati University and India Statistical Institute, Delhi Centre, op. cit., Chapter 4.
11. No evaluative study of the extent and the pace of implementation is available. However, various newspaper reports suggest that the progress is very slow.
12. *The Assam Tribune*, Guwahati, June 14, 2001.
13. Report of the Committee on Clause Seven of Assam Accord, op. cit., p. 2.

13

Socio-Economic Development of Majuli: A Preliminary Study

Background

Majuli situated in the upper reaches of the river Brahmaputra in the Assam valley is the biggest river island in the world. The island was formed with change in the course of the river Brahmaputra and its tributaries in 1671. Dr. John Peter Wade (1792-93) in his book, *An Account of Assam* observed: "Majuli then was constituted with 13 (thirteen) chapories or small islands intersected by channels of communication by boat between the Dihing and Lohit, which in reality, it converges into a cluster of islands and in addition to these, numerous smaller islands are found along the whole streams. Some of these always overflowed in the season of inundation, others occasionally only; all possess a stratum of rich soil above a deeper layer of sand or soft clay" (pp. 369-372 cited in the Report on Majuli Island by Office of the Additional Chief Engineer, Upper Zone, FC Department).

The island has occupied a very special place in the history and culture of the Assamese people ever since Sankardev established Majuli as a seat of Vaishnavite religion in the last decade of the 15th century.

As noted earlier, the landmass is known to exist since 1671 Over the years, its size contracted from 1200 sq kms in 1853 (Mr. A.J. Mefat Mills of the British East India Company) to just 880 sq kms in 1993 (Brahmaputra Board as cited by E.F. Muller, May 1996) through erosion. An area of 40 sq kms is estimated to have been eroded between 1974 and 1993.

The fast diminution in landmass through erosion and frequent floods has threatened the very existence of Majuli, the largest river island and the seat of Assamese/Vaishnavite culture. The Majuli Protection and Development Council formed recently has urged upon authorities at different levels for its protection. At another level, it has initiated a study on the development of Majuli under the sponsorship of the Planning Commission. As is well known, the data required for studying the development of an administrative unit at the level of subdivision are scanty. Nevertheless, this study addresses itself to study:

- The demographic features of the subdivision.
- The social and economic profile.
- The level and pattern of economic development.
- The development potentials.
- The constraints that hinder the full utilization of its development potentials. and finally, indicates
- The areas that call for policy interventions in addition to suggesting the types of information that are required to make a more complete policy-oriented study.

Data

The socio-economic data at the level of sub-division are not available in published form. Population census does collect and compile demographic and some other data even at the village level. But the report in respect of Majuli against the 2001 census is still to be published officially due to some reason best known to the authorities. However, critical analysis of the available data with specific recommendations for the purpose of this study, a schedule was prepared to collect data on a few variables through the courtesy of the office of the SDO (Civil), Majuli. The study based on very limited data would inevitably be somewhat sketchy. Nevertheless, it attempts to provide a broad outline of the potential parameters that call for detailed examination, carrying out specific field surveys.

Demographic Profile

Majuli is one sub-division under Jorhat district of Assam. For administrative purposes, the sub-division has been divided into three Mouzas/Revenue blocks.

The population of Majuli rose from 35,000 in 1901 to 1.35 lakhs in 1991 and to 1.53 lakhs in 2001. It recorded a growth of 1.8 per cent per annum during 1971 to 1991 and 2.4 per cent per annum during 1991-2002. There are 923 females per 1000 male population in Majuli in 1991 and 926 in 2001. It was a significant improvement over 858 in 1971. Female to male-ratio, though improved to 926 females for 1000 males in 2001 from the corresponding ratio of 858 in 1971 falls far short of the desirable ratio. One of the observed reasons is the outflow of male population in search of employment and shelter.

Majuli is predominantly a tribal subdivision, which has been declared as the ST reserved Legislative Constituency of Assam. Scheduled Tribe population constituted 42.2 per cent of the its population in 1991. Scheduled Caste population comprised another 14.0% of the Majuli inhabitants in the same year. In other words, SC and ST population together accounted for more than half (56.2%) of Majuli's total inhabitants.

Social Development

There was one primary and middle school for every 112 children in the age group of 0-14 in 1991. The teacher-pupils ratio was 1:33.4 at the primary school level and 1:21.7 at high school level. Even with a favourable teacher-pupil ratio, the rate of literacy in Majuli was 49.3 per cent, which falls below the state's average.

Four dispensaries, 34 sub centres and three primary hospitals catered to the health needs of 135,000 people of Majuli in 1991. One doctor, on an average, takes care of the health of 5641 people in the same year. For every thousand population there are less than three hospital beds. As against these health infrastructures, the infant mortality stood at 69 per 10,000 persons and maternity mortality at 50 per 10,000.

Economic Profile

The participation rate of the labour force was 55 per cent for males and 35% for females in 1991. The occupation pattern of the workforce is shown in the following table.

Table– Occupation Pattern as Per Census of 1991 (%)

Farmers	64.0
Agricultural labour	1.6
Non-Agri. Labour	6.0

Traders	8.3
Government employees	6.3
Self-employed	1.3
Unemployed	12.5

The occupation pattern clearly shows that Majuli is predominantly an agrarian economy. 64.1 per cent of its work force had cultivation as the main occupation and 1.6 per cent were agricultural labourers in 1991. The occupation that came next in importance was traders, though with a far lower share at 8.3 per cent. It was followed by government employees at 6.3 per cent and non-agricultural labourers at 6.0 per cent.

Agriculture and Allied Activities

Given the importance of agriculture for the means of livelihood of the people of Majuli, it will be useful to discuss the characteristics of the sector. As was mentioned earlier, frequent floods and erosion are the annual features of Majuli. During one single year, for example, floods occurred six times for the duration ranging from 2 to 10 days between June and September 2000-01.

Of the total cultivable land of 27,824 hectares, only 322 hectares were irrigated in 1997 leaving 98.8 per cent of Majuli's cultivable land unirrigated. There was a large patch of 4838 hectares, which remained as wasteland.

While oil seeds, lentils, sugarcane, wheat and jute are grown, paddy, rabi and kharif remains the most predominant crop. Even this mono crop is grown using the traditional method of cultivation. Farmers are wary of adopting more costly modern methods of cultivation mainly because of high risk and uncertainties arising from frequent floods and erosion. The following facts clearly bring this out. Only 1,756 hectares of land were subject to double cropping The area under high yielding variety (HYV) 390 hectares in kharif and 1,200 hectares in rabi in 1997-98. Similarly, the use of fertilizer was limited to only 110 quintals during kharif and 610 quintals during rabi in the same year. Only a very insignificant portion of 129 hectares in kharif and 410 hectares during rabi were ploughed with the help of tractors. Even so, Majuli produces a considerable amount of marketable surplus of rice and mustard (1,208 tons).

The prospects, constraints and the thrust areas of the agricultural sector is analysed as follows:

The cropping pattern in the island: Unlike in other areas of Assam, rabi crop and only *Ahu* paddy are more important than the normal kharif crop as can be seen from land utilisation.

Area under rabi crops like pulses, peas, oilseeds and others = 11,975 hectares

Early ahu paddy = 3,915 hectares

Area under kharif: Sali paddy = 11,500 hectares

This variation from the state's pattern is mainly because *Sali* paddy is subject to huge uncertainties in terms of regular floods, water logging, pest infection etc. in Majuli. Greater reliance on rabi crops result in higher production of oil seeds and pulses. . High yielding variety of seeds of such rabi crops would raise productivity and much larger marketable surplus.

One very important feature of cultivation in Majuli is that crops are raised using solely organic manure. It is because organic alluvial deposition to the extent of 4"-6" thick layer makes the cultivable land highly fertile and renders any use of fertilizer unnecessary. This type of soil also requires less labour in ploughing–sometimes even zero tillage–and yet yields bumper crop. This means that no chemical fertilizer and pest control chemicals are used for cultivation and thus the area is free from the chemical hazards, degradation of the soil, environment pollution, health hazards, etc. that are associated with cultivation in most parts of the world.

Constraints on Agricultural Development

To sum up, the agricultural development of Majuli is hindered by several factors. Frequent floods, silt and sand deposition, water stagnation after floods, heavy pest/disease infestation in post flood situation, inadequate and untimely supply of seeds, lack of irrigation facilities, poverty of farmers and inability and unwillingness of farmers to adopt new technology and lack of credit facilities are major ones.

In the face of such constraints farmers take to rabi crops and even produce considerable marketable surplus of crops such as oil seeds and pulses. But farmers do not get incentive prices for lack of access to the market in the absence of transport facilities, suitable storage facilities or oil extraction/processing units. Thus non-availability of marketing and storage facilities stands as high risk factors for farmers in receiving incentive prices that could induce them to produce larger marketable surplus.

Adequate transport by way of activating the motor boat system linking the urban centres/towns like Jorhat on the other side of the Brahmaputra would open up market outlets for the surplus farm products of Majuli. Such market access would make several agro-processing units in Majuli viable. Once production and market are linked up, farmers will receive incentive prices. Then imparting training of farmers towards better farm practices and newer technology would further strengthen the economic base of the agriculturally predominant Majuli.

Allied Activities

Forests: Majuli does not have any significant forest cover. However, social forestry has covered an area of 240 hectares. According to the source, only an area of 50 hectares could be brought under forests. Forest cover of suitable species could withstand the frequent flood ravages and thus could yield some ecological and economic benefits. Moreover, cultivation of high yielding variety of bamboo on the banks of the river Brahmaputra, will be resourceful for the steady growth in both ways; economic and afforestation to prevent erosion.

Mines and Mineral Resources: Majuli does not have any mineral resources and mines. However, it has recently been reported that Oil India Limited has discovered two wells in the island. However, recurring devastation of road connectivity, oil could not set up drilling till 2002. If it were so, this would bring up new sources of income and employment.

Horticulture: Horticulture is another agriculture-allied activity that contribute to incomes generation, to an extent, in Majuli. We will examine one by one the strength and potential of these activities.

Majuli grows a wide variety of vegetables and fruits. Vegetables were grown on 615 hectares of land in 1999-2000. Onion and garlic are most widely grown covering 457 hectares accounting for three –quarter of the total area under vegetables.

Other horticultural crops were grown on 921 hectares of land in 1999-2000. Some examples of types of such crops are banana pineapple, arcanut, black pepper, Assam lemon, turmeric and ginger. While data are not available, one can surmise that most of these horticultural crops do not go beyond home consumption and the local market. The important point to flag is that with proper market access, several of these horticultural crops could be a good source of income in Majuli. Marketing facility accompanied by credit availability can be expected to induce the growers to produce these horticultural crops on a commercial basis.

But the most promising factor in the Majuli Island is the abundance of medicinal herbs and shrubs, which have been bestowed by nature, and are still to be explored. Some of the medicinal herbs have very high market potentiality. Commercial harvesting of these herbs will open up opportunities for both income and employment generation in the island. The table indicating the range of medicinal herbs and shrubs and their uses is available with the author.

Livestock: Animal husbandry can provide an important potential source of income for the inhabitants of Majuli. Farmers rear cattle, buffaloes, goats and pigs. In fact the cattle density is very high in Majuli. It is roughly worked out at four per household. But crossbreeds are very few (only 143 in number) despite the fact of having five insemination centres. But, it is noteworthy to mention that due to abundant availability of grassland and open fields, one can get the purest and very high quality of milk at Majuli, which may leave a record mark in the scale. Pigs are next in importance. Pig density is worked out at more than one per household. What is worth noting is that more than one-third of the pig population seems to be cross breeds. Goats and buffaloes, in that order, are other types of animals that farmers of Majuli rear. These facts suggest that with proper marketing facilities, animal husbandry could be promoted as a viable source of income generation with no investment for animal feed.

People of Majuli do poultry farming, to an extent. Birds that are popular are fowls and ducks, in order of importance. But only an insignificant portion of these birds is of the high breed type. As a result, the productivity is very low. Fowls and ducks respectively lay, on an average, 37 and 24 eggs a year.

Piggery: There is a very good prospect for piggery. The tribal inhabitants of Majuli have piggery as an economic activity. Nearly 34,030 families have taken up pig farming. But trading is confined to the local market only.

But pig farming as adopted in Majuli lacks a scientific approach. There is no marketing facility nor does Majuli have any processing facility. As a result, piggery has not yet become an economically profitable activity.

Efforts towards creating marketing facilities followed by a scientific approach of farming and establishing processing units will help generating income and employment of the tribal people who are already familiar with pig farming.

Pisciculture: Pisciculture is another main source of livelihood for the Majulians. There are a large number of wetlands (*bils*) as can be seen from the list below.

The list of some important wetlands (*Bils*) of Majuli:

Borchali Bil	Dighali Bil	Nadua Bil
Bidha Kata Bil	Komon Bil	Garukhuti Bil
Kakarikata Bil	Bhereki Bil	Sakali Bil
Phutuka Bil	Solmara Bil	Jor Bil
Tekelia Bil	Kachariboka Bil	Nai-Da Bil
Gogalar Doba Bil	Borbila Bil	Magur mara Bil
Param Bil	Nalani Bil	Chapori Gaon Bil
Deuri Bil	Bokajan Bil	Bhakati Bil
Manihari Bil	Phulani Bil	Naldoba Bil
Khetai Maharani Bil	Barbill Bil	Tarua Bil
Geleki Bil	Chengeli Mari Bil	

Pisciculture can give a boost to the socio-economic scenario of the island with the introduction of appropriate technology and support to the farmers for better marketing opportunities. Proximity to the river Brahmaputra and many water bodies in and around, Majuli should naturally be a big fish-producing centre. Due to the lack of market access and other supporting infrastructure, it has not emerged so. There are only two government and 62 private fisheries in the sub-division. Its fish production was estimated at 5,269.8 tonnes in 1997-98. It works out to 389.3 kgs per head. The per capita production of this size is too high to be consumed within the sub-division. This suggests that a part of production finds market outlets in Jorhat and other nearby towns across the river Brahmaputra. Local producers are yet to get a remunerative price owing to lack of proper linkup and marketing facilities. Transport costs being high, small producers are unable to take their produce to distant markets. In that case, middlemen would reap more than the normal margin, fish being highly perishable.

Fishery has a very good potential in Majuli for the following favourable factors:

1. Abundance of all types of fish.
2. Availability of natural fisheries.
3. Directly or indirectly, it is the major livelihood for the people of Majuli.
4. Trading of both raw fish, and salting fish.

But as indicated above, lack of quick transportation facilities, exploitation by middlemen thus depriving the producers of the right price and lack of quality processing and upgradation of the skill for the salted fish have hindered the emergence of pisciculture as an effective means of livelihood to at least those who are associated with this activity.

To make pisciculture a viable economic activity at Majuli efforts should be directed towards the following:

1. Establishment of a systematic marketing chain.
2. Creation of cold storage facility.
3. Introduction of quick transportation facility.
4. Establishment of direct link with consumers.
5. Adoption of cooperative method for both, production and marketing.

Secondary Sector

Activities in the secondary sector are mostly at the household and cottage level. According to the information available for 1997, Majuli had 11 SSI units, one agro processing unit and 13 miscellaneous household enterprises. At the household and cottage level, sericulture, handloom, handicrafts such as cane and bamboo crafts, jute, woodcrafts, boat making and potteries are largely secondary activities that provide income and employment. There are 15 cane and bamboo units, 16 jute units, 130 woodcraft units,

29 potteries, 45 mat and 13 'pati' making craft units. Majuli has 13,520 private owned handlooms and 228 handlooms in the cooperative sector. However, special emphasis has to be given to the handicraft and handloom sector of Majuli as it plays a vital role in the socio-economic scenario of the island.

The Vaishnavite culture (Satra Culture) and the way of life at Majuli have given birth to some of the rare phenomenal handicrafts such as mask making which is unique from its type, in other parts of the country. Devastating floods have taught the people of Majuli to coexist with the natural calamities and developed the skill of boat making.

Emphasis on the handicraft sector of Majuli in the most organized way will certainly enhance the economic condition of the people.

Drawbacks: The raw materials for the predominant handicrafts of Majuli are abundantly available. But the raw materials are not properly used. Appropriate training and upgrading skills, marketing inclusive of product design according to consumers' preference and market linkage can give a boost to the handicrafts in Majuli. If tourism is developed several crafts can become economically viable activites.

Handloom: In Majuli women and even young girls are at least familiar with the traditional method of weaving clothes. Tribal flok weave a unique tribal design in their clothes. But lack of financial support for inputs, market linkage, upgradation of weaving technology and the required skill stand as obstacles to the emergence of handloom as a effective means of livelihood in Majuli.

Tertiary Sector

The tertiary sector comprises 1,729 shops and establishments, 58 repair units in addition to 7 banks, some transport, government establishments and educational institutions. Given the location of Majuli, water transport provides the only link with the rest of the state. Around the island, there are 14 'ghats' from where 16 private owned boats and four government owned ferries operate for carrying men and materials to and from Majuli.

Seven bank branches provide financial services in the sub-division. They collected public deposits to the tune of Rs. 1,214.3 lakhs and disbursed Rs. 519.3 lakhs as loan advances in 1997.

Levels of Living

The per capita household consumption expenditure is worked out at Rs. 1,583.2 for 1997, which is considerably low compared with the state's average. So is the cereal consumption expenditure per head at Rs. 164.7.

Safe drinking water is available in 181 villages but there is none of this bare minimum facility in more than one-quarter of the villages (25.7 per cent).

One telephone is available for 681 persons or there are 199 telephones for 244 villages of Majuli.

Concluding Remarks

Sustainable development is defined as a pattern of social and structural economic transformations (i.e. development), which optimizes the economic and societal benefits available in the present, without jeopardizing the likely potential for similar benefits in the future. A primary goal of sustainable development is to achieve a reasonable and equitably distributed level of economic well-being that can be perpetuated continually for many human generations. Sustainable development implies using renewable natural resources in a manner, which does not eliminate or degrade them, or otherwise diminish their usefulness for future generations. It further implies using non-renewable (exhaustible) mineral resources in a manner, which does not unnecessarily preclude easy access to them by future generations. Sustainable development also requires depleting non-renewable energy resources at a slow enough rate so as to ensure the high probability of an orderly society transition to renewable energy sources.

Our democratic governance, comprising cooperative federalism, commitment to decentralization, an independent judiciary, a vigilant media, and an engaged civil society, provide the enabling framework to attain the objectives of sustainable development. Yet the dynamics of having a population of one billion people being sustained on a comparatively low natural resource base poses an enormous challenge. Sustained efforts in addressing this challenge have shaped our strategy that is specific to our social and economic context but is, at the same time, consistent with global concerns and initiatives. This study outlines the broad contours of our strategy.

The above discussion has brought out, to the extent the data collected permitted, a sketch of the economy of Majuli, the world's largest island and Assam's great Vaishnavite heritage. Despite its incomplete picture, the study has served two important purposes. First, it could identify the potentials for economic development that the present pattern of economic activities indicated and the probable constraints that impeded their full realization. Second, it could identify the data requirement for a more complete analysis that could be useful for development policies. The important limitation is that the consistency and validity of the data used in the study could not be ascertained. Perhaps a follow-up study could aim at that.

The most persistent problem that Majuli, has been confronting originates in erosion and frequent floods. This has acted as a threat to the life and property of its inhabitants. This has also hindered economic development by way of imparting risk and uncertainty that eventually retard motivation to invest. Unless the problem of erosion and floods are properly tackled, the economic development of Majuli can be addressed only partially.

The very location of Majuli puts it at a great disadvantage in terms of geographical isolation and connectivity with the rest of the state. Its economic implications manifest themselves in terms of inadequate transport facilities and following this-high transport cost and poor market access for its marketable surplus.

The assessment of the Majuli economy has clearly established that agriculture and allied activities provide the means of livelihood for this tribal sub-division. Because of high risk and lack of market access, farmers are not geared to producing much marketable surplus. However, diversified crops including some cash crops that farmers grow are highly promising. With proper infrastructure such as irrigation and credit facilities accompanied by a conducive environment for incentive prices, farmers can be induced to raise productivity of their farms. For lack of data on land distribution, it cannot be said whether that would automatically raise the income level for all associated with agriculture.

From the pattern of livestock activities currently prevailing it appears that several livestock related activities such as dairy and piggery could be economically viable. Market outlets ensuring incentive prices and adoption of modern technology would be necessary conditions for their commercial success.

Fishery appears to have all the potentials for being a highly profitable activity. But for that, there must be appropriate marketing infrastructure including cold storage.

Handlooms and sericulture could also emerge as commercially successful activities. For that to happen there has to be technology shift and production has to be oriented to consumer preference.

This can be said even in the case of cane and bamboo crafts, potteries and other handcraft products, too. Improvement in technology, consumer preference driven products would ensure higher productivity and better marketability.

On the whole, both social and economic infrastructures are absolutely inadequate. Transportation facilities in addition to frequent flood are serious handicaps. The former has added to transport cost of the marketable surplus of various products while the latter hinders long-term investment. The transport problem could be addressed by developing cheaper water transport and by providing for warehouse and cold storage. Lack of proper marketing infrastructure is another stumbling block to Majuli's economic development. It stands in the way of inducing producers to maximize their marketable surplus. There seems to be a large potential for enlarging it in regard to different agricultural products, fish, milk, handloom and handicraft products.

One strategy could be to promote tourism packaging imaginatively. Majuli's clean air and cultural heritage together with water sports are attractions. If it could be developed, it would boost demand for local products, which in turn would spur farmers and other small producers to maximize their output. It would, however, be necessary for craftsmen and weavers to produce according to consumers' preferences.

The suggestions made above are of a tentative nature for the simple reason that the analysis is incomplete as indeed the case in the present study since the available data do not enable one to have firm basis for drawing conclusions. A proper follow-up study based on a well-designed survey would go a long way for working out a good strategy for Majuli's development.

Annexure I: Data of Majuli

Source: www.jorhat.nic.in

Item	*Ref. Year*	*Unit*	*Jorhat sub-divison*	*Majuli sub-division*	*Jorhat district*
1	*2*	*3*	*4*	*5*	*6*
Area and Administrative Unit					
Total Geographical Area	1971	sq. k.m.	1934.7	924.6	2859.3
Urban Area	1971	sq. k.m.	65.4	Nil	65.4
Rural Area	1971	sq. k.m.	1869.3	924.6	2793.9
Revenue Circle	1998	No.	4	1	5
No. of Towns					
Municipalities	1998	No.	1	Nil	1
Town Committee	1998	No.	1	Nil	1
Census Town	1991	No.	1	Nil	1
No. of Villages					
Villages (inhabited)	1991	No.	608	207	815
Villages (uninhabited)	1991	No.	15	37	52
Gaon Panchayat	1995-96	No.	91	20	111
Police Station	1998	No.	7	3	10
Police Outpost	1998	No.	14	3	17
Fire Station	1998	No.	3	-	3
Assembly Constituency	1998	No.	5	1	6
Population					
Total Population	1991	No.	735828	135378	871206
Male	1991	No.	385195	70410	455605
Female	1991	No.	350633	64968	415601
Rural Population	1991	No.	602801	135378	738179
Male	1991	No.	312463	70410	382873
Female	1991	No.	290338	64968	355306
Town & Town Committee	1991	No.	79360	Nil	79360
Male	1991	No.	44013	Nil	44013
Female	1991	No.	35347	Nil	35347
SC Population	1991	No.	46451	19278	65729
Male	1991	No.	24133	10133	34266
Female	1991	No.	22318	9145	31463
ST Population	1991	No.	47709	57357	105066
Male	1991	No.	24313	29052	53365
Female	1991	No.	23396	28305	51701
Jorhat Urban Aglo(City)	1991	No.	112030	Nil	112030
Mariani Town Committee	1991	No.	21002	Nil	21002
Estimated Population	1998	No.	-	-	1018400

1	*2*	*3*	*4*	*5*	*6*
Density	1991	per sq km	380	146	306
Urban	1991	per sq km	2047	Nil	2047
Rural	1991	per sq km	323	146	246
Sex Ratio	1991	per 1000 male	910	922	913
Literate Population	1991	No.	410439	66748	477187
Male	1991	No.	239028	41658	280686
Female	1991	No.	171411	25090	196501
Urban Literates (including outgrowth area)	1991	No.	92729	Nil	92729
Rural Literates	1991	No.	317710	66748	384458
Population 0 to 6 Years	1991	No.	116881	25737	142618
Total Workers					
Urban					
Male	1991	No.	36158		36158
Female	1991	No.	5399		5399
Rural					
Male	1991	No.	142278	31848	174121
Female	1991	No.	68485	15376	83861
Classification of Workers					
Cultivators	1991	No.	95536	36968	132484
Agricultural Labour	1991	No.	15031	938	15969
Livestock Forestry & Fishery	1991	No.	57524	440	57964
Mining & Quarrying	1991	No.	1628	11	1639
Manufacturing/Processing etc in Household Industry	1991	No.	1825	1433	3258
Manufacturing/Processing etc Other than Household Industry	1991	No.	9640	264	9904
Construction	1991	No.	5312	384	5703
Trade & Commerce	1991	No.	20752	1761	22513
Transport, Storage & Communication	1991	No.	7675	250	7925
Other Workers	1991	No.	37411	4770	42181
Marginal Labourers	1991	No.	27831	6754	34585
Non-Workers	1991	No.	455677	81405	537082
Community Development Block-wise Population					
Jorhat Dev. Block	1991	No.	167831		167831
East Jorhat Dev. Block	1991	No.	74334		74334

1	*2*	*3*	*4*	*5*	*6*
Central Jorhat Dev. Block	1991	No.	73240		73240
Jorhat NW Dev. Block	1991	No.	131703		131703
Kaliapani Dev. Block	1991	No.	70986		70986
Titabor Dev. Block	1991	No.	138374		138374
Majuli Dev. Block	1991	No.		81984	81984
Ujani Majuli Dev. Block	1991	No.		53394	53394
EDUCATION					
Primary Schools	1996	Nos.	1126	425	1551
Middle Schools	1996	Nos.	219	97	316
High School (Provincial)	1997	Nos.	141	67	208
Higher Secondary Schools	1996	Nos.	21	2	23
College	1996	Nos.	11	3	14
Law College	1998	Nos.	1	-	1
Engineering College	1998	Nos.	1	-	1
Polytechnic College	1998	Nos.	1	-	1
ITI	1998	Nos.	1	-	1
Agriculture University	1998	Nos.	1	-	1
Home Science College	1998	Nos.	1	-	1
B.T. College	1998	Nos.	1	-	1
Homeopathic College	1998	Nos.	1	-	1
MEDICAL & HEALTH					
Civil Hospital	1997-98	No.	1	Nil	1
Other Hospitals	1997-98	No.	4	Nil	4
Primary Health Centres	1997-98	No.	6	1	7
Rural Hospitals	1997-98	No.	3	1	4
Mini Health Centres	1997-98	No.	15	4	19
State Govt. Sub-Centres	1997-98	No.	14	1	15
State Dispensaries	1997-98	No.	8	4	12
Family Welfare Centres	1997-98	No.	103	37	140
No. of Beds (State Hospitals)	1997-98	No.	308	36	434
Doctors (Allopathic) Govt.	1997-98	No.	109	18	127
Doctors (Homeo) Govt.	1997-98	No.	3	1	4
Doctors (Ayurvedic) Govt.	1997-98	No.	6	3	9
Nurses & Midwives	1997-98	No.	119	14	133
Para Medical Personnel	1997-98	No.	56	9	65
No. of Villages with Drinking Water Facility (Deep Tubewell)	1995-96	No.	165	16	181

1	2	3	4	5	6
AGRICULTURE					
Land Utilization (provisional)					
Total Cropped Area	1997-98	Hect.	-	-	166276
Net area shown	1997-98	Hect.	-	-	120940
land upto Non-Agri Uses	1997-98	Hect.	-	-	81627
Barren & Unculturable	1997-98	Hect.	-	-	21060
Permanent Pastures and Other Grazing Lands	1997-98	Hect.	-	-	4406
Land under Misc. tree Crops & Groves Excluded in Net Area	1997-98	Hect.	-	-	9364
Cultivable wasteland	1997-98	""	-	-	7910
Area Irrigated	1995-96	""	2708	224	2932
Area under Important Crops					
Autumn Paddy	1997-98	Hects	5020	350	5370
Winter Paddy	1996-97	Hects	78000	6340	84340
Summer Paddy	1996-97	Hects	450	2	452
Wheat	1996-97	Hects	750	2400	3150
Mustard	1996-97	Hects	2800	7000	9800
Sugarcane	1996-97	Hects	500	100	600
Other Rabi Pulses	1996-97	Hects	985	4595	5580
Potato	1996-97	Hects	1900	1200	3100
Production of Important crops					
Autumn Rice	1997-98	Tonnes	6728	277	7005
Winter rice	1996-97	Tonnes	141214	9580	150794
Summer Rice	1996-97	Tonnes	765	3	768
Wheat	1996-97	Tonnes	999	3175	4174
Other Rabi Pulses	1996-97	Tonnes	391	2211	2602
Sugarcane (in cane)	1996-97	Tonnes	1829	387	2216
Potato	1996-97	Tonnes	15090	7814	22904
Average Yield Rate					
Autumn Paddy	1997-98	Kg/Hect.	1362	804	1326
Winter Rice	1996-97	Kg/Hect.	1838	1534	1815
Summer Rice	1996-97	Hg/Hect.	1701	1701	1701
Wheat	1996-97	Hg/Hect.	1332	1323	1323
Other Rabi Pulses	1996-97	Hg/Hect.	396	481	466
Mustard	1996-97	Hg/Hect.	480	363	396
Sugarcane	1996-97	Hg/Hect.	37236	39389	37595
Potato	1996-97	Hg/Hect.	7942	6512	7388

FOREST AREA					
Reserved Forest Area	1997-98	Sq. Kms.	272	Nil	272
1	*2*	*3*	*4*	*5*	*6*
Proposed Unreserved					
Forest Area	1997-98	Sq. Kms.	Nil	Nil	Nil
Non-Surveyed Forest	1997-98	sq. Kms	No	Nil	Nil
Forest Production					
Timber	1997-98	Cu Mts	130.778	Nil	130.778
Plywood	1997-98	Cu Mts	Nil	Nil	Nil
Other Wood	1997-98	Cu Mts	22.705	Nil	22.705
Straw	1997-98	1000	800	Nil	800
Social Forestry Area	1995-96	Hect.	16.00	25.00	41.00
Social Forestry Area					
on Road	1995-96	Kms.	0.50	Nil	0.50
INDUSTRY					
Registered Factory	1996-97	No	N.A.	N.A.	95
Registered Industry	1995-96	No	59	13	72
Industrial Estate	1995-96	No	1	Nil	1
No. of Sheds under					
Industrial Estate	1995-96	No	29	Nil	29
Commercial State	1995-96	No	2	1	3
Shed under Commercial					
Estate	1995-96	No	6	4	10
Total Sheds	1995-96	No	35	4	39
TEA INDUSTRY					
No. of Tea Estatea	1995	No	101	Nil	101
Total Area under 55 Nos					
Reported Tea Estates	1995	Hect.	24274	Nil	24274
Planted Area	1995	Hect	12761	Nil	12761
Tea Production	1995	Kgs.	18801753	Nil	18801753
Registered Labour on —					
Roll	1995	No	20179	Nil	20179
FISHERY					
Registered Beel	1997-98	No	9	17	26
Unregistered Beel	1997-98	No	17	90	107
Area under Registered					
Beel	1997-98	Hect.	N.A.	N.A.	958
Area under Un-					
registered Beel	1997-98	Hect.	N.A.	N.A.	597
Fish Production	1997-98	Tonnes	N.A.	N.A.	5805
Important Fish from					
Outside the State	1997-98	Tonnes	2806	Nil	2806

1	2	3	4	5	6
BANK					
Scheduled Commercial Bank	1996	No.	61	8	69
Total Deposit	1996	Rs. in Lakhs	N.A.	N.A.	254.72
Total Credit	1996	Rs. in Lakhs	N.A.	N.A.	8615
No. of Banks in Rural Area	1996	Rs. in Lakhs	41	8	49
Regional Bank	1996	No.	N.A.	N.A.	16
Deposit	1996	Rs. in Lakhs	N.A..	N.A.	1365
Credit	1996	Rs. in Lakhs	N.A..	N.A.	608
Cooperative Societies					
No. of Societies	1995-96	No.	634	133	767
No. of Members	1995-96	No.	181106	10864	191970
Shared Capital	1995-96	Rs.	54136225	901300	55037525
Working Share Capital	1995-96.	Rs.	25510650	852840	26423490
ROAD COMMUNICATION					
National Highway	1998	Kms.	59	Nil	59
State Highway	1998	Kms.	110.60	27.08	137.68
Main District Road	1998	Kms.	142.70	82.36	225.06
NEC Road	1998	Kms.	30.31	Nil	30.31
Border Road	1998	Kms.	66.25	Nil	66.25
Other PWD Road	1998	Kms.	1025.61	33.87	1059.48
Total Length of PWD Road	1998	Kms.	1334.47	143.31	1477.78
Total Surfaced Road	1998	Kms.	254.55	1.94	256.50
Total Gravelled Road	1998	Kms.	1079.92	122.37	1202.29
Total Earthern Road	1998	Kms.	Nil	19.09	19.09
RAILWAY					
Total B.G. Route	1998	Kms.	89	Nil	89
Total M.G. Route	1998	Kms.	Nil	Nil	Nil
Airport	1998	No.	1	Nil	1
Inland Water Transport	1998	No.	2	3	5%
SERICULTURE					
Total No. of Sericultural Village	1995-96	No.	305	133	438
Number of families Engaged in Sericulture					
Eri	1995-96	No.	7721	5534	13255
Muga	1995-96	No.	1812	61	18

List of Existing Satras in Majuli

Auniati
Garamur
Dakhinpat
Bengena-ati
Bhogpur
Natun Kamalabari
Uttar Kamalabari
Natun Samaguri
Purani Samaguri
Saru Garamur
Dakhinpat Grihasthi
Dighali
Belosudhia
Adhar
Bihimpur
Narasinha
Malual
Sakala
Matiabari
Sarjan
Dikhow Mukhia Alengi
Madhay Kamalabari Satra
Ahatguri Satra
Alege Madarguri Satra
Natun Sakala Satra
Alengi Satra
Bar Alengi Satra
Dikhow Mukhia Bah Jengani Satra

14

Service Delivery and Governance*

Growth and Development Debate: Idea of Human Development

The link between economic growth and development was a subject of global discussion during the second half of the 20th century. By the early 1960s, economic growth had emerged as the goal as well as indicator of national progress in many countries. The process of development, as the World Bank defines, aims at raising the per capita Gross National Product or the income and average material well-being of the people of a country. This 'quantitative change or expansion in a country's economy' implies economic growth while economic development is more holistic encompassing qualitative change. While economic growth or enhancement of income per capita is the goal by itself, economic development is only the means rather than an end, the end being the well-being or welfare of a country's citizens. The concept of human development has evolved from the development debate of the above type in the 1970s and 1980s.

The specific concept of human development as introduced aims at eliminating the confusion between means and ends and focusing on human beings. Human development is all about "expanding the richness of human life, rather than simply richness of the economy in which human beings live. It is an approach that is focused on creating fair opportunities and choices for all people". (UNDP, HDR, 1990)

---

* Keynote Address: National Conference on Social Sector Development and Governance Issues, November 29, 2015 at Krishna Kanta Handique State Open University.

Social Services and Human Development

Social sector services together with income constitute the basic constituents of human development. Social sector services include services such as education, health, administration, housing, water and sanitation and social security measures while the human development index takes into consideration income, education and health indicators.

Social sector service outcomes depend on (a) availability of and access to infrastructures and (b) utilization of the infrastructures. The former is physical while the latter is behavioural. For example, the availability of a school or a health centre within an accessible distance is a necessary condition but not sufficient for education or health outcome. The outcome will depend on whether or not households send their children to school or use the health institutions. It is easier to create the physical infrastructures, if the required fund is available. It is more challenging to make the people utilize the available infrastructures since non-availing of the facilities is the result of behaviour or the decision of the households. It requires understanding of the factors lying behind such a decision of households and imagination to design an effective policy instrument. Conditional cash transfer programme (Bolsa Familia) introduced in Brazil is a good example of innovative public policy to influence household behaviour towards a desirable social outcome.

It may be mentioned that if income is reasonably high for everyone in the society, people themselves would largely take care of their health and also their children's education needs. The government's role will be limited to taking care of those parts of social sector services which are of the nature of public goods with high externality. But in reality, the income distribution is highly skewed necessitating higher government interventions in providing social sector services, particularly, health and education services. In a society like ours where the income level is low as well as unequally distributed, the role of government and the quality of governance becomes crucial. In short, good governance is imperative as much for growth and development as for human development.

Social Sector Spending and Human Development

Government expenditure on social sector services in the North Eastern states is generally much higher than most other states in the country. For example, apart from Assam, the per capita expenditure on the social sector during 2005-10 ranged from Rs. 8,294 in Arunachal Pradesh to Rs. 4,451 in Tripura against the mean expenditure of Rs. 3,022 for the non-special category states. However, Assam's per capita expenditure of Rs. 2,503 on the social sector was lower than the non-special category states' mean expenditure. A similar picture emerges if social sector expenditure as percentage of GSDP is considered.[1] When the expenditure on social sector is decomposed into education and health, Assam spent the highest share of 51.52 per cent on education in 2011-12 among all the states in the country. Other North Eastern states also allocated a large portion of social sector expenditure on education ranging from 43.96 per cent in Nagaland and Tripura to 33.9 per cent in Arunachal Pradesh in the same year. On health also North Eastern states spent in the range of 18.5 per cent (Manipur) to 11.2 per cent (Assam) of their total social sector expenditure in 2011-12.

But the deployment of resources for the social sector is not equally matched by the delivery of social sector services. It is reflected in the fact that the North Eastern states ranked very low in terms of the human development index. What is more, their ranks slipped over time. That is what is brought out by a recent study[2] by NIPFP (2014) which assessed human development across Indian states over three decades from 1983 to 2011. The study has placed most North Eastern states in the bottom segment. Four of the North Eastern states, Meghalaya, Manipur, Assam and Arunachal Pradesh, in the same order, were ranked 20 or above among the 28 states while the other four–Mizoram Tripura, Sikkim and Meghalaya in the range of 13 to 19 in 2011-12. Worse still, except for Tripura which improved marginally by one rank, ranks of the other North Eastern states in human development attainment deteriorated hugely between 1983 and 2011-12.

Obviously, deteriorating HDI suggests falling social sector outcomes in relative terms. Many factors could be responsible for such an outcome. But one of the crucial factors that contributes to poor social development outcomes is governance.

Governance

What is governance? The World Bank has defined governance as "the manner in which power is exercised in the management of a country's economic and social resources."[3] Three aspects of governance that the Bank has identified are: "(1) the form of the political regime; (2) the process by which authority is exercised in the management of a country's economic and social resources for development; and (3) the capacity of governments to design, formulate and implement policies and discharge functions.[4]

It may be added that governance is now understood in a wider perspective: it "refers to new processes, methods, or ways of governing where government is one of the actors in the process of governance along with civil society and the private sector. The government has to steer, support and guide as opposed to command and control, direct provision of public services and to act as a standalone institution of governance"[5].

Good governance presupposes rule of law which means equal treatment of all citizens while framing and implementing rules. The importance of rule of law cannot be overstressed. It creates an enabling environment for improved performance of an economy/society. In this sense, rule of law can be called foundational factor. Institutionally, it calls for a political system with independent legislatures, strong executive and free judiciary. In a liberal democracy like ours, good governance should have the following properties: participation, transparency, accountability, efficiency, decency and fairness.[6]

Barriers to Good Governance

In a hugely unequal society accompanied by high illiteracy and rampant poverty, the rule of law is a great challenge. Whether in the domain of legislature or of executives or of the judiciary, the people at the bottom layer do not get equal space or treatment. In other words, the rule of law treating all citizens is a huge challenge. Even in regard to judiciary, the adage that all are equal in the eyes of law is a mere notion and what happens in reality is people with money can buy justice. Again, political interference can and in fact does bend law or its execution and even the judiciary.

The use of public resources for personal gains, which is what corruption is, is a big barrier to good governance. Corruption has encompassed government agencies, market institutions and even civil society. Such all-pervasive corruption has eaten into the vitals of the country. It has led to devastating results in terms of not realizing targeted goals and poor quality of service delivery and sub-optimal or inefficient use of resources. Similarly, nepotism in terms of family, sectarian, ethnic/community and regional connections have undermined the principles of merit and equality of opportunity. The end result is that poverty perpetuates, transaction cost rises, and service delivery suffers and finally distrust between those who govern and those who are governed spreads, all leading to disorder across the society.

When it comes to corruption in the North East, India Corruption Report 2008 classified the eight states in terms of the levels of corruption into four categories[7]: the level of corruption is alarming in Assam and Nagaland; very high in Meghalaya and Sikkim; high in Arunachal Pradesh and Manipur and moderate in Mizoram and Tripura. Conceding that such measurement is sensitive to the data and methodology used, the broad inference that the corruption is very pervasive in the North Eastern states is inescapable. In an environment of rampant corruption, service delivery will be poor and the human development index is bound to deteriorate in the North Eastern states as it indeed did in the last three decades.

Fragmented society in terms of ethnicity, religion, caste, class and gender is another impediment to good governance. Such fragmentation is a fertile ground for discrimination in employment and service provisioning.

Government capacity to govern is constrained by factors like weak management and control system, corruption and nepotism and politicization of the bureaucracy and judiciary.

Finally, when bureaucracy is responsible for service delivery, one has to note that its objective function is to maximize power and not to optimize service delivery. How do they maximize power? They maximize power by colluding with politicians, by explicit or implicit networking among its members, exercising wide discretionary powers and closely guarding and not sharing the information relating to decision-making with the civil society.

Towards Good Governance and Service Delivery

Good governance depends on the capacity of the government to perform effectively its various roles such as "policy formulation and coordination; monitoring and evaluation; performance management and accountability for results; budget and expenditure management"[8] and so on.

The maintenance of law and order, which is the core of good governance, creates an enabling environment for peace, security, improved service delivery and economic performance. It also enables the civil society and the private sector, the other two actors of governance in the present context to play their respective roles effectively.

Equally important is that the mobilzation and deployment of resources for desirable social outcomes should be accompanied by matching attention to good policy design and effective implementation.

In the process of implementation, an external agency should be put in place to monitor whether the scheme/project is being executed as per design, whether materials being used as stipulated, and whether the project is progressing as per schedule and finally to suggest whether any course correction is needed. Similarly, there should be an independent agency to evaluate projects from its design to execution/implementation essentially for corrective actions in future policy formulation and project design. Social audit as provided under MGNREGA has demonstrated the usefulness of external monitoring and evaluation.

In this technology era, various opportunities have opened up for improving transparency and efficiency in service provisioning and delivery by promoting e-governance using IT and IT enabled services. In Chhattisgarh, just to cite an example, localized kiosks have been put in place in easily accessible locations to provide various services such as birth, death and cast certificates to the people without their making rounds to government offices. Young people from amongst the educated unemployed youths are engaged to run these kiosks and authorized to charge a stipulated fee for every service delivered.

Some state governments have introduced "Citizens' charter" to deliver certain services in a time-bound framework. The Delhi Right of citizens to time-bound delivery of services 2011 is a step in right direction. At another level, the Right to Information Act 2005 which was passed by the Parliament in 2005 and came into effect from October 13, 2005 has empowered the citizens in a substantive way. It has enhanced the accountability of the government to the people.

There are also some other initiatives to improving governance. For example, at the "Make in India" workshop organized in December 2014, state governments and Union Territories agreed to a 98–point action plan for business reforms[9]. These reform measures relate to the following eight areas: (i) Setting up a business; (ii) Allotment of land and obtaining construction permit; (iii) Complying with environment procedures; (iv) Complying with labour regulations; (v) Obtaining infrastructure related utilities; (vi) Registering and complying with tax procedures; (vii) Carrying out inspections and (viii) enforcing contracts. While assessing the progress made by the states and UTs about a year later, the North Eastern states have been ranked at the bottom among the 32 states and UT; the topmost rank among the North Eastern states is given to Assam at 22.

Decentralized governance is ideal for good governance and service delivery. Local governments like panchayats are better placed to discharge certain localized functions efficiently. Being closer to the people, they can assess people's preference more realistically and can plan accordingly and deliver the services in a cost effective manner. Their functioning can be expected to be more transparent and accountable to the people. One can expect a higher degree of people's participation in the decision-making process. Given these advantages of local self-government, the decentralized governance should be strengthened for good governance and service delivery.

Finally, I would like to conclude this chapter by narrating an incident that brings out how good governance works. It happened long years ago in the 1980s and it was told to me by a Member of the Planning Commission. The story goes as follows. The Member accompanied by the Chief Engineer, Irrigation went to see an irrigation project in a remote part of Haryana. Immediately after they reached the guest house, a large group of farmers came to see the Chief Engineer. He went to meet the farmers and came back in no time. The Member was curious to know as to how he could manage to satisfy the crowd in such a short span of time. The Chief

Engineer explained that he found out from them the reason why they came. They came to complain that a few irrigation nooks in their fields do not discharge an adequate quantity of water. He assured them that an engineer would come within the next 48 hours and set them right. They were satisfied and dispersed. He further added, if he would not deal with the issue this way, some of them would go to the MLA or the concerned Minister and place their problem before him. Given the priority accorded to agriculture, it was given to know to all concerned that farmers' problems have to be tackled on the highest priority basis. The implication is that if the Chief Engineer had not addressed the problem at his level, the concerned Minister would have called him and instructed him to deal with it forthwith and report back to him. In a situation such as this, it is less stressful for him to address the problem at his level.

In a nutshell, this real life incident brings out the very essence of good governance and the resultant quick service delivery: participation, transparency, accountability and efficiency.

NOTES

1. For detailed analysis of social sector expenditure and its impact, see Goswami, Binoy (2015)," Impact of Social Sector Expenditures by Government on Health and Educational Attainments" in Mishra, R.K. and Anand Akundy, *Indian Social Sector: Trends and Issues,* Academic Foundation, New Delhi, 2015 and Goswami, Binoy and M.P. Bezbaruah (2011), "Social Sector Expenditure and Their Impact on Human Development", *Indian Journal of Human Development,* Vol. 5, No. 2.
2. Mukherjee, S.D. Chakraborty and S. Sikdar (2014), (Mimeo) Three Decades of Human Development Across Indian States: Inclusive Growth or Perpetual Disparity, NIPFP, Working Paper No. 2014-139.
3. The World Bank (1992), Governance and Development, As quoted in Borbora, Saundarjya (2015), Governance and Institutional Reforms, Presidential Address at 17th NEEA Conference, RGU, October 30, 2015, p. 5.
4. Ibid.
5. Borbora, op. cit., p. 4.
6. For further discussion see, Borbora, Saundarya, op. cit., p. 8.
7. Op. cit., p. 12.
8. Borbora, p. 10.
9. See, World Bank, KPMG, CII and FICCI, Assessment of State Implementation of Business Reforms, September 2015, pp. 9-10.

15

'Crisis' in the Tea Sector: A Study of Assam Tea Gardens*

I. Introduction

The tea industry in India is said to be facing a severe crisis, particularly after the disintegration of the Soviet Union, the largest importer of Indian tea. However, over the past decade, domestic consumption of tea has increased at a faster rate than production—at a steady rate of around 15 to 20 million kgs annually. The steady increase in domestic demand and the inability of the tea sector to enhance production has resulted in a decline in tea exports. India's share in global export of tea has declined drastically in the recent period. The decision of the government to allow cheaper tea imports from Bangladesh and Sri Lanka, according to tea producers, has only deepened the crisis (Bhowmik, 2002). However, the fall in the price of tea was observed in India as well as in other tea producing countries (Kumar et al., 2008).

Several recent studies and reports have reported the growing labour unrest and worsening living conditions of labourers in the tea gardens (Misra, 2002; Khawas, 2006). While low labour productivity is frequently cited as the main reason behind the crisis faced by the sector[1], other variables such as inability to expand the area under cultivation, ageing of the tea-bushes[2], inadequate replanting of bushes, inadequate investments in plant modernization and labour welfare measures[3], and traditional, cost-ineffective management practices have also contributed towards the near-stagnation of production (Sivaram, 2000; Bhowmik, 2002).

This chapter attempts to analyse the trends in production and employment in the tea sector in India at a disaggregated level. The

* Jointly with Deepak K. Mishra, Vandana Upadhyay. Published in the *Indian Economic Journal*, Vol. 56(3), October-December, 2008.

focus is on Assam, one of the significant producers of tea in India.[4] While much of the discussion on the impact of globalization on tea sector revolves around trends in tea auction prices and exports, the present study looks at the post-reform changes in production and labour use in the tea-producing districts of Assam. In Section II the trends of tea production in India and in Assam has been discussed. The growth performance of the tea sector in terms of growth of area, production, and yield has been discussed at a disaggregated level. In the following section the trends in labour-use and employment has been discussed. Trends in the growth of labour productivity and employment elasticity in different districts have also been discussed in this section. Summary of findings and concluding remarks have been placed in the final section.

II. Growth of Tea Production in India and Assam

There has been a phenomenal growth of tea gardens in India, particularly since the 1990s, mainly due to increase in the number of small tea growers in various states such as Assam, Himachal Pradesh, Tamil Nadu and Kerala.[5] Tea production in India, which started during the colonial period, expanded rapidly since 1870. The British East India Company and later the colonial government supported the expansion of the tea plantations in Assam and elsewhere through a series of legislative and institutional support (Behal and Mohapatra, 1992; Dasgupta, 1992; Siddique, 1995). During this period, there was a steady growth in area under tea plantation; there were many improvements in the technology of tea production; significant gains in productivity were also achieved, although there were periods of crises because of war and political instability (Karmakar and Banerjee, 2005).

During the post-independence decades, area, production and yield of tea have registered a steady increase. Taking a three-yearly moving average, it is found that production and yield have suffered a serious setback since 1998, although the area under tea has expanded due to increase in small tea gardens (Figure 1). The growth performance of tea in India comes out in clearer terms, when the variations in growth performance among decades are taken into account. While for the entire period of 1950-2004, growth rate of production has been close to 2.4 per cent, area has expanded at a rate of less than one per cent per annum. Thus, the major contribution to growth in production has come from rise in productivity. It is important to note that the highest increase in production as well as yield was recorded in the 1970s. While the highest growth rate in area under tea has been registered during the 1990s, this is the decade when growth of production was at its lowest and yield has shown a negative growth (Table 1). Although the trends in the growth of area, production and yield could have been influenced by the inclusion of small gardens since 1998, even for the period 1998- 2004, all these findings—viz. of slow growth of production, negative growth of yield, and comparatively high growth rate of area—also hold good.

Figure 1: Index Number of Area, Production and Yield of Tea in India: 1950-2004

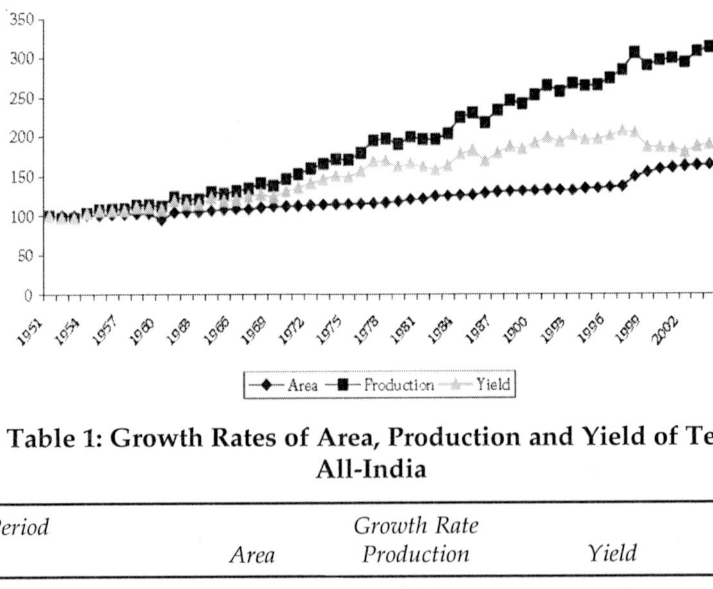

Table 1: Growth Rates of Area, Production and Yield of Tea: All-India

Period		*Growth Rate*	
	Area	*Production*	*Yield*
1951-1960	-0.08	1.81	1.44
1961-1970	0.81	2.01	1.19
1971-1980	0.63	3.05	2.41
1981-1990	0.87	2.88	1.98
1991-2000	2.09	1.73	-0.35
1991-2004	2.13	1.50	-0.62
1950-2004	1.53	0.63	-0.88
1998-2004	0.90	2.38	1.48

Note: Growth rates are compound growth rates.
Source: Calculated from data provided in *Tea Statistics, 2004*.

Growth of Tea Production in States of India

The major tea-producing states of India are Assam, West Bengal, Tamil Nadu and Kerala.[6] The growth performance of tea in these states has been highly uneven. Among all the major tea-producing states, the growth rate of area under tea production has been highest in the 1990s. As it has already been pointed out earlier, this high growth in area has been possible partly because of the increase in the number of small tea growers, mainly in Tamil Nadu and Assam. But the growth rate in area continues to be high in many of the states even during the last sub-period under study, i.e. 1998-2004 (Table 2).

In terms of trends in growth of production of tea, for both Assam and West Bengal, the 1970s was the best period, among the five post-reform decades under study. While growth rates of production have been considerably low in almost all the major tea-producing states, for Assam it was the worst. Among the southern states, growth in tea production was negative in Kerala and was exceptionally low in Tamil Nadu. The important aspect of the growth performance of the states in the recent years is the remarkably poor performance in production in Assam, as well as north India as a whole during 1998-2004.

The 'crisis' in the tea industry, or to be more precise, the productivity-related aspect of the crisis, comes out in bold relief when the growth rate of yield of tea is compared across various states and group of states for different decades under consideration (Table 2). For the states of Assam and West Bengal, the 1970s was the decade of highest growth in yield per hectare. At the all-India level, however, growth of yield was higher in the 1990s than the previous decade, because of the high growth of yield in the southern states. Again, the growth rate of yield has been observed to be negative at the all-India level as well as in north India, while in south India it has registered a very low growth during 1998-2004. Of the sixteen tea-producing states, growth in yield was negative in as many as seven states during this period, while in major tea-producing states like West Bengal, Tamil Nadu and Karnataka it was abysmally low. To put the record straight, the crisis in the tea industry is primarily a crisis of falling productivity, than anything else.

Table 2: Growth of Area, Production and Yield of Tea in Major Tea-Producing States of India

Period		*Assam*	*West Bengal*	*North India Total*	*Tamil Nadu*	*Kerala*	*South Total India*	*All India*
1951-1961	A	0.42	0.39	0.33	-0.2	1.82	0.85	0.11
	P	1.94	0.99	1.59	4.66	4.37	4.57	2.13
	Y	1.52	0.6	1.26	4.86	2.51	3.68	1.66
1961-1971	A	1.17	0.68	0.96	0.57	-0.65	-0.07	0.79
	P	2.07	1.9	1.97	3.76	0.78	2.43	2.19
	Y	0.89	1.21	1	3.18	1.43	2.51	1.38
1971-1981	A	1.08	0.6	0.89	0.68	-0.46	0.1	0.70
	P	3.15	2.11	2.79	2.21	1.09	1.75	2.75
	Y	2.05	1.5	1.88	1.52	1.56	1.64	2.05
1981-1991	A	1.4	0.82	1.11	0.41	-0.26	0.1	0.84
	P	2.76	1.93	2.55	5.29	3.44	4.54	2.94
	Y	1.34	1.1	1.42	4.86	3.71	4.44	2.08
1991-2001	A	1.18	0.84	1.36	6.95	0.63	4.30	2.20
	P	1.25	1.87	1.46	0.99	-0.25	0.6	1.67
	Y	-0.19	1.02	0.1	-5.57	-0.88	-3.54	-0.53
1991-2004	A	1.18	0.87	1.26	5.34	0.52	3.33	2.13
	P	0.65	2.52	1.26	2.39	-0.55	1.46	1.50
	Y	-0.53	1.64	0	-2.8	-1.07	-1.81	-0.62
1998-2004	A	1.29	1.28	1.49	3.02	0.16	1.99	1.53
	P	-1.15	1.71	-0.21	3.57	-0.98	2.12	0.63
	Y	-2.41	0.42	-1.68	0.53	-1.14	0.14	-0.88

Note: Growth rates are compound growth rates.
Source: Calculated from data provided in *Tea Statistics*, various years.

One important aspect of the declining productivity growth in tea plantation is the inadequate replanting of bushes. The desired annual rate of replanting is 2 per cent (Bhowmik, 2002). However, in north India[7], the present annual rate of replanting is less than 0.3 per cent. Again the growth of area under replantation has been negative during 1991-2000 at the all-India level as well as in north and south India separately. When we consider the area under replantation as a percentage of total area under tea plantation, the dismal performance becomes all the more glaring (Table 3). In terms of area under extension there has been a robust growth during 1991-2000 in north India, probably due to the growth of small tea plantations in Assam.

Table 3: Growth of Area Under Extension, Replacement and Replantation

Growth Rate in the Period	*1961-1970*	*1971-1980*	*1981-1990*	*1991-2000*	*1961-2001*
Area under Extension (North)	3.66	5.83	2.68	4.41	0.79
Area under Replacement (North)	-0.82	10.05	-2.71	13.08	1.93
Area under Replantation (North)	-13.16	0.12	0.77	-0.03	0.12
Area under Extension (South)	8.74	0.09	5.57	-9.97	-0.81
Area under Replacement (South)	-4.62	-1.99	26.85	-10.09	5.97
Area under Replantation (South)	12.60	-11.25	12.46	-30.11	-0.89
Area under Extension (All-India)	4.03	5.20	2.81	3.14	0.84
Area under Replacement (All-India)	-0.99	9.59	-1.73	12.81	2.09
Area under Replantation (All-India)	-12.22	-0.28	1.39	-1.14	0.13
Area under Tea Plantation (All-India)	0.80	0.63	0.96	2.07	0.90
Percentage of Area under Extension to Total Area under Tea Plantation (All-India)	3.19	4.54	1.83	1.05	-0.06
Percentage of Area under Replacement to Total Area under Tea Plantation (All-India)	-1.77	8.90	-2.67	10.53	1.18
Percentage of Area under Replantation to Total Area under Tea Plantation (All-India)	-12.92	-0.91	0.42	-3.14	-0.77
Percentage of Area under Extension, Replacement and Replantation to Total Area under Tea Plantation (All-India)	-1.73	3.21	0.84	0.96	-0.21

Note: Growth rates are compound growth rates.
Source: Calculated from data provided in *Tea Statistics*, various years.

Growth Performance of Tea in Assam: A District-Level Analysis

As it has already been mentioned that in terms of expansion of area under tea, there has been a significant growth in Assam in recent years, so much so that when we consider the growth rates for the post-independence decades, the 1990s comes out as the most favourable decade for gains in terms of area. For a plantation crop like tea, this is presumably a significant positive development in view of the declining forest cover, declining land-man ratio as well as competition for land among alternative crops and alternative industries. However, the regional and spatial concentration of this expansion of area needs careful investigation, as much of the new land under cultivation has come through the small tea plantations. The district-level analysis of growth in area, production and yield of tea in Assam has been restricted to the period 1980 to 2004, for reasons of data availability. It is clear that the 1990s have been a favourable decade for expansion of area both in north as well as in the south, but this expansion was highly concentrated in a few pockets. For example, in the 1980s growth of area in Assam was much higher in Goalpara and Sibsagar districts, while the high growth of the 90s has been confined to Dibrugarh and Sibsagar in Assam. The high growth rates in the districts closely follow the growth pattern of small tea gardens. Even if the last sub-period under study, i.e. 1998-2004 is considered, the high growth in area is noticed in Goalpara, Dibrugarh and Sibsagar (Table 4).

The trends in growth of production of tea reveal the stagnation of production performance at the district level (Table 4). For the entire period under study, i.e. 1980- 2004, growth rates were higher in the southern states in general and Tamil Nadu in particular, compared to that of Assam and West Bengal. The districts of Assam, which have experienced a relatively better growth in production, include Cachar, Sibsagar, and Goalpara. Coming to growth in various sub-periods, in the 1980s almost all the tea-producing districts of Assam registered a growth of more than two per cent per annum. Growth rates of tea production were particularly high in Goalpara, Sibsagar and Darrang. During the 1991-2000, however, not only that growth of production at the state-level slowed down considerably, of the seven districts under study, growth was negative in two; while in two others it was negligible. When growth in production during 1991-2004 is taken into account, the dismal performance on the tea production front becomes even more visible in all the districts of Assam, except Dibrugarh (including Lakhimpur). More importantly, growth performance has further worsened during 1998-2004. In as many as six of the seven districts, as well as for Assam as a whole, growth rate of production of tea has been negative (Table 4).

Table 4: Growth of Area, Production and Yield of Tea in Districts of Assam

Period		*Darrang*	*Goal-para*	*Kamrup*	*Dibru-garh*	*Now-gong*	*Sibsagar*	*Cachar*	*Assam*
1980-2004	A	0.62	0.96	0.16	1.97	0.48	1.55	-0.33	1.16
	P	1.23	1.89	0.5	1.69	1.44	1.92	2.06	1.79
	Y	0.6	0.91	0.35	-0.27	0.95	0.35	2.39	0.61
1981-1990	A	1.32	3.98	1.36	1.35	1.32	2	0.86	1.39
	P	3.58	3.74	2.79	2.03	2.77	3.5	2.73	2.89
	Y	2.23	-0.22	1.4	0.66	1.43	1.46	1.85	1.48
1991-2000	A	0.31	0.57	-0.81	3.37	0.19	1.32	-1.51	1.44
	P	-0.34	0.62	-0.97	1.28	0.4	2.76	2.52	1.47
	Y	-0.65	0.05	-0.16	-2.02	0.21	1.42	4.09	0.03
1991-2004	A	0.25	1.08	0.01	3.28	0.36	1.64	-0.45	1.65
	P	-0.3	0.36	-0.77	1.62	-0.78	1.2	0.72	0.95
	Y	-0.55	-0.7	-0.78	-1.62	-1.14	-0.44	1.18	-0.69
1998-2004	A	0.24	1.66	0.9	1.88	0.65	1.18	0.71	1.22
	P	-0.49	-0.65	-1.87	1.49	-3.51	-2.63	-3.75	-0.75
	Y	-0.73	-2.27	-2.75	-0.38	-4.13	-3.77	-4.43	-1.95

Note: Growth rates are compound growth rates.
Source: Calculated from data provided in *Tea Statistics*, various years.

This poor performance also gets reflected in the district level estimates of growth in yield per hectare. While yield improvement has not been at the desired level since the 1980s itself, the relative performance of the districts of Assam was much better in the 1980s than in the 90s (Table 4).

During 1991-2000 growth of yield slumped in as many as three of the seven districts in Assam. If a longer period of 1991-2004 is taken into consideration, negative growth was recorded in six districts, and in the latest sub-period of 1998-2004, growth was negative in all the districts of Assam. Growth rate of yield per hectare has declined considerably during this period in West Bengal, and apart from Tamil Nadu, other southern states have also suffered heavily on the productivity front.

Another important issue relating to productivity in the tea plantation system is the age distribution of the tea plantations. The age of tea bushes has significant implications for productivity as older bushes gradually become less productive. Generally bushes that are more than 50 years old are considered to be less productive. As a share in total plantations the area under older bushes (i.e.

Table 5: Production, Labour Employed and Production Per Labour in Tea Producing Districts and States of India: 1980-2004

Districts/	*TE 1982*			*TE 1992*			*TE 2002*			*TE 2004*		
States	*P*	*L*	*P/L*	*P*	*L*	*P/L*	*P*	*L*	*P/L*	*P*	*L*	*P/L*
Darrang	606	866	700	810	1029	787	778	1162	670	797	1181	674
Goalpara	3 8	6 4	605	5 5	7 6	726	6 3	9 6	659	6 0	9 9	612
Kamrup	3 9	6 8	590	4 7	8 3	580	4 5	9 0	500	4 4	9 3	474
Dibrugarh*	1227	1667	736	1533	1914	801	1749	2145	815	1822	2169	840
Dibrugarh	1227	1667	736	1450	1773	817	1658	2004	828	1736	2028	856
Lakhimpur	0	0	0	8 3	140	595	9 1	142	640	8 6	141	610
Nowgong	9 1	143	640	120	176	681	118	190	621	115	192	597
Sibsagar#	711	1760	404	1019	2140	476	1252	2278	550	1122	2300	488
Sibsagar	707	1261	561	951	1542	617	1197	1597	750	1075	1605	669
N.Cachar	0	0	0	5 4	5 8	0	5 5	104	528	4 7	106	445
K.Anglong	0	0	0	0	1 7	0	1 9	4 5	429	2 0	4 8	417
Cachar	305	500	610	407	598	680	496	681	728	433	695	624
Assam	3016	4567	661	3989	5490	727	4521	6111	740	4413	6188	713
W.Bengal	1316	2165	608	1532	2482	617	1851	2561	723	2007	2607	769
North India	4372	6914	632	5595	8151	686	6475	8843	732	6538	8963	729
Tamil Nadu	657	861	764	1112	996	1116	1322	2664	497	1540	2700	571
Kerala	481	711	677	607	729	832	664	779	853	618	857	724
Karnataka	3 4	3 9	878	4 2	4 1	1032	5 4	3 9	1404	5 5	4 3	1284
South India	1172	1611	728	1761	1767	997	2040	3482	587	2213	3600	615
All India	5545	8525	651	7356	9917	742	8515	12324	691	8750	12563	696

Note: i P= Production in Hundred Thousand Kgs; L = Average Daily No. of Labour Employed in Hundreds; and P/L = Production per Labour in Kgs; TE= Triennium Ending. i i * Including North Lakhimpur District; # Including North Cachar and Mikir Hills.
Source: *Tea Statistics*, various years.

those older than 50 years), has changed from 34 per cent in 1980 to nearly 29 per cent in 2002, presumably because of growth of small gardens in recent years. However, this data fails to indicate the trends in the larger tea gardens separately. It is important to note that in Assam the share of bushes of less than 5 years increased substantially from around 8 per cent during the late 80s and the early 1990s to 12 per cent in 2002. Among the districts of Assam, the share of older bushes was higher in districts like Darrang, Cachar, Dibrugarh and Lakhimpur in 1980, while in 2002 the districts having a higher share of older bushes were Lakhimpur, Cachar and Nowgong. Thus in spite of a remarkable increase in the tea plantations in Assam, primarily because of the expansion of area under small tea gardens, the share of area under older bushes has not declined very sharply. Another aspect of the inter-district variations in the age distribution of bushes is that share of older bushes is relatively high in districts where the share of large tea gardens is also high. For example, the share of large tea gardens continues to remain high in districts like Kamrup, Nowgong, Darrang and Lakhimpur. Precisely in these districts, it is found that the share of older bushes also remains relatively high. This indicates the possibility that larger tea gardens have not been investing enough in planting new bushes. If this inference is found to be true[8] then it implies that lack of investment in productivity enhancing technologies could be at the bottom of the crisis faced by the tea sector.

III. Trends in Labour-Use and Employment

The production process in the tea sector, particularly in the tea plantations, is highly labour-intensive. The tea sector provides direct employment to around 12.6 lakh workers in India, apart from providing direct sustenance to another 12.3 lakhs people, who are the dependents of the workers. Around six lakhs were employed in the tea gardens of Assam in 2004. There has been a steady growth of employment in absolute terms in the tea gardens of Assam. Along with increase in the volume of production, and in recent years, with the expansion of area under tea gardens there has been a greater demand for labour. The triennial average of labour employed increased from 4.6 lakhs at the end of 1982 to nearly 6.2

lakhs at the end of 2004 (Table 5).

To find out the extent of employment growth, and the spatio-temporal variations in it, the growth rates of average estimated labour employed in the districts of Assam as well as in major tea producing states of India have been presented in Table 6, for four distinct time periods. For the entire period under study, the table shows that employment has grown at a higher rate at the all India level than in Assam. South India as a whole and Tamil Nadu in particular has recorded substantial growth in employment during 1980-2004. In northern states, Assam has a higher growth rate of employment than West Bengal and all the other states taken together. Within Assam, higher employment growth has been witnessed in districts like Goalpara and Cachar. When the growth differentials during the two decades of the 1980s and 90s are taken into consideration, it is clear that employment growth suffered serious setbacks during the latter decade in Assam, but continued to show a higher growth rate at the all-India level, owing to an exceptionally high expansion of employment in Tamil Nadu. In Assam, the only districts where employment growth improved in the 90s as compared to the earlier decade were Goalpara and Kamrup; in all others, and particularly in Sibsagar and Nowgong it declined substantially. When a relatively longer view of employment scenario is considered, during 1991 to 2004, it is found that in Dibrugarh that includes Lakhimpur, Nowgong and Sibsagar, growth of employment was less than one per cent during this period. The worrying aspect on the employment front gets manifested in the fact that for the latest period under consideration, i.e. 1998-2004, employment has grown at a rate of less than one per cent per annum in all the districts of Assam, except in Goalpara and Kamrup. Although at the all-India level, growth of labour employed has been relatively robust during this period, mainly on account of the tremendous expansion of employment in Tamil Nadu, in Assam the growth rate has decelerated to 0.87 per cent per annum. It is important to note that this slowing down of employment growth in Assam has occurred in the backdrop of increase in the area under tea as a result of expansion of area by small tea growers.

Table 6: Growth of Employment

Districts/States	Time Period				
	1980-2004	1981-1990	1991-2000	1991-2004	1998-2004
Darrang	1.49	1.95	1.35	1.17	0.84
Goalpara	1.89	0.91	1.36	1.32	1.42
Kamrup	0.83	-1.37	1.47	2.03	1.23
Dibrugarh*	0.92	1.30	0.96	0.93	0.90
Nowgong	1.28	3.50	0.27	0.29	0.49
Sibsagar#	1.01	1.87	0.00	0.59	0.94
Cachar	1.51	2.96	1.85	1.38	0.75
Assam	1.43	2.06	1.08	1.06	0.87
West Bengal	0.74	1.94	0.08	0.36	0.97
Others Total	-0.58	-0.27	1.91	0.86	-0.69
North India	1.18	1.98	0.72	0.80	0.87
Tamil Nadu	5.38	1.67	10.02	10.64	10.44
Kerala	0.74	0.38	0.55	1.36	3.47
Karnataka	0.03	0.88	-1.30	0.21	3.67
South India	3.71	1.11	6.68	7.42	8.06
All-India	1.76	1.82	2.02	2.29	2.53

Note: i) All growth rates are compound growth rates.
ii) * Including North Lakhimpur District; # Including North Cachar and Mikir Hills.
Source: Computed from the data provided in *Tea Statistics*, various years.

Figure 2: Trends in Labour Per Hectare: 1980-2004

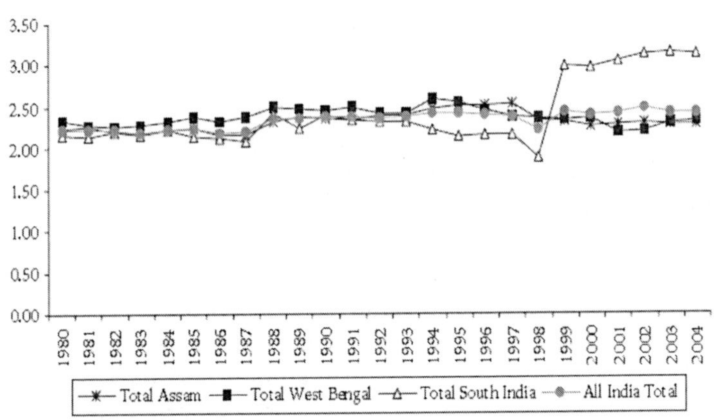

Source: *Tea Statistics*, various years.

Spatio-Temporal Variations in Labour Absorption

To understand the changing dimensions of labour absorption in the tea gardens, the trends in labour-use per hectare has been analysed with respect to inter-district and inter-state variations. In 2004, labour per hectare was higher in South India than that in north India; it was remarkably high in Tamil Nadu than in other major tea producing states. Labour per hectare has been consistently lower in Assam than in West Bengal. Labour use in Assam increased from 2.24 in 1980 to around 2.52 in 1995-1997. After 1998, possibly because of inclusion of the small tea growers, it has gone down to 2.27 per hectare in 2004. The gap between South India and Assam has gone up substantially in the post-1998 period (Figure 2). At the district level labour employed per hectare, in 2004, was relatively high in Darrang, Lakhimpur, Goalpara and Kamrup, while districts having a lower labour per hectare of tea included Dibrugarh, Sibsagar and Cachar.

So far as long- term changes in labour per hectare are concerned, during 1980-2004, there has been insignificant growth at the all-India level as well as in Assam, and a negative growth in West Bengal. Among the districts of Assam, Dibrugarh, that includes Lakhimpur, experienced a negative growth rate while in Sibsagar it was very low. In the 1980s labour per hectare increased at a rate of 0.7 per cent in Assam, while in the next decade there was a negative growth of 0.36 per cent. Both Dibrugarh and Sibsagar registered negative growth rates. During 1991 to 2004 apart from Kamrup and Cachar, labour per hectare either declined or grew at a very slow pace. Three districts namely Dibrugarh, Nowgong and Sibsagar experienced negative growth in labour per hectare, while it was as low as 0.2 per cent in Goalpara. Assam, West Bengal, other states of north India and Karnataka have registered negative growth during this period. During 1998 and 2004, however, there has been some recovery of growth of labour per hectare at the all-India level, primarily because of a spur of employment per hectare in south India in general and Tamil Nadu in particular. The situation in Assam and West Bengal continues to be grim. As many as four out of the seven districts under consideration, registered a negative growth in labour per hectare, while others experienced very low growth (Table 7).

Table 7: Growth Rate of Labour Per Hectare

Districts/States	*Growth Rates in Period*				
	1980-2004	*1981-1990*	*1991-2000*	*1991-2004*	*1998-2004*
Darrang	0.86	0.62	1.03	0.92	0.60
Goalpara	0.91	-2.94	0.78	0.24	-0.24
Kamrup	0.68	-2.69	2.30	2.02	0.33
Dibrugarh*	-0.64	0.41	-2.34	-2.31	-1.00
Nowgong	0.79	2.14	0.08	-0.07	-0.17
#Sibsagar	0.27	0.18	-0.52	-1.10	-3.58
Cachar	1.84	2.08	3.41	1.84	0.04
Assam	0.26	0.67	-0.36	-0.59	-0.34
Darjeeling	1.32	0.90	2.47	1.62	1.09
Terai†	-0.24	4.30	-5.14	-4.67	-2.84
Dooars+	-0.13	0.67	-0.45	-0.27	0.07
W.Bengal	-0.04	1.16	-0.69	-0.91	-0.56
Others Total	-2.51	0.21	-11.18	-8.57	-5.37
North India	0.12	0.83	-0.69	-0.81	-0.53
Tamil Nadu	1.66	1.11	2.00	3.89	7.58
Kerala	0.45	0.67	-0.26	0.84	3.34
Karnataka	-0.58	0.46	-1.98	-0.25	3.51
South India	1.45	0.94	1.77	3.28	6.20
All-India	0.45	0.85	-0.07	0.17	1.04

Note: i) All growth rates are compound growth rates.
ii) Dibrugarh* Including North Lakhimpur District; # Including North Cachar and Mikir Hills; † Including West Dinajpur;
+ including Cooch Behar district.
Source: Computed from the data provided in *Tea Statistics*, various years.

Growth in Labour Productivity

In terms of average production per labour, Assam has recorded a higher labour productivity compared to the all-India average, except for the triennium 1990-1992 (Table 8). Within the districts of Assam, Dibrugarh recorded the highest labour productivity during 1982-2004. When the growth rate of labour productivity during this period is considered, Assam's labour productivity has increased at a level of only 0.4 per cent per annum. The performance of four districts namely, Darrang, Goalpara, Kamrup and Nowgong has been incredibly dismal on this front. However, in all these districts except Nowgong, labour productivity had increased comfortably during the 1980s. It was precisely during the 1990s that the labour productivity growth slumped in many of the districts of Assam and during 1991 to 2004 in as many as five of the seven districts the state experienced deceleration in labour productivity growth. During the last six years, i.e. 1998 to 2004, there has been a substantial deterioration in labour productivity in almost all the major tea-producing states of India. The districts of Assam have experienced a considerable decline in growth of labour productivity (Table 9).

Table 8: Output Per Labour in Districts of Assam

Districts/States	*District Output Per Labour as% of All-India Average*				*District Output Per Labour as% of Assam's Average*			
	TE 1982	*TE 1992*	*TE 2002*	*TE 2004*	*TE 1982*	*TE 1992*	*TE 2002*	*TE 2004*
Darrang	107	106	97	97	106	108	90	95
Goalpara	93	98	95	88	92	100	89	86
Kamrup	91	78	72	68	89	80	68	66
Dibrugarh*	113	108	118	121	111	110	110	118
Dibrugarh	113	110	120	123	111	112	112	120
Lakhimpur	-	80	93	88	-	82	87	86
Nowgong	98	92	90	86	97	94	84	84
Sibsagar#	62	64	80	70	61	65	74	68
Sibsagar	86	83	109	96	85	85	101	94
N.Cachar	-	-	76	64	-	-	71	62
Karbi Anglong	-	-	62	60	-	-	58	58
Cachar	94	92	105	90	92	94	98	88
Total Assam	101	98	107	102	100	100	100	100

Note: i) * Including North Lakhimpur District; # Including North Cachar and Mikir Hills.
ii) TE= Triennium Ending, the figures are average for the three years.
Source: Computed from the data provided in *Tea Statistics*, various years.

Employment Elasticity in the Tea Sector

During the 25-year period, employment elasticity with respect to output in Assam has been estimated to be 0.75, which is much higher than that of West Bengal but is lower than that of south India (Table 10). As expected employment elasticity has come down in the 1990s compared to the 80s. At the district level with the notable exception of Goalpara, it has declined for all the districts during the 90s. However, employment elasticity has become negative in Assam during 1998 to 2004. In Darrang, Goalpara, Kamrup, Nowgong and Sibsagar (excluding North Cachar), it has become negative. This captures the implication of crises of low productivity in the tea sector for labour households in Assam. Increasingly they find it difficult to get absorbed in the tea sector, their traditional sources of livelihood. Field investigations in three tea producing districts of upper Assam reveal a distinct pattern in the changing employment situation in the gardens.[9] There has been a clear move towards gradual casualization of the tea labour force. Tea gardens, in an attempt to cut down expenses, are increasingly substituting permanent workers by casual labour. In many gardens there has been virtually no expansion of the permanent workers in spite of increase in area under plantation. The labour market situation in the tea labour market is such that it puts labour at a disadvantage while allowing flexibility on the part of the employer. The market fluctuations in labour demand conditions have largely been absorbed by one segment of the labour force.

Table 9: Growth of Labour Productivity

Districts/States	*Growth Rates of Labour Productivity*				
	1980-2004	*1981-1990*	*1991-2000*	*1991-2004*	*1998-2004*
Darrang	-0.26	1.60	-1.66	-1.46	-1.32
Goalpara	0.00	2.80	-0.73	-0.95	-2.05
Kamrup	-0.33	4.22	-2.40	-2.75	-3.07
Dibrugarh*	0.37	0.25	0.33	0.71	0.62
Nowgong	0.16	-0.71	0.13	-1.06	-3.98
Sibsagar#	0.66	1.88	1.67	0.32	-0.65
Cachar	0.54	-0.23	0.66	-0.65	-4.47
Assam	0.35	0.80	0.40	-0.10	-1.62
West Bengal	0.98	-0.61	2.00	1.95	1.17
Others Total	5.77	6.65	1.78	2.86	4.92
North India	0.63	0.49	0.94	0.58	-0.67
Tamil Nadu	-1.37	5.12	-7.11	-7.10	-5.74
Kerala	0.65	2.93	0.82	-1.14	-5.12
Karnataka	2.17	1.47	4.14	2.02	-3.11
South India	-0.69	4.23	-4.46	-5.08	-5.40
All-India	0.32	1.26	-0.28	-0.73	-1.79

Note: i) All growth rates are compound growth rates.
i) * Including North Lakhimpur District; # Including North Cachar and Mikir Hills.
Source: Computed from the data provided in *Tea Statistics*, various years.

Table 10: Employment Elasticity with Respect to Output

Districts/States	*Employment Elasticity with Respect to Output*				
	1980-2004	*1981-1990*	*1991-2000*	*1991-2004*	*1998-2004*
Darrang	0.825	0.517	-0.166	-0.501	-0.101
Goalpara	0.887	0.422	2.427	1.847	-0.262
Kamrup	-0.108	-0.144	-0.166	-0.526	-0.254
Dibrugarh*	0.718	0.689	0.289	0.405	0.322
Dibrugarh	0.587	0.617	0.295	0.408	0.339
Lakhimpur	-	-	0.148	0.185	0.007
Nowgong	0.653	0.863	0.182	0.018	-0.089
#Sibsagar	0.622	0.362	0.615	0.487	0.337
Sibsagar	0.413	0.331	0.045	0.119	-0.089
N.Cachar	-	-	2.783	1.349	1.461
Karbi Anglong	-	-	-	-	0.248
Cachar	0.568	0.693	0.578	0.312	-0.123
Total Assam	0.752	0.660	0.533	0.700	-0.377
Darjeeling	-0.252	-0.122	-0.172	-0.177	0.089
Terai	0.369	0.769	-0.007	0.049	0.145
Dooars	0.273	0.289	-0.026	0.083	-0.057
West Bengal	0.358	0.655	-0.022	0.124	0.198
North India	0.627	0.691	0.295	0.457	0.057
Tamil Nadu	1.046	0.194	2.805	2.681	0.835
Kerala	0.258	0.182	0.152	-0.199	-1.097
South India	0.942	0.194	1.904	2.608	1.380
All-India	0.779	0.520	0.817	1.234	0.049

Note: *Including North Lakhimpur District; # Including North Cachar and Mikir Hills.
Source: Computed from the data provided in *Tea Statistics*, various years.

IV. Conclusion

This study brings out important characteristics of the tea sector in Assam in a comparative perspective. The analysis of growth performance of the tea sector clearly brings out the fact that declining productivity in the sector at the all-India level gets manifested much more sharply in the tea gardens of Assam than in any other states or region. Within Assam, while there have been some gains in terms of area in a few districts, the dismal performance in productivity growth has been all pervasive, particularly in the last few years.

For the period 1980-2004, employment has grown at a higher

rate at the all-India level than in Assam. Although at the all India level, growth of labour employed has been relatively robust during 1998-2004, mainly on account of the tremendous expansion of employment in Tamil Nadu, in Assam the growth rate has decelerated to 0.87 per cent per annum. As many as four out of the seven districts in Assam under consideration, registered a negative growth in labour per hectare, while others experienced very low growth. Although labour productivity had increased relatively comfortably during the 1980s in Assam, during the 1990s its growth slumped in many of the districts of Assam. During the six-year period 1998 to 2004, however, there has been a substantial deterioration in labour productivity in almost all the major tea-producing states of India.

Employment elasticity has come down in Assam in the 1990s compared to the 80s. At the disaggregated level, it has declined in almost all the districts during the 1990s. What is worse, it has become negative in Assam during 1998 to 2004. All these features of the labour market in Assam, in a situation of falling growth in productivity as well as in employment, have significant implications for labour households dependent on the tea sector. Increasingly, they find it difficult to get absorbed in the tea sector, their traditional sources of livelihood.

The uniqueness of the labour market in Assam's tea plantation in its historical legacy of migrant labourers being brought along with their families to ensure availability of cheap labour for the sector, the supply side is governed by a set of factors that impart the characteristics of a reserve army of labour. In contrast, the demand side of the labour market is highly responsive to the market conditions. The market fluctuations in labour demand conditions have largely been absorbed by the supply side of the labour force.

Although this study is not addressed to investigating the nature and causes of the crisis facing the Indian tea sector, some of the findings of the study do provide important clues towards understanding the underlying causes behind it. It is interesting to note that the 'crisis' in the tea sector is reflected neither in shrinkage of production nor in declining prices and sale in the domestic market. Domestic consumption of tea in India has, in fact, gone up from an average of 518 million kgs during 1990-92 to 714 million kgs in 2002-04. Production of tea in the country has also gone up from an average of 726 million kgs to nearly 870 million kgs during the same period. If there was any crisis of tea, it could be seen in the loss of export share. India's share in global tea exports has declined from 17.20 per cent in 1992 to nearly 12 per cent in 2004. In absolute terms, India's tea export declined from 208 million kgs in the triennium ending 1991-92, to 183 million kgs in the triennium ending 2003-04. This means that the fall of export was more than compensated by a considerably larger rise in domestic consumption; an increase of domestic consumption by 196 million kgs as against the fall of export by only 25 million tonnes during the triennium ending 2003-04. It is for this reason that the price of tea in the domestic market could more or less maintain an upward trend.

It is true that imports have increased from nearly 1.37 million kgs in 1992-93 to nearly 15 million kgs during the triennium ending 2003-04, but then it constitutes only 2.4 per cent of domestic consumption in India. Imports made inroads in the Indian market partly because of fluctuations in domestic prices and partly because of cheaper import prices. However, it is doubtful whether cheaper imports on its own could be cited as a major cause of the crisis facing the tea industry. The more substantive reason is near lack of investment possibly because traditional/older firms in view of much more promising investment avenues elsewhere started treating the tea sector as a residual avenue for investment. While growing competition from newer foreign competitors both in global and domestic markets has led to the loss of export share, lower productivity due to lower investment could be the main contributory factor behind the crisis.

NOTES

1. Kumar et al. (2008) report that export competitiveness of Indian tea, as measured through the export performance ratio, fell sharply during the late 1990s, although the trend was reversed through corrective measures in the form of promotional efforts of the government in the recent years.
2. Normally the tea bush achieves its prime in terms of output of green leaves from the age of 5 to 30 years. In 2002, 35 per cent of tea bushes in India were over 50 years, which is considered as the uneconomic

phase of tea bush. In Assam, 29 per cent of tea bushes were over 50 years old (Bhowmik, 2002).

3. For a discussion on the evidences showing the relationship between investment in the health and welfare of workers on labour productivity in the tea sector, see Sivaram, 2000.
4. According to 2004 figures, Assam produces around 52 per cent of the total tea produced in India and employs around 56 per cent of the labour force working in this sector. Assam's share in total area under tea was also around 52 per cent of the total area under tea in India in the year 2004.
5. This has also altered the regional distribution and concentration of tea gardens. While the south Indian states accounted for nearly 80 per cent of tea gardens in the early 1980s in 2004 their share has come down to 47 per cent. After the inclusion of small tea gardens in the data on total tea gardens since 1998, the share of Assam has jumped from less than 7 per cent to 30-35 per cent in recent years.
6. In addition to these, tea is grown in a limited way in Himachal Pradesh, Uttarakhand, Karnataka and Tripura. In recent years tea has been introduced in some non-traditional areas like Arunachal Pradesh, Manipur, Nagaland, Meghalaya, Mizoram, Sikkim, Orissa and Bihar.
7. During the period 2002-04, the area under replantation, was nearly 0.2 per cent of the total area under plantations in north India as well as all-India levels.
8. Such an inference can be conclusively proved only when we have separate data on the age distribution of tea bushes in the relatively large tea gardens. In the absence of such data, it is not possible to put the argument in definite terms.
9. For details, see Sarma, Mishra and Upadhyay, 2008.

REFERENCES

Behal, Rana P. and Prabhu Mohapatra (1992). "Tea and Money versus Human Life: The Rise and Fall of the Indenture System in the Assam tea Plantations 1840-1908", *The Journal of Peasant Studies* 19(3-4): 142-171.

Bhowmik, Sharit K. (2002). "Productivity and Labour Standards in Tea Plantation Sector in India", in A. Sivananthiran and C.S. Venkata Ratnam (eds.), *Labour and Social Issues in Plantations in South Asia: Role of Social Dialogue*. ILO–SAAT and IIRA, New Delhi.

Dasgupta, Ranjit (1992). "Plantation Labour in Colonial India", *The Journal of Peasant Studies* 19(3-4): 173-197.

Karmakar, K.G. and G.D. Banerjee (2005). "The Tea Industry in India: A survey", Occasional Paper 39, Department of Economic Analysis and Research, National Bank for Agriculture and Rural Development, Mumbai.

Khawas, Vimal (2006). *Socio-Economic Conditions of Tea Garden Labourers in Darjeeling Hills.* New Delhi: Council for Social Development.

Kumar, P., P.S. Badal, N.P. Singh and R.P. Singh (2008). "Tea Industry in India: Problems and Prospects", *Indian Journal of Agricultural Economics* 63(1): 84-96.

Misra, U. (2002). "Assam Tea: The Bitter Brew", *Economic and Political Weekly* 38, July 19.

Sarma, Atul, Deepak K. Mishra and Vandana Upadhyay (2008). Occupational Mobility of Plantation Sector Labour in Assam: Determinants and Implications. Project report submitted to the National Tea Research Foundation, Kolkata.

Siddique, M.A.B. (1995). "The Labour Market and the Growth of the Tea Industry in India: 1840-1900", *South Asia* 18(1): 83-113.

Sivaram, B. (2000). "Productivity Improvement and Labour Relations in the Tea Industry in South Asia", Working Paper.

Geneva: Sectoral Activities Programme, ILO.

16

Understanding the Rural Transformation Process: Story of My Village and Beyond

Back in my village for some days in 2000, I asked myself three questions. First, was there a significant improvement in the levels of living of the people of my village over the years? Second, if there were, what were the processes that led to the outcome? Third, could the insights from the exercise form the basis of a more general approach to rural transformation?

I intended to take a view, though not rigorously, of the inter-temporal change in the level of living of the people of my village, Hatirpithi of Chamata, which is around 90 kms away from Guwahati. Without going into the details of the exercise, I would like to indicate the initial conditions against which the exercise was made and the broad methodology adopted.

Briefly speaking, a cluster of settlements inhabited by four different castes and two religious groups in and around the village formed the study unit. Not more than 15 per cent of the households had relatively large land holdings and the rest were small and marginal farmers or landless. Sharecropping was the dominant feature of the land tenure system. Cultivation and caste-based occupations were the main source of livelihood.

As for the broad methodology, a base line scenario in respect of a few important indicators of levels of living of the villagers around 1960 was constructed essentially from my memory recall and validated by cross checking with several better informed people. The current/terminal level scenario, i.e for the year 2000, on the corresponding indicators was drawn on the basis of the information obtained from a set of informed people in the locality.

Village Economy: Then and Now

In the base year, only paddy was grown twice–but once rather casually–in a year. Vegetables, oil seeds etc. were grown mainly for self-consumption. As was then, so is now, irrigation facilities do not exist although a deep tube well was installed but remained mostly out of operation. Unlike in the base year, high yielding variety of seeds are now widely used. Perhaps for lack of irrigation facilities, fertilizers are rarely used. Land tenure system characterized by sharecropping is still prevalent. Landholdings have become smaller due to division and sub-division.

Over these four decades, demographic transition as reflected in smaller average family seems to have taken place, to a varying degree though, across different castes and religious groups. Labour force has also undergone a change in terms of the rising number of literates and occupation diversification, to an extent. Such changes seem slower in the case of low castes and the Muslim community.

Educational institutions have come up within a reasonable proximity, even if the majority of them seem to be of indifferent quality. So are the health services. But the extent of utilization varies with factors such as income level and family motivation. Road conditions have improved, even if these are still kaccha. Rural electrification has reached less than 20% of the households. Housing and sanitation have perceptibly improved particularly for the well off section.

What is striking is that the percentage of households that could not afford a couple of meals a day is now significantly low, though calorie and nutrition contents of food consumption could not be assessed. There has emerged a considerably large segment of low middle-income population over the years. Yet the rate of accumulation or productive investment in farm and/or any other activities that impart growth dynamism is slow.

These positive changes took place over a long period of four decades. They are, however, directional changes but the extent of their significance in quantitative terms could not be ascertained. Further, the observations based on an inter-temporal exercise as above obviously overlooked the impact on the levels of living due to seasonal fluctuations that are associated with rain-fed agriculture.

Understanding the Process

What processes contributed to these positive outcomes? On the basis of close interactions with a cross section of population covering both intelligent observers and actual actors at the grass root level, it was possible to identify four broad forces that contributed to the improvement in the people's lives.

First, the expansion of government and government promoted activities particularly since the planning era, made it possible for some villagers to get regular employment, though largely at the lower end in government and semi-government activities such as public institutions, cooperatives and schools within the locality and/or in the nearby town or in Guwahati. This section could have a steady income, even if not high, in the majority of cases. Nevertheless, it impacted their consumption level and pattern.

Further, such job migrants of the initial period had one important characteristic: most of them did not shift to their place of work but remained rooted in their village homes and looked after their dependents including the education of their siblings. They also improved the conditions of living by way of constructing better houses and improving sources of drinking water. Their interactions and exposures with urban living slowly impacted the consumption pattern at their village home, too.

Second, this pattern of migration induced local level demand for newer products and services in the village itself. On the weekends or whenever they came home, they brought with them some of the commodities usually found a place in the urban consumption basket. This had also a demonstration effect on their neighbours' preferences. In the process, urban items began to enter the rural consumption basket. This, in turn, induced non-farm activities such as shops, rice husking units. A PWD road, though only a gravelled and poorly maintained one, connecting the village to Guwahati and other emerging urban centres and regular transport service facilitated the above described migration process and strengthened the market linkage.

Third, market linkage became stronger when a daily evening market instead of a bi-weekly Haat/Bazar further away from the village came into place around the bus station. It served as a regular outlet for disposable goods. The local demand mostly from salaried people with a regular stream of income, the land owning class, people engaged in more profitable activities, etc. boosted the growth of non-farm activities. The daily evening market also induced people to produce whatever they could using their slender productive assets more intensively and bring to the market for sale even if not in large quantity.

Kakati Sir's–Khagen Kakati, a B.Sc. teacher of Chamata High School, (now Higher Secondary)–model farm in the 1950s in close proximity to my village demonstrated the efficacy of improved method of cultivation and supplied quality seeds and seedlings of various rabi crops. That motivated big, small and even marginal farmers to adopt better seeds and new methods of cultivation. The availability of a daily market acted as a booster.

But these producers later faced a new problem. With a growing number of farmers adopting improved methods of cultivation particularly in regard to vegetables, a situation of excess supply occurred at times resulting in price crash as it happens in all agricultural products that do not enjoy support prices. In such situations, farmers did not receive incentive prices.

Fourth, the emergence of a cluster of non-farm establishments around the daily market spurred various demand-induced services such as shops, means of transport like rickshaws later graduated to auto-rickshaws and various repairing services such as bicycles, radios, etc.

Learning Some Lessons

What do we learn from these processes of change overtime? We could find that:

- The rural economy of my village, perhaps of many other villages, has graduated from the stage of self-sufficiency to one of producing market surplus and economic agents such as farmers have become price sensitive.
- Road connectivity has facilitated the evolution of market centres and market linkages.
- Regular market centres together with a steady stream of income of the local and migrant salaried class and dispersed farm income have given a fillip to the growth of both farm and non-farm activities.

- Access to new technology and the proper demonstration of its efficacy have induced even illiterate small and marginal farmers to adopt them and motivated them to use more productively even their small productive assets.
- Herd effects resulting in producing more of the same crops as in the case of vegetables by many have led to excess supply affecting realization of incentive prices.
- Uncertain weather conditions in the absence of adequate irrigation infrastructure, lack of land tenure reforms have impeded capital accumulation, farm investment and crop diversification in favour of high value crops.
- Allied activities like animal husbandry, fisheries, etc. have attracted attention but have not taken off partly because of risk averse behaviour and partly because of non-availability of cattle and poultry feed in the case of animal husbandry and fingerlings in the case of fisheries.
- Non-availability of easy credit, market infrastructure, irrigation, timely supply of seeds and seedlings, uncertain power supply, poor road and transport and the failure of the government functionaries to connect with the economic agents like farmers have acted as major stumbling blocks to the sustained agricultural prosperity and non-farm sector growth.
- Rural youths, particularly the educated ones, are averse to taking up cultivation as an occupation. More remunerative non-farm activities and urban destination in search of jobs even humble ones attract them more.

In short, reforms of land tenure, adequate and quality rural and market infrastructure, market linkage, accessibility to new technology and its demonstration, easy credit and proper interface of different agents of change could boost agricultural growth and through its multiplier effects spur the dynamic growth of non-farm activities including agro-processing.

Suggesting a General Approach

Could these insights suggest a general approach to rapid rural transformation?

To begin with, it should be recognized that the rural population can be classified into the following broad categories on the basis of the means of income generation: (i) those who own large productive rural assets in the form of land; (ii) those who have land but not of viable size–small and marginal farmers; (iii) those who do not own land and have only labour to sell–landless labour; (iv) those with skill such as carpenters and masons; (v) those who are self-employed in the non-farm sector and (vi) those who are employed in government, semi-government and other establishments and earn a regular stream of income and (vii) those who come under non-workers.

Viable land owning category benefits from crop loan, Kisan Credit card, KVIC, Margin Money Scheme, other micro credit and normal bank credit. Those without productive rural assets may benefit but temporarily from employment-oriented schemes such as Employment Assurance Scheme, PM's Gram Sadak Yojana and Indira Awas Yojana. Similarly, schemes like PMRY, SJSRY, SGSY, SHG and other special target group micro-credit schemes are meant to benefit marginal asset holders. The realization of benefits from these schemes, even if temporarily, depends on whether the implementation actually reaches out to the target groups.

Given the dependence of an overwhelmingly large segment of the rural population on agriculture and allied activities, the development of this sector is a crucial determinant of rural transformation. The question is how to stimulate agricultural growth in a way that would strengthen linkage with non-farm activities through its feedback effects.

High growth of this sector essentially depends on three factors: shift to higher technology and to high valued crops; farm infrastructure such as irrigation, market infrastructure like cold storage facility, rural roads and availability of credit with ease and on time and market linkage that facilitates disposal of marketable surplus at incentive prices.

Proper land tenure reforms and land consolidation, on the one hand and minimization of risk due to floods and vagaries of nature either through crop insurance and flood prevention will attract private investment in the farm sector. That will also provide the required incentive to adopt new technology and new crops. The demonstration of their efficacy and profitability will be essential as the model farm mentioned earlier, did.

This can be said in the case of other allied activities of agriculture such as fishery, animal husbandry, horticulture and forest farming. These activities are land intensive and eminently suitable for the North Eastern states both for reasons of soil and demand conditions. Their growth will give a fillip to the growth of rural non-farm activities. But technology adoption and market linkages are crucially important for this to happen.

Rural connectivity in terms of road and communication together with other infrastructure such as stable power supply, good schools, quality health institutions, drinking water and sanitation facilitate market linkage as also non-farm income and employment.

Interface of progressive producers with technology providers, concerned government functionaries, marketing experts, development financiers such as NABARD and NEDFi and experts providing technology options for storage and preservation of different products to be followed by proper monitoring will spur growth in these activities.

With change in the composition of the rural labour force in terms of having more educated members, this type of interface is eminently useful. Combined with Kiosk/internet-based computer information centres such interface workshops has the potential of unleashing the productive forces. It can spur the growth of agro-processing industries such as food processing, cattle feed and poultry feed units, dairy, organic farming, forest farming, ornamental fish farming, floriculture, seed farming and organic manure.

As Dr. Jayanta Madhab, Adviser to the Government of Assam observed on the opportunities of rural development with particular reference to Assam:

"The opportunities are there; the market is here; unutilized manpower is abundantly available; bank's credit deposit ratio being low, banks are under pressure to increase lending; therefore money is available; unutilized land is available and water is plentiful". But he did not address the question: even though all these opportunities were all there for long, why is it that the Assam economy continues to decelerate and the rural poverty is far higher than even the national average level? If we know the answer to this question, we have the key to rapid rural transformation.

In the light of what President A.P.J. Abdul Kalam stated in his convocation address at GB Pant University of Agriculture and Technology on November 17, 2003, I submit that four types of connectivity: (i) Physical connectivity in the form of road, transportation, and power; (ii) electronic connectivity in the form of reliable telecommunication, internet and information technology services (iii) knowledge connectivity in terms of technology and its demonstration in addition to good educational and training institutions and (iv) market connectivity that would ensure incentive prices to farmers and others would impart dynamism in rural transformation in general and agricultural growth in particular.

High agricultural growth through its output, income, consumption and investment feedback effects or in technical jargon, through multiplier effects, would stir growth in non-farm activities and thus stimulate rapid rural transformation.

Index